I0821977

Friends on the Way

Friends on the Way

Jesuits Encounter Contemporary Judaism

Edited by Thomas Michel, S.J.

Fordham University Press
New York 2007

Library of Congress Cataloging-in-Publication Data

International Colloquium of Jesuits in Jewish-Christian dialogue (3rd : 2005 : Zug, Switzerland) Friends on the way : Jesuits encounter contemporary Judaism / edited by Thomas Michel.—1st ed.
p. cm.—(The Abrahamic dialogues series)
Includes bibliographical references and index.
ISBN 978-0-8232-2811-9 (cloth : alk. paper)
1. Catholic Church—Relations—Judaism—Congresses.
2. Judaism—Relations—Catholic Church—Congresses.
3. Jesuits—Congresses. 1. Michel, Thomas F., 1941– II. Title.
BM535.1486 2005
261.2′6—dc22

2007034059

Printed in the United States of America
09 08 07 5 4 3 2 1
First edition

Contents

Preface

Thomas Michel, S.J.

The papers in this volume were delivered at the Third International Colloquium of Jesuits in Jewish-Christian dialogue, which was held at Bad Schönbrunn in Zug, Switzerland, from July 18 to 23, 2005. This was the third colloquium in a series of meetings of Jesuits involved in dialogue with Jews. The first seminar was held in Krakow, Poland, in December 1998, and the second in Jerusalem in June 2000.

In each case, the venue dictated the theme. In the first seminar, "Jesuits and Jews: Towards Greater Fraternity and Commitment," held in Krakow less than forty miles from the Nazi concentration camp of Auschwitz and the death camp of Birkenau, the papers focused on the Jesuit involvement and responsibility in the long history of anti-Semitism in Europe which culminated in the Holocaust. At its beginnings, the Society showed greater openness and acceptance toward the Jews than did many in the Church. The first generations of Jesuits were influenced by the positive attitude of Ignatius, who "wished he had been Jewish so that he would have had the honor of being from the same race as Jesus and the Virgin Mary," as Marc Rastoin notes in his historical essay in this volume. A surprising number of the early Jesuits, including Laínez, the second general, and Polanco, Ignatius's personal secretary, were from families of *conversos*, or Christians of Jewish descent, at a time when such were prohibited from entering most religious orders.

However, as time went on, the Society of Jesus succumbed to the prejudices of the day, and the doors of the Society were eventually closed to candidates of Jewish blood. In the two centuries since the restoration of the Society of Jesus in 1814, the Jesuits on occasion even took the lead in fomenting anti-Semitic feelings and policies in the Church and in society, as happened in the Dreyfus affair in France the 1890s and in the editorials of Rome's influential *La Civiltà Cattolica* in the 1930s. The papers of the first Jesuit seminar were delivered mostly by Jesuits and focused on this ambiguous and often shameful history of anti-Semitism to which Jesuits too often made a significant contribution.

The second colloquium was held in Jerusalem two years later on the theme "The Significance of the State of Israel for Contemporary Judaism and Jewish-Christian Dialogue." On this occasion, the speakers were almost all Israeli Jews, who represented various points of view on the meaning of the Jewish state in Israel for Jewish self-understanding and relations with those outside the Jewish community. Some of the speakers were members of the Knesset, while others were rabbis, peace activists, settlers, and representatives of women's movements. The picture was completed by the voices of Muslim and Christian Israeli Arabs and Palestinians. For the first time in this series of colloquia, the proceedings were later published by the Jesuit Secretariat for Interreligious Dialogue.

The third colloquium, at which the papers in this volume were delivered, was held in a Jesuit retreat house and conference center in Zug, Switzerland. The theme of this colloquium was "The Importance of Modern Jewish Thought for Jewish-Christian Dialogue" and focused on the writings of modern Jewish thinkers in the Diaspora and the significance of their insights for Jewish-Christian relations. This topic provided a broad scope for the Jesuit researchers, who took up the ideas of rabbis such as Heschel and Soloveitchik, biblical exegetes such as Sternberg, Alter, Fishbane, and Levinson, philosophers such as Arendt and Lévinas, and the literary critic Harold Bloom.

Although these colloquia were planned as study sessions for Jesuits involved in dialogue with Jews, in every case the Jesuit participants were accompanied throughout by Jewish scholars. In Krakow, Rabbi Leon Klenicki, then assistant director of the Anti-Defamation League of B'nai B'rith, took part in the whole seminar and delivered a moving testimonial to the victims on a bitterly cold overcast day in Auschwitz. In Jerusalem, the participants were invited to the Shalom Hartman Institute, took part in Shabbat services in various synagogues, shared in the Shabbat meal in homes, heard from various currents of Judaism—Orthodox, Conservative, and Reform—as well as from secular Jews, and visited the "old" Yad Vashem Holocaust memorial (the new Yad Vashem is described in this volume). In Switzerland, the Jesuits were accompanied by Zurich's Rabbi Tovia Ben-Chorin and Professor Harold Kasimow of Grinnell College, whose contributions appear in this volume, and the academic sessions were supplemented by visits to the Institute of Jewish-Christian Research at the University of Lucerne and the Jewish-Christian House of Learning in Zurich.

What was the point of these colloquia? Since the time of the Second Vatican Council document *Nostra Aetate*, and to a lesser extent even before, there had always been some Jesuits in dialogue with Jews. Augustin Bea and John Courtney Murray at the time of the council, and since the council, Paul Beauchamp in France, James Bernauer in the United States, Francesco Rossi de Gasperis in Italy, and Stanisław Musiał in Poland were pioneers in this work, often as "single fighters" without much opportunity to share perspectives and take common initiatives. The purpose of bringing Jesuits together in colloquia was so that they could share the fruits of their research, encourage one another in their apostolic commitments, and reflect together on how they might best enrich and transform the Jesuit Order and the Church by the insights gained from their study of Judaism and their personal experiences with Jews.

All this is an effort to contribute positively to the Church's commitment to dialogue with Jews. Jesuits admit that their history toward Judaism has been checkered, at times heroically countercultural but perhaps more often silently approving the prejudices of their day or even fomenting and perpetuating hatred toward the Jews. However, in the Thirty-Fourth General Congregation of the Society of Jesus, held in 1995, interreligious dialogue was recognized as one of the distinguishing marks of Jesuit mission, and within that apostolic work, dialogue with the Jews was given a special importance. I conclude with the words of the Congregation:

> Dialogue with the Jewish people enables us to become more fully aware of our identity as Christians. Since the publication of *Nostra Aetate* in 1965, the Catholic Church has radically renewed the Jewish-Christian dialogue after centuries of polemics and contempt in which our Society shared. To enter into a sincere and respectful relationship with the Jewish people is one aspect of our efforts to think with and in the Church. (*Documents of the Thirty-Fourth General Congregation*, Decree Five, 12 [149])

Friends on the Way

Introduction

Harold Kasimow

> Dialogue with the Jewish people holds a unique place. The first covenant, which is theirs and which Jesus the Messiah came to fulfill, has never been revoked. A shared history both unites us with and divides us from our elder brothers and sisters, the Jewish people, in whom and through whom God continues to act for the salvation of the world. Dialogue with the Jewish people enables us to become more fully aware of our identity as Christians. Since the publication of *Nostra Aetate* in 1965, the Catholic Church has radically renewed the Jewish-Christian dialogue after centuries of polemics and contempt in which our Society shared. To enter into a sincere and respectful relationship with the Jewish people is one aspect of our efforts to think with and in the Church.
>
> *Decree 5: Our Mission and Interreligious Dialogue*[1]

This remarkable statement from the 1995 Jesuit meeting in Rome represents, in my view, the true spirit of the Second Vatican Council and of the magnificent document *Nostra Aetate*, "The Declaration on the Relationship of the Church to Non-Christian Religions," which states that "The Catholic Church rejects nothing that is true and holy in these religions."[2] Then follows an extraordinary statement that urges all Christians to "acknowledge, preserve, and encourage the spiritual and moral truths" found in other world religions.[3] This revolutionary document is remarkable because for the first time in two thousand years, the Church rejected the accusation that the Jews were collectively to blame for the crucifixion of Jesus. The document clearly states that "the Jews still remain most dear to God."[4] This document was constantly on the lips of Pope John Paul II, the most influential promoter of interfaith dialogue in the twentieth century, who really understood the importance of *Nostra Aetate*. I know of no other person in the world who has devoted more time and energy to making *Nostra Aetate* a reality.

John Paul II made it very clear that it was the duty of religious leaders to promote, in the words of *Nostra Aetate*, "unity and love among men."[5] He was convinced that lack of love for people of other faiths has in the past been a factor for conflict and even war. It is of the utmost importance that interfaith dialogue, which can become a path to friendship and love, must become a priority for all religious leaders. John Paul II consistently singled out the Jesuits to ask them to make interreligious dialogue a priority for the third millennium.

The most powerful Jesuit pioneer of interfaith dialogue in our time was Augustin Cardinal Bea, the architect of *Nostra Aetate*, who was responsible for steering this revolutionary declaration through the council. My teacher, Rabbi Abraham Joshua Heschel, the major Jewish advisor to Cardinal Bea, had deep respect and admiration for him. After reading Cardinal Bea's book *The Church and the Jewish People*, Heschel wrote, "Cardinal Bea's wisdom, courage, and pioneering effort in the cause of interreligious understanding will be remembered with esteem by future historians."[6] Heschel was inspired by the piety and ecumenical spirit of Cardinal Bea and other Christians. In a 1966 address Heschel stated: "Jewish-Christian relations have improved beautifully. There is certainly a new atmosphere and increasing mutual esteem. . . . [N]ow Christians are discovering that there is a religious voice and a human voice in the Jew."[7]

Even before the Second Vatican Council, many Christians, especially Catholics, began to see Heschel as the most profound spiritual Jew of his time. Thomas Merton claimed that Heschel "is the most significant spiritual (religious) writer in this country at the moment. I like his depth and his realism. He knows God."[8] Reinhold Niebuhr, the most prominent Protestant theologian of the twentieth century, spoke of Heschel as "the most authentic prophet of religious life in our culture,"[9] while for Martin Luther King Jr., Heschel was "one of the truly great men of our day and age . . . indeed a truly great prophet."[10] And at our conference I was thrilled when Stanislaw Obirek, from Poland, the land of Heschel's birth, called Heschel "a real prophet." After reading the brilliant papers by James Bernauer and Marc Rastoin and learning about the painful history between the Jesuits and the Jews, it seems almost miraculous that it was the Jesuit journal *America* that dedicated an entire issue to Heschel soon after he died. The idea for this special issue came from John C. Haughey, S.J., an associate editor, who stated: "Anyone who knew [Heschel] sensed the depth of his exposure to the Presence of God. . . . One event in the twentieth century that Christians were happily affected by was Abraham Joshua Heschel."[11] The editorial explained that a special issue was being devoted to Rabbi Heschel because "no Christian who ever entered into conversation with Professor Heschel came away without having been spiritually enriched and strengthened."[12]

Since the end of the Second Vatican Council, December 8, 1965, the Jesuits have been at the forefront of interreligious dialogue not only with Jews but also with Buddhists, Hindus, Muslims, and members of other religious traditions in different parts of the world. Jews will never forget Stanisław Musiał, S.J., for his help in negotiating the relocation of a Carmelite convent from near Auschwitz and his persistent attacks on anti-Semitism in the Catholic Church; Thomas Michel, S.J., the secretary of the Jesuits for Interreligious Dialogue, has made significant contributions to Catholic-Muslim relations; and Jacques Dupuis, S.J., was the leading Catholic thinker of our time in the area of the theology of religions. Perhaps the most enriching and transforming religious path that the Jesuits have been in dialogue with has been Buddhism in Japan. Many of the leading Zen teachers in the world have been Jesuits, including Hugo Enomiya-Lassalle, Niklaus Brantschen, Thomas Hand, and Robert Kennedy, to name only a few. These Zen teachers and many more all made the journey to Japan to train under Yamada Koun Roshi of the Kamakura San-un Zendo. They went to Kamakura not to become Buddhists but to become better Christians. Yamada Roshi told them that he was not trying to make them Buddhists but to empty them in imitation of "Christ, your Lord."[13] Robert F. Drinan, S.J., after attending a Zen *sesshin* with Robert Kennedy, wrote: "After the retreat . . . I experienced Asian wisdom combined with Christian illumination. I found God in a new way. I became a new man with deeper insights, and more importantly, a better Christian."[14] With regard to the Jesuits' involvement in Buddhist-Christian dialogue and Zen training, the superior general of the Society of Jesus, Peter-Hans Kolvenbach, S.J., wrote: "Jesuits and other Christians have found Zen to be a valuable instrument for progressing in the spiritual life. . . . By coming to focus on the present moment through the practice of the techniques of Zen meditation, the Christian can become aware of God's immediate loving presence."[15]

I have been involved in interfaith dialogue, especially with Christians, Muslims, and Buddhists, since 1972, when I began teaching in the Department of Religious Studies at Grinnell College in Iowa. During a year of teaching in Japan, I had the good fortune to meet with many Buddhist priests and with a number of Jesuits from Sophia University in Tokyo, including the Jesuit scholar of Buddhism Pier P. Del Campana and the Jesuit Zen master Kakichi Kadowaki, author of the well-known work *Zen and the Bible*.[16] During the 1990s I also participated in a number of sesshins at San-un Zendo in Kamakura. It was therefore a double joy for me to be invited to the Third International Jesuit Congress on the theme of "The Importance of Modern Jewish Thought for Jewish-Christian Dialogue." First, I feel greatly honored to be the only Jewish academic to have been invited to participate in the conference. But I felt even greater joy when I arrived at the conference at Lassalle-Haus in Bad Schönbrunn in Zug, Switzerland, and soon came to realize that it was named after Fr. Hugo Enomiya-Lassalle. The Lassalle-Haus was founded by Pia Gyger and Niklaus Brantschen, who became a Zen teacher under the direction of Yamada Koun Roshi at San-un Zendo, the place where I also trained. The current director of Lassalle-Haus, Christian Rutishauser, one of our Jesuit hosts, who is also immersed in Buddhist-Christian dialogue, presented a fascinating comparison of Ignatian spirituality and the thought of Rabbi Joseph B. Soloveitchik, the preeminent Orthodox Jewish theologian and talmudic scholar of the twentieth century.

Since Pope Benedict XVI's election, there has been some question about his commitment to interreligious dialogue, but I think these concerns are misplaced. In May 2001 the Pontifical Biblical Commission issued the significant document *The Jewish People and Their Sacred Scriptures in the Christian Bible*, signed by the new pope, who was then Cardinal Joseph Ratzinger.[17] At the time he was the prefect of the Congregation for the Doctrine of the Faith and the president of the Pontifical Biblical Commission. Cardinal Ratzinger singled out the following passages from the document in his preface:

> Without the Old Testament, the New Testament would be an incomprehensible book, a plant deprived of its roots and destined to dry up and wither. . . .[18] Christians can and ought to admit that the Jewish reading of the Bible is a possible one. . . . [They can] learn much from Jewish exegesis practiced for more than two thousand years, and, in fact, they have learned much in the course of history.[19] Statements are fully in accord with the teaching of Pope John Paul II, and I believe they can help bring healing between Jews and Christians at this critical time in our history.

For me the Third International Jesuit Conference was an incredible event not only because the presentations were insightful and intelligent but also because they attempted to clarify how Jews define their own religious tradition. With regard to the request by both Holy

Fathers for Jews and Christians to join in biblical study, I found Fr. Jean-Pierre Sonnet's essays particularly helpful. Historians of religion have pointed out a very special affinity between Judaism and Christianity. These are the only two traditions that share a common text: the Hebrew Bible. Today scholars have presented us with many examples of the exegetical encounters that took place between the Church Fathers and the rabbis and how they influenced each other.[20] Fr. Sonnet's deep probing into traditional and contemporary Jewish interpretations of their sacred texts shows how enriching this can be for Christian students of these sacred scriptures. His essays show that a dialogue between Jewish and Christian interpreters of sacred scriptures will enable them to penetrate more deeply into some of the most cryptic passages of these texts.

The essays in this volume also deal with Abraham Joshua Heschel and Joseph Soloveitchik, the two most influential and profound Jewish thinkers of the twentieth century. What I find most fascinating is that although Heschel's and Soloveitchik's views of the Jewish tradition are radically different, Heschel representing the Hasidic mystical vision of Judaism, and Soloveitchik representing the rationalistic Lithuanian tradition, there are strong affinities between their spirituality and Ignatian spirituality. Each essay in the volume helps to illuminate other central Jewish themes, including a creative essay by David M. Neuhaus on how Christians are presented in the new Yad Vashem Museum, Israel's national Holocaust memorial.

In his essay "An Ignatian Perspective on Contemporary Jewish Spirituality," Donald Moore, S.J., tells one of my favorite Hasidic tales. In this tale Eizik, son of Rabbi Yekel, travels from Krakow to Prague in search of treasure. He ultimately discovers, after meeting with a Christian, that the treasure is in fact buried in his family's home in Krakow. Father Moore presents us with the traditional interpretation of this tale: "There is something that can be found only in one place, that great treasure known as the fulfillment of existence. It is found in the place where one stands here and now." Father Moore points out that "these Hasidic insights closely parallel the apex of Ignatian spirituality, and in a sense the apex of all Christian spirituality: the grace of finding God in all things."

I think it would be consistent with this conference to see this story in a different light. The story teaches us that we can develop a deeper relationship with our own tradition after an encounter with a member of another tradition. For after all, Rabbi Eizik found the treasure only after his meeting with a stranger, a member of a different religious community.

Acknowledgments

I want to express my deep gratitude to Stanisław Obirek and Tom Michel for inviting me to be part of the Third International Congress of Jesuits in Dialogue with Jews. I am grateful to the participants, all of whom are devoting their lives to the service of others, for making me feel welcome and encouraging me in my belief that genuine interfaith dialogue between members of different religious traditions can be enriching. I would also like to express my heartfelt gratitude to Peter Du Brul for his wonderful essay "The Genius and the Wisdom of Harold Bloom" and for taking a special walk with me on the day we visited the Jesuit church in Lucerne, Switzerland.

From Windfall to Fall: The *Conversos* in the Society of Jesus

Marc Rastoin, S.J.

Over the past two decades, historians have studied Ignatius Loyola's relations with the Jews.[1] Their studies have demonstrated that Loyola was so favorably disposed toward them that he wished he had been Jewish so that he would have had the honor of being from the same race as Jesus and the Virgin Mary.[2] Such sentiments reveal how much he differed from a Spanish culture in which hostility toward Jews and *conversos* grew steadily in the first half of the sixteenth century. It is also well known that Diego Laínez, one of the first ten companions, arguably the most outstanding after Ignatius, and his successor as father general, came from a *converso* family.[3] Recent books on the history of the first Jesuits recall this particular feature of the Society: its acceptance of recruits from Jewish origin.[4] They also narrate how this tolerance ended at the Fifth General Congregation in 1593 due to the combined efforts of the Spanish Crown and the majority of Spanish Jesuits themselves.[5] The assembled fathers decreed:

> The ministries of our Society are exercised with greater fruit in the general quest for the salvation of souls in proportion to the distance. Ours are from those human situations that can prove offensive to others. Those, however, who are descended from

> parents who are recent Christians have routinely been in the habit of inflicting a great deal of hindrance and harm on the Society (as has become clear from our daily experience). . . . The entire congregation then decided to decree, as is affirmed by this present decree, that in no case is any one of this sort, that is to say, one of Hebrew or Saracen stock, henceforth to be admitted into the Society. And if by error any such will have been admitted, he should be dismissed as soon as the impediment will have been shown to exist, at whatever time before profession it becomes known, after first notifying the superior general and awaiting his reply.

The fathers offered an "apostolic" explanation for their decision. It was not necessary for the Society to recruit its members from all races. "Rather," the decree continued:

> It is more suited to the greater glory of God and the more perfect pursuit of the end it [the Society of Jesus] proposes to itself that it possess workers who are very acceptable to other nations throughout the world and who might be more freely and reliably employed in the Church of God by those people whose good or ill will towards us (as Father Ignatius, of happy memory, says) has much influence to open or to keep closed out access to the divine service and the help of souls.[6]

The same congregation, after unnamed participants appealed for reconsideration, confirmed the decree.[7]

Nonetheless, some issues require further examination.[8] Why did the *conversos* join the Society? From which families did they come? Where did they work as Jesuits? Indeed, how many were there? What factors influenced their decisions to enter the Society? What caused a decline in the number of *conversos* entering the Society? In this short paper, I shall propose some tentative answers to those thorny questions.

Why did the *conversos* join the Society? To this question a very short answer could easily be given: the Society was the only order they could join. But it would be better to take a second look. The adoption of the statutes regarding *limpieza de sangre* reached their peak toward the end of the 1540s. In particular, all of Spain was influenced by the decision of Juan Martinez Guijeño (better known as Siliceo), Archbishop of Toledo, to adopt the statutes and the eagerness with which he implemented them.[9] Most religious orders had either already adopted the prohibitions or were in the process of doing so.[10] On the contrary, Loyola directed the Society to pursue a entirely different policy; he was not convinced that the rejection of *conversos* in any way served God. If a candidate was fit for the apostolic life as envisioned by the founder, no question of origin should hinder his entrance. On this Ignatius was adamant. Reporting on Ignatius's stormy conversation with the archbishop of Toledo, the Jesuit Francisco de Villanueva said the proud archbishop made it clear that he would consider admitting the Society into his archdiocese only if it adopted the *limpieza de sangre*.[11] Because the archbishop had various objections to the Society, including his conviction (influenced by Dominican theologian Melchior Cano) that the *Spiritual Exercises* were heretical, and because, as primate of Spain, his endorsement would facilitate the Society's work in Spain, the offer was tempting, but Ignatius refused to accept any accommodation on this point.[12]

Not all Spanish Jesuits supported Loyola. Antonio de Araoz,[13] Loyola's cousin, frequent resident at the Spanish court, and the first provincial of Spain, strongly opposed the acceptance of *conversos* into the Society.[14] Despite his wide influence, Araoz bowed to Loyola even though he remained unconvinced by the arguments.[15] Another influential Jesuit with tendencies opposed to Ignatius's policy was Simão Rodrigues, provincial of Portugal and one of the first ten companions.[16] At the end of 1551 he ordered that *conversos* not be accepted into the Society in India and did so in such a way as to give the impression that the command had come from Ignatius himself. Francis Xavier implemented the instruction for a brief period until a counterorder arrived from Rome.[17] Between 1548 and 1558, because of Loyola's resolution, the doors of the Society remained open to *conversos*.[18]

The attitude of Juan de Ávila to the Society testifies to Loyola's openness. A major religious leader in Spain and widely regarded as a saint during his lifetime, Juan de Ávila evangelized Andalucía, the south of Spain, which had been reconquered in 1492. He had numerous disciples, many of whom were, like himself, *conversos*.[19] On the verge of founding a new religious order, Juan de Ávila instead wrote to Ignatius Loyola upon hearing of the Society and its policies. The understanding between the two was immediate. Consequently many of Ávila's disciples entered the Society.[20] Three of the more famous disciples were the influential author Gaspar de Loarte, who worked mostly in Italy, Diego de Guzmán, who also worked in Italy,[21] and Luis de Santander, who joined as a priest in 1554.[22] Both Loarte and Santander were *conversos*.

A trickier question is the motivation of the *conversos* for joining the Jesuits. Did they join because they wished to enter religious life or did they specifically want to join the Jesuits? What or who influenced them to join? Two elements must be distinguished. First, why were there so many priests among the *conversos* entering the Jesuits? And second, what were the main features of their spirituality (if we can identify them)? Before trying to provide an answer to those questions, we must examine more closely the social identity of the *conversos*.

It would be misleading to think of the *conversos* as a unified body. First, there were great differences between the Portuguese and the Spanish *conversos*. And even within Spain, as the Spanish historian Dominguez Ortiz noted, there was a difference between north and south. *Conversos* from Aragon, Catalonia, and part of Castilla la Vieja were much more integrated into society than those from the south. Their number was smaller, and they often came from families who had converted decades before the ordeal of 1492.[23] Many more of them had contracted marriages with *cristianos viejos* before the statutes were effectively implemented. Dominguez Ortiz noted the paucity of cases of *Judaizantes* before the Inquisition in the north in comparison with the southern cities of Seville, Córdoba, and Toledo. Generally speaking, Spanish *conversos* came from old Christian families. Almost all came from the big urban centers (e.g., Juan de Polanco, Toledo, Acosta) and very often were from powerful and rich merchant families. Their families encouraged university studies, and many of the first Spanish recruits had graduated very successfully (Laínez, Toledo, Alfondo de Pisa). Many were already priests when they joined the Society (Loarte, Pedro Ramon, Santander, Toledo), or deacons (Henrique Henriques).[24] *Conversos* who entered as laymen were quickly ordained and sent to teach or to exercise important offices within the Society. Some (e.g., Acosta, Toledo, and Pisa) were among the first instructors at the Collegio Romano; some (e.g., Polanco, Loarte, Santander, and Ramon) were professed of the four vows.

The situation was quite different in Portugal. *Conversos* there came from families much more attached to Judaism. Many Portuguese Jews had accepted forced exile from Spain in 1492 in order to remain Jews.[25] Among the twenty or so *conversos* mentioned by name by Father Wicki, one, Gomes Vaz, had two grandparents who had been burnt at the stake. Almost all came from very humble social backgrounds. The Jews who had emigrated to Portugal from Spain were generally the most observant and the poorest; they were those who had been able to sell their small shops and possessions in the four months allowed by the king of Spain.[26] Portuguese *conversos* were accordingly usually poorer than Spanish *conversos*. In Portugal almost half the *conversos* entered the Society as brothers (Fernão de Narbona, Gaspar Rodrigues, Luis de Almeida), even if some were ordained after some years of apostolic work in Japan or in India (e.g., Bartolomeu dos Santos, Antonio Fernandes, Antonio Dias). When they pronounced vows, they were often spiritual coadjutors. Rarely were they appointed as rectors or superiors. If they did assume such positions, there were extenuating circumstances, such as terrible persecutions (Pedro Gómez in Japan in 1590), or because there was no other candidate. Nonetheless, even in these instances, their appointments sometimes provoked tensions within the community.[27] As early as December of 1574, Alessandro Valignano,[28] Jesuit Visitor to the Far East, asked that no more *conversos* be sent to India because there were then so many that the Society was falling from favor among the Portuguese in Asia. The door was beginning to close against the *conversos*.[29]

Where did they work? We have seen that Ignatius was ready to admit that in Spain and Portugal the popular shame attached to the *conversos* made it difficult for them to work in their homeland. He suggested, in case their origin was known, that they be sent to work in another country.[30] The missionary impetus of the Society provided both a wonderful occasion for the *conversos* to live and work freely outside their homeland and a powerful appeal to their authentic Christian missionary feelings. But unfortunately, as we have already seen, the Portuguese colonies quickly became as hostile to them as the homeland they had left. This situation prompted superiors to request a change of policy. Some *conversos* (e.g., Polanco, Toledo, Loarte, Pisa) worked in Italy; others went to America (Acosta), to Germany (Ferdinando de Jaén) or Italy and northern Europe, to the Middle East (Giovanni Baptista Eliano),[31] and obviously to India and Japan. Some entered the Society in those non-European countries after having worked as merchants or doctors (Almeida, Narbona), painters (Manuel Alvares) or musicians (Antonio Belo). In cases where they were already in their thirties or forties, they joined as brothers.

As Spanish and Portuguese institutions took root in the colonies, and with the progressive development of the Inquisition overseas and the entrance into the Society of more and more sons of the noble families, Jesuit authorities in Spain and Portugal became increasingly reluctant to admit *conversos*. In 1584 the Portuguese provincial congregation decreed that it would admit no more *conversos*.[32] That decree was not sudden. From the end of the 1560s, pressure to forbid admission to *conversos* was strong throughout the Society but especially in Portugal. By 1575 Italy and eastern Europe were the only possible fields of activity for *conversos*. But even within Italy, perhaps because of the increased presence and influence of Spanish Jesuits during the generalates of Diego Laínez and Francis Borgia,[33] this door was also closing. By the death of Laínez, most of the professors at the Collegio Romano and more than half the professed Jesuits in Italy were Spaniards, creating a growing resentment among the Italian Jesuits.

Why then did the formal decree of the Fifth General Congregation come only in 1593? The text of the *Constitutions*[34] and the clear will of the first superior generals,[35] especially the clearly expressed desire of Ignatius, were a powerful barrier to any change. As soon as he heard of the decree, Pedro de Ribadeneira, a close companion during Ignatius's life, protested strongly, arguing that this decree was a shameful betrayal of Ignatius's manifest will.[36] The decree eliminated an important sign of the Society's independence from the Spanish Crown and other earthly powers. This was only one of the first battles[37] in a war that would last till the royal decree of March of 1767, which expelled all Jesuits from Spanish territories. Then many old charges—for example, Jesuit conspiracies against the king, the wealth and power of the Society, the illegitimacy of the fourth vow, and Jesuit ambitions in South America (some of these charges date back to the sixteenth-century controversies)—were again arrayed against the Society.

Jesuit desire to win more respect in the Iberian world resulted in the Society's capitulation in the face of powerful adversaries. The Society hoped to ingratiate itself with the king and thus protect its apostolates within Spain.[38] Juan de Ávila had predicted that only two issues could possibly destroy the Society: the acceptance of too many ill-suited candidates, and the adoption of *limpieza de sangre*. Ribadeneira, in his defense of the Society's traditional openness, reminded Jesuits of Ávila's prophecy. Perhaps we should interpret the suppression of the Society as a belated fulfillment of the prophecy.[39]

How many *conversos* were there during Acquaviva's tenure as general? It is obviously almost impossible to answer this delicate question precisely. In Spain the presence of so many *conversos* prompted critics to disparage the Society as an order of Jews.[40] Even if the question of *limpieza* had been asked prior to admission,[41] the answer was usually not recorded and preserved. Moreover, surnames cannot always provide clues because some *conversos* had very common Spanish names or, indeed, had changed their residences and their names.[42] We can even note changes of names after someone had joined the Society: Jerónimo Concha became Cuenca and Fernão de Narbona became Nuñes.[43] A Jesuit's origins usually became a matter for concern only after rumors began to circulate. These rumors prompted the Jesuit's superiors either to defend him or to transfer him. As long as there were no suspicions and no complaints, there was no need to raise the issue of someone's origins.

To limit publicity, Jesuits used coded language or foreign expressions. Antonio Araoz referred to *conversos* as "*la gente verriac*" in his plea to Loyola that the Society adopt the statutes of *limpieza.* "*Verriac*" is the Basque word for "new."[44] Father Wicki demonstrated how letters from India sometimes used Greek letters within the Latin text to conceal a Jesuit's origins or employed the antiphrasis "*viscayno*," Basque people.[45] The last requires some explanation. It was well known that the only region of Spain with scarcely any *conversos* was the Basque country (as Ignatius recalled during his trial by the Spanish Inquisition).[46] Thus the description of a Jesuit whose name clearly revealed that he was from another part of Spain as a "*vizcayno*" indicated that he was a *converso.*[47] It is as if one were to say today, "The problem of Patrick Murphy is his Italian origin," the reader initiated in the code will automatically supply "Irish origin."

Despite these problems, we can approximate the number of *conversos* within the Society. If we consider, for example, the Spanish Jesuits mentioned by John W. O'Malley, S.J., in *The First Jesuits*, approximately a fifth—eight of thirty-seven—were *conversos.* This would surely be a maximum in those first years of the Society. According to Father Wicki, approximately one tenth (20 of 197) of the Jesuits in the Indian province in 1565 were *conversos*. All but two were Portuguese. The two Spanish provinces most concerned with the issue were Toledo and Andalucía. The first had attracted many university students immediately after their graduation. The second accepted many of Juan de Ávila's disciples after he and Loyola had reached an agreement in 1555.[48] O'Malley has pointed out that approximately 25 percent of candidates for the Society in Spain in 1562 entered at the Jesuit house in Alcalá. Around the same period, Alcalá and two other university cities, Salamanca and Valencia, produced nearly 50 percent of Spanish vocations.[49] Because many *conversos* attended the universities, the last social organizations within Spain to enforce the statutes, and many more were among Ávila's disciples, some candidates for the Society must have been *conversos*. But how many? If we extrapolate from O'Malley's data, nearly 20 percent of the provinces should be *conversos*; if we use Wicki's, 10 percent. There were 165 Jesuits in the province of Toledo in 1565 and 176 in Andalucía. That would make twenty or so men for each province. The proportion should not be surprising.[50] Not only were *conversos* very numerous in the cities where the Society was establishing itself but they belonged to the social classes attracted to the Society. They came from very large and pious families. Consider the following three examples. Diego Laínez entered in the Society, as did two of his brothers. One of his sisters was a Clarisse.[51] Astráin cites the Acosta family, which gave five sons to the Society, and the Dueñas, which gave four. They were all from the college of Medina del Campo.[52]

Now we can return to the first question: Why were *conversos* so enthusiastically drawn to this new order? Of course, as we mention above, *conversos* had few options, since the majority of religious orders and congregations denied them access. But *conversos* did not simply select the Society by default. There were aspects of Jesuit life and spirituality that appealed to them. *Conversos* strongly resented Spanish obsession with "*el punto de honor*"[53] and wanted to return to the spirit of the Gospel. Eager to demonstrate the depth of their faith in the face of the suspicions of the "old Christians," *conversos* often became priests and nuns.[54] They encouraged contemporary spiritual revivals, including that of the *alumbrados*.[55] Aspects of their cultural, intellectual,[56] and spiritual[57] background disposed them toward the Society of Jesus.[58] The reaction of Juan de Ávila is especially revealing in that regard,[59] and the proof of it is that those men who joined as priests were among those who best embodied the Ignatian spirit even if they were already mature when entering. We need only mention G. de Loarte, F. Vasquez, or L. de Santander.[60] In contrast, some Spaniards who joined as laymen took much more time to discover the spirit of the Society, as we see with A. de Oviedo, A. Araoz, or even Francis Borgia.[61]

The *conversos* represented a fantastic opportunity for the young order, a windfall that Ignatius was happy to receive. They provided a good number of talented scholars who helped to establish the fame of the Collegio Romano, among whom we can count the first Jesuit cardinal, F. de Toledo. Among their ranks were some of the most courageous missionaries in India and Japan, catechists, preachers, and men of leadership. Let us not forget the man Ignatius thought the most suited to replace him and who in fact would become the second general of the Society, Diego Laínez. It is striking to note that the first theologian of the Roman college and cardinal (Toledo), the first historian and biographer of St. Ignatius (Ribadeneira), the first secretary and historian of the Society (Polanco), the first successor of St. Ignatius as general (Laínez), and the first well-known Jesuit philosopher (Suarez) were all of *converso* origin.[62]

Certain points emerge from this examination of *conversos* in the early Society:

1. Many *conversos* were attracted to the Society because of their desire for a religious life learned, devout, and rooted in an evangelical spirituality.
2. *Conversos* were warmly welcomed into the Society for an extremely brief period. Their admission in Spain peaked between

1549 and 1559, declined through the 1560s, and became almost negligible in the 1570s and 1580s.

3. Although all *conversos* were subject to the same treatment by society at large, they differed among themselves on the basis of social class, national origins, and so on.
4. In the face of strong pressure, especially in Portugal and in some circles in Spain, the Society tried to deal with the problem by accepting *conversos* but sending them abroad for their formation. Between 1573 and 1593, intensified pressure resulted in increased restrictions on their acceptance, until the congregational decree barred them completely.[63]
5. The question of the *conversos* was intertwined with the complex issue of the Society's relations with the pope and the Spanish king. The Society's acceptance of *limpieza de sangre* proved that, despite its loyalty to the pope,[64] it remained disposed to specifically Iberian issues and prejudices.[65] In the midst of a major constitutional struggle, at a congregation summoned to evaluate his generalate, Acquaviva bowed to pressure[66] and accepted the policy of *limpieza de sangre* for the sake of unity within the Society and the preservation of normal governance.

Appendix: Jesuits of Jewish Origin in the Early Society

We attempt in this table to list Jesuit *conversos*,[67] well aware that the Society kept no record of this information and, indeed, tried to hide the data in order to avoid problems.[68] Among those whose origin is certain or strongly asserted (87), I distinguish here two groups: the first includes the Spaniards (52);[69] the second, the Portuguese (31) and others (4 Italians).

Name	*Origin*	*Birth*	*Entrance*	*Activity and Degree*	*Death*
José de Acosta[70]	Medina del Campo	1540	1554	Priest and professed; writer, professor, missionary provincial of Peru	1600
Bernardino de Acosta[71]	Medina del C.	?	1554	Priest and professed; missionary in Mexico	1615
Cristobal de Acosta	Medina del C.	?	1554	Died as scholastic	1571
Diego de Acosta	Medina del C.	1535	1552	Professor of theology in Rome; provincial of Andalucía	1585
Jerónimo de Acosta[72]	Medina del C.	?	af. 1554	Priest and professed	1606
Luis de Alcázar[73]	Seville	1554	1568	Priest and exegete	1613
Vasco Baptista[74]	Beira	1550	1563	Professor	1596
Alonso de Castro[75]	Seville	1552	1566	Priest	1637
Gaspar de Castro	Seville	1554	1568	Priest and preacher	1592
Melchior de Castro[76]	Seville	1555	1571	Priest	1599
Antonio Francisco de Critana[77]	Almodóvar del Campo	1548	1569	Priest and missionary	1614
Bartolomeo de Dueñas[78]	?	?	?	Priest	1640
Bernardo de Dueñas[79]	Medina del C.	?	1554	Brother	1592

Gabriel de Dueñas	Medina del C.	?	1554	Priest	1605
Gaspar de Dueñas	Medina del C.	?	1554	Priest	1585
Juan de Dueñas[80]	?	?	?	Priest	1599
Mateo de Dueñas	Medina del C.	?	1554	Priest	1579
Juan Bautista Ferrer[81]	Malaga	1526	1576	Priest	1584
Miguel Ferrer	Malaga	1536	1562	Priest	1608
(Pedro) Paulo Ferrer[82]	Malaga	1529	1559	Professor	1618
Pedro Gómez[83]	Antequera	1535	1553	Priest and professed; theologian in Japan	1600
Jerónimo (Romano) de la Higuera[84]	Toledo	1538	1562	Priest and professed	?
Juan Jerónimo[85]	Cabra	1545	1562	Priest and preacher	1605
Cristoforo Laínez[86]	Almazán	1528	1547	Priest; twice dismissed, twice reaccepted	1592
Diego Laínez[87]	Almazán	1512	1540	Professed; second general of the Society	1565
Marco Laínez[88]	Almazán	?	1540	Scholastic; first Jesuit to die after the approbation of the Society	1541
Balthasar de Loarte[89]	Medina del C.	1512	?	Priest; died in Plasencia	1580

Name	*Origin*	*Birth*	*Entrance*	*Activity and Degree*	*Death*
Gaspar de Loarte[90]	Medina del C.	1498	1554	Priest; professed; writer, preacher, superior in Italy	1578
Juan de Loarte	?	?	?	Brother; died in Seville	1583
Gabriel Oliveira (or d'Oliver)[91]	Plasencia	c. 1534	bf. 1564	Spanish; arrived in Goa 1565; spiritual coadjutor 1584	1599
Esteban de la Palma[92]	Toledo	1566	?	Priest	1636
Gabriel de la Palma[93]	Toledo	?	?	Priest	1594
Luis de la Palma[94]	Toledo	1559/1560	1575	Priest and provincial	1641
Diego Pareja[95]	?	?	?	Priest; left c. 1598	?
Alfonso de Pisa[96]	Toledo	1528	1553	Priest and professed; doctor, professor in Rome, Germany, and Poland	1598
Alonso de Polanco[97]	Burgos	1551	1570	Priest; "memorialista"	1599
Francisco de Polanco[98]	?	?	?	Brother	1635
Juan Alfonso de Polanco[99]	Burgos	1515[100]	1541	Priest; professed; secretary of the Society 1547 to 1573; vicar of the Society 1573	1576
Pedro Ramon[101]	Zaragoza	1549	1570	Priest; martyr in Japan	1611

Alexandre de Rhodes[102]	Avignon	1583	1612	Priest and missionary	1660
Pedro de Ribadeneira[103]	Toledo	1526	1540	Priest and profesed; first historian of the Society[104]	1611
Alfonso Roman[105]	Toledo	1520	1549	Priest and professed; provincial	1598
Luis de Santander[106]	Seville	1527	1554	Priest and professed; superior	1593
Balthasar de Santofimia[107]	Seville	1543	1563	Priest	1594
Cyrpriano Suarez (known as Soares)[108]	Ocaña	1524	1549	Professor of rhetoric; professed	1593
Francisco Suarez[109]	Granada	1548	1564	Priest and professed; famous theologian and philosopher	1617
Pedro Tercero[110]	?	?	?	Priest	1615
Francisco de Toledo[111]	Córdoba	1534	1558	Priest and professed; professor in Rome 1559; first Jesuit cardinal 1593	1596
Inácio Tolosa[112]	?	?	?	Priest and missionary in Brazil	1611
Francisco Vásquez[113]	Ávila	1534	1557	Priest and professed; novice master and superior	1603

Name	*Origin*	*Birth*	*Entrance*	*Activity and Degree*	*Death*
Rodrigo de Vida[114]	?	?	bf. 1629	Priest	1689
Ignacio Yáñez de Ávila[115]	Baena	1555	1575	Priest and professed; professor	1621

This second group contains the Portuguese (as well as four Italians). It lists thirty-five Jesuits.

Name	*Origin*	*Birth*	*Entrance*	*Activity and Degree*	*Death*
Luis de Almeida[116]	?	?	c. 1560	Merchant and surgeon; joined in Japan as brother; admitted by C. de Torres	1583
Manual Álvares[117]	Portugal	1527	1549	Priest; famous painter; joined in Portugal and worked in Goa after 1562	1571
Gaspar de Araújo[118]	?	?	?	Priest; dies in Brazil	1603
Antonio Belo[119]	?	1534	1561	Admitted by Quadros in Goa, priest, professor of music, and confessor	1571
Afonao de Castro[120]	Lisbon	1520/1525	bf. 1548	Priest 1549; martyr in the Moluccas	1558
Antonio Dias[121]	?	?	1551	Joined as brother; ordained; minister in Goa	1581

Giovanni Baptista Eliano (or Romano)[122]	Rome	1530	1551	Priest; missionary in the Middle East (Egypt, Lebanon); writer, linguist	1589
Antonio Fernandes[123]	?	?	bf. 1557	Brother; missionary in Ethiopia 1557 to 1593; ordained priest by Oviedo	1593
Jorge Fernandes[124]	?	?	?	In India	1580
Cristovã de Figueiredo[125]	?	?	1563	Admitted by Quadros	?
Manuel Gomes[126]	?	?	?	Priest; sent to Bassein	1591
Francisco Henriques[127]	?	?	?	Priest and professed	1590
Henrique (or Enrique) Henriques[128]	Vila Viçosa	1520	1545	Professed of three vows 1560; missionary in India	1600
Manuel Lopes[129]	Oporto	1525	1545	Priest and professed	1603
?Lopes[130]	?	?	?	Jesuit	?
Pedro Méndes[131]	Vila Viçosa	1558	1575	Priest and missionary	1643
Paolo Mentuato[132]	Morrovalle	1539	c. 1557	Novice	1557
Ferñao de Narbona[133]	?	c. 1536	1557	Joined as brother; pharmacist; worked in Goa	1579

Name	*Origin*	*Birth*	*Entrance*	*Activity and Degree*	*Death*
Miguel dá Nobrega[134]	?	?	1550	Joined in Goa; priest in India	1558
Lourenço Pinheiro[135]	?	?	?	Priest	1590/1591
Andres Pinto[136]	Lisbon	1595	1617	Priest and professed	1654
Alessandro Possevino[137]	Mantova	?	?	Scholastic	1591
Antonio Possevino[138]	Mantova	1533	1559	Priest and professed; preacher and missioinary in Italy, France, and Poland	1611
Enriquez de Quadros[139]	Tangier	1561	1579	Brother	1623
Gaspar Rodriques[140]	?	?	1548	Brother; admitted by Xavier in Goa	1552
Aires Sanches[141]	Lisbon	c. 1527	1562	Joined in Japan; ordained in Macao 1579–1580; good preacher in Japanese	1590
Duarte de Sande[142]	Guimarães	1547	1562	Priest and professed; worked in Goa	1599
Bartolomeu dos Santos[143]	?	c. 1540	1557	Joined as a brother; ordained; worked in Cochin; professed of three vows 1598	1610
Gonçalo Simoes[144]	?	?	?	Priest; master of novices	1626

Manuel de Távora[145]	Coimbra	1534	1552	Admitted by Barzeus in Goa; missionary in the Moluccas, Rome, and Brazil; dismissed 1578	?
Hernando de Torres[146]	Portugal	1537	1569	Brother	1588
Antonio Vaz[147]	Leiria	?	1548	Joined in Goa; ordained 1551; missionary in the Moluccas and India; spiritual coadjutor 1597	1605
Gaspar Vaz[148]	Chaves	1555	1572	Priest and theologian	1596
Gomes Vaz[149]	Serpa	1542	1562	Joined in Portugal as brother; in Goa 1564; priest 1568; professor of theology; professed 1584 in Goa	1610
Manuel da Veiga (Vega)[150]	Coimbra	1549	1569	Priest and professed; theologian	1640

Reflections on the Dialogue between Jew and Non-Jew in the Bible and in Rabbinic Literature

Rabbi Tovia Ben-Chorin

> The Lord your God will keep for you the covenant and the *hesed*.
>
> —(Deut. 7:12)

Dialogue between God and man and between man and man is a foundational element of the Tanach (Jewish Bible). It derives in the first instance from the relationship of the deity to humankind as such, and later, specifically to the Children of Israel. This relationship is expressed not only by means of verbal revelation, which is directed exclusively to individuals, but by the very possibility of discourse and dialogue with the deity, which itself derives from the concept of *brith* (covenant).

The first biblical covenant comes into being after the Flood. "I will maintain My covenant with you: never again shall all flesh be cut off by the waters of a flood, and never again shall there be flood to destroy the earth" (Gen. 9:11). A careful look at this chapter reveals not only God's obligation to man but also man's obligation to God, an obligation that is expressed in a number of basic mitzvoth (commandments), later referred to in rabbinic parlance as the seven Noachite Commandments (Tos Av. Zara 8).

The covenant is in essence the transformation of the basic discourse into mutual obligation, formulated in covenantal terms. What underlies the covenant is obligation/commitment which includes responsibility to the partners in the covenant, be they family members, friends, master and slave, or any other form of belonging in which commitment plays a role. Covenantal dialogue has a unique base in the connection between God and Noah (as an individual and also as representative of all humanity) and between God and the People of Israel at Sinai. It reflects mutual obligation accompanied by many mitzvoth that relate to the relationship between man and man—be he a Jew, that is, "son of the Sinaitic covenant," or a non-Jew, that is, "son of the Noachite covenant"—and of course, between man and the divine.

There is no specific expression or phrase in the Tanach that is in any way similar to the word "dialogue." And the question then presents itself: How is it that a book based upon what God says to man and man's turning to God, through direct speech, prayer, ritual, poetry, music and the like, a book in which the covenant between God and the universe is so fundamental, appears not to contain any definitive expression for the concept of dialogue?

Rabbi and professor of archaeology Nelson Glueck wrote his doctoral dissertation in German on *Das Wort Hesed im altestamentlichen Sprachgebrauche als menschliche und göttliche gemainschaftsgemässe Verhaltungsweise.*[1] A study of this dissertation, as well as of the entry *Hesed* in the *Biblical Encyclopedia*, written by Yizhak Heinemann, enables the reader to delve into the fine points of this concept: "*Hesed* . . . does not reflect purely legal relationships but rather the existence of the spiritual connection which grows out of the covenant . . . good deeds without any expectation of recompense."[2] Thus *hesed* is in many instances found coupled with the words *truth* (*emet*) and *faithfulness* (*emuna*). As Heinemann points out, the concept of *hesed* expanded from something directed toward the Children of Israel to a concept directed toward all humanity, finding its ultimate expression in the words of the Prophet Micah (eighth century BCE): "He has told [*higeed*] you, O man, what is good and what the Lord requires/expects [*doresh*] of you: only to do justice and to love *hesed* (deeds of loving kindness) [goodness] and to walk modestly with your God" (Mic. 6:8). It must be emphasized that the prophet addresses himself here to his audience not as members of his nation but as part of humankind.

The two verbs that precede the instruction itself—*NGD* (to tell, explain) and *DRSh* (to require, expect)—are verbs of encouragement and do not carry the same weight as *ZIVA* (command). *Hesed* includes an element of affection for the other, without which there can be no *hesed* relationship. Therefore Martin Mordecai Buber, the great Jewish existentialist of the twentieth century, translates *hesed* by the Old German word *huld*, which implies something of sympathy, empathy, finding favor, friendliness, a positive spirit, affection, cordiality, loyalty, and devotion, all of which are human qualities that cannot be commanded. *Hesed* in speech and deed can be realized only through "telling" and "expecting." The covenant, insofar as it is based upon mutual agreement, is the formal aspect of *hesed*. Through *hesed* I can relate to my partner in covenant, even when he is not my equal; without *hesed* we cannot be true covenantal partners. A true covenant cannot be forced. Rather it is an expression of the desire of the partners to establish a relationship. Therefore the highest expression of covenant lies not in the commandments but rather in the system of *hesed* created between/among the partners.

Dialogue based upon covenant plays a most central role in Buber's teaching. The great innovation of this preeminent thinker is his view that the dynamic of the dialogue exists outside the world of the mitzvoth. He still retains the concept of the ethical and moral teaching whose source is the divine, but there is a total relinquishing of both the ethical ritual as well as the purely ritual commandments. This approach, which is problematic in my eyes, was offered some two thousand years ago by another Jew, Paul/Saul. The latter placed in the center, as a replacement for the mitzvoth, the belief in an individual figure incorporating within itself all of the mitzvoth as well as the belief in Resurrection and the coming of the Messiah, while Buber accepts Micah's three-pronged principle without any substitute for mitzvoth. (It is beyond the scope of this paper to deal with the concept of love as it relates to *hesed* and covenant, on the one hand, and its implications for the two Jews, Paul and Buber, on the other hand. However, it is related to our discussion through Micah, who speaks of the need to "love *hesed.*")

The Tanach also provides us with an example of *hesed* between tribes or nations. When King Saul is instructed by Samuel to destroy the most dangerous enemy of Israel, the Amalekites, we find the following: "And Saul said to the Kenites, 'Come, withdraw at once from among the Amalekites, that I may not destroy you along with them; for you showed *hesed* to all the Israelites when they left Egypt'" (1 Sam. 15:6).

The dialogue with the non-Jew, the stranger, is obviously also an outcome of the influence of the Wisdom Literature in the Tanach. It bears testimony to the connection with the outside surrounding world from Mesopotamia to Egypt and later on with the Hellenistic world. That this dialogue was also extremely important for the Sages can be seen from the arguments as to which of the Wisdom Books should be included in the biblical canon and which should be excluded. The inclusion of some of the books testifies to a spiritual connection and a truthful, nonapologetic discourse with those around them. In the Book of Proverbs, mention is even made of two non-Jewish wise men, Agur, son of Jakeh (Prov. 30:1), and Lemuel, king of Massa (Prov. 31:1). Earlier on, mention was also made in the Book of Kings of famous wise men from Mesopotamia and Egypt (1 Kings 5:11)

An example of the spiritual connection achieved through wisdom between a Jewish wise man and a non-Jewish person seeking his wisdom, that is, the Queen of Sheba, is illustrated in the description of the latter's visit to King Solomon in Jerusalem, described in great detail in 1 Kings 10. Wisdom is not only a matter of the spirit; it also finds expression in the magnificent wealth that the "wise one" accumulates. In addition, it enhances and expands his reputation. If he is a king, it strengthens his position (1 Kings 23:24). It should be noted, by the way, that this combination of wealth and wisdom (in that order, in the passage in Kings) eventually led to Solomon's downfall. His great wealth brought with it many foreign wives. "In his old age, his wives turned away Solomon's heart after other gods, and he was not as wholeheartedly devoted to the Lord his God as his father David had been" (1 Kings 11:4). At the end of his days, Solomon's fabled wisdom did not sustain him, personally or in the administration of his kingdom, and the result was not long in coming.

In the book of Leviticus, we find reference to the connection and the special relationship to the foreigner arising out of the experience of Egypt: "The stranger who resides with you shall be to you as one of your citizens; you shall love him as yourself, for you were strangers in the Land of Egypt: I the Lord am your God" (Lev. 19:34). The Jewish dialectic again comes to expression in the Bible in connection with the relationship to the stranger.

On the one hand, we find clear laws limiting the contact with the non-Jew as much as possible, mainly through the prohibition against intermarriage and the dietary laws. This is one side of the coin. The other side of the coin is represented in the dialogue between the Children of Israel and the non-Jews who attach themselves to the Jewish people that we find in the second Isaiah after the destruction of the First Temple, which speaks of "the foreigners who attach themselves to the Lord, to minister to Him and to love the name of the Lord, to be His servants" (Isa. 56:6). Isaiah clearly speaks here of free association without any expectation of actual conversion. (The rabbis later did interpret these verses to mean conversion, despite the fact that the concept of conversion does not exist in the Tanach). Verse 6 continues: "all who keep the Sabbath and do not profane it, and who hold fast to My covenant," which is in fact a partial repetition of verse 2 in the same chapter: "Happy is the man who does this, the man who holds fast to it; who keeps the Sabbath and does not profane it, and stays his hand from doing any evil."

What is the connection in the mind of the prophet between refraining from profaning the Sabbath and refraining from doing evil, which is the goal of all morality? Is there something inherent in the Sabbath that counteracts evil? In order to prevent the doing of evil, action is required. Looking at Genesis 2, verses 1 to 3, we see that on the Sabbath, on the day on which He ceased to create, something new was added nonetheless: "blessing" and "sanctification," two powerful elements that are indeed the counterbalance to evil. By his very nature, man is a creature with a strong impulse for action, which must be curbed on the Sabbath. (I would dare to say that it would appear that even the Holy One, Blessed be He, at least from the human perspective, can also not totally desist from "doing" on the Sabbath.) The blessing and sanctifying that God "does" on the seventh day (Sabbath) bring us full cycle to Genesis 1, verse 1, when the "spirit" of God swept over the water. In total opposition to the later rabbinic Halakhah, which prohibits the non-Jew from keeping the Sabbath, Isaiah turns to all mankind with the instruction to keep the Sabbath and refrain from doing evil. The keeping of the Lord's Sabbath on the part of all mankind contributes to the balance between spirit and matter in the world of creation. It is a clarion call to all humanity.

Rabbinic Literature

The best known example of dialogue between Jews and non-Jews in rabbinic literature is that which takes place between R. Judah the Prince (often referred to simply as Rabi) and Antoninus. The time frame of this dialogue is noteworthy: namely, after the destruction of the Second Temple in Jerusalem in 70 CE. There is a very interesting parallel between the above and the prophetic universalism that developed after the destruction of the First Temple in 586 BCE and the experience of the Babylonian Exile. This Antoninus is in fact representative of several Roman caesars. In essence, what is important here is that these stories or legends attest to the fact that philosophical and theological discussions were current within the Jewish intellectual strata. It is not even the identity of the characters that is important but rather the fact that despite the nearly total destruction of the land of Israel as a result of the failure of the Bar Kochba rebellion (132–135 CE), the dialogue with the non-Jews continued. They even went so far as to question whether there might even be those among them who were deserving of Olam HaBa (the World to Come). Indeed, the rather astonishing opinion of the Tanna R. Yehoshua (third-generation Tanna, 80–120 CE), in the face of the Roman experience, is as follows: "There are righteous people among the nations who have a place in the world to come" (Tos San. 13:2).

Returning to the conversations between Rabi and Antoninus (B. San 91a(b); B. Avoda Zara 10a(b)), the discussions relate to such diverse matters as the administration of the state, body and soul, and the reign of the Evil Inclination. Other references are to discussions between R. Yohanan ben Zakkai, the founder of the academy at Jabne after the destruction of the Second Temple, and one of the Roman rulers, Contaricus. The latter argued with R. Yohanan about whether Moses was a knowledgeable, dependable treasurer or possibly a thief, based upon the fact that the numbers of the Levites mentioned in different parts of the Pentateuch differ one from another. (The same discussion is reported in brief in the J Talmud San., chap. 1, at the end of the chapter.) Yet another question (J Talmud San., chap. 1, end of Halacha 2): "Hegemon Agnatos asked R. Yohanan" about the law with respect to a bull—known to be dangerous—which kills a man or a woman. The law determines that the bull shall be stoned and its master put to death as well (Exod. 21:29):

> He [R. Yohanan] said to him [the Hegemon]: "The accomplice of a thief is like the thief." And when he came out, his students said to him, "You pushed him away with a reed, [i.e., your response was not convincing] since surely the bull does not have the knowledge or the understanding which man has, when he provides direct or indirect support to thieves. What would you say to us?" He said to them: "It is written, the bull shall be stoned and his master put to death. As the death of the master, so the death of the bull. Just as the death of the master would require 23 [judges], in order to examine and investigate the case, so with the bull as well: examination and investigation by 23."

Three things can immediately be derived from this short narrative. First, discussions took place with non-Jews. Second, the students were also included in these discussions or were at least witness to them. Given that the teachers were seen as role models for their students, the very fact of their presence delivers the message that the dialogue with non-Jews was to be cultivated. Third, the dialogue did not have to be based upon detailed halakhic thinking but should attempt to come to terms with and make use of the other's way of thinking, which emphasized the philosophical basis of the law rather than the practical law from which the philosophy is derived. In the internal Jewish discussion, on the other hand, the teacher made use of a distinctively halakhic argument.

> Traditions have been preserved regarding four discussions between R. Akiva and Titus Annius Rufus or Turnosrufos (various spellings possible), the Roman high commissioner in Judea during the Bar Kochba rebellion, the same person who later gave the command to torture R. Akiva to death. And it is precisely with Akiva that he is supposed to have discussed the attributes of the Holy One, Blessed be He, the nature of His Providence and His Sovereignty in this world, as well as the nature of and reasons for the mitzvoth (B. Baba Batra 10a; Genesis Rabba 11:5; Tanhuma, Teruma 3; Tazria 5). There is even a legend that states that the wife of the said Turnosrufos converted to Judaism and married R. Akiva, who became wealthy through her (B. Avoda Zara 20a). In addition, there are stories that connect R. Joshua ben Chanina and Adrianus Caesar in Rome, who were said to have discussed matters of faith and the Torah commandments (B. Hullin 59b[60a]), as well as a disputation between the same sage and the Sabi (wise men) of Athens (B. Berachot 8b).

Let us conclude this survey by returning to the seven Noachite Commandments (as extrapolated from Tos. Avoda Zara 8). The children of Noah were commanded to follow seven precepts, one positive: 1. judges (establishing a system of law); and the rest prohibitive: 2.

avoda zara (idol worship); 3. invoking God's name in a curse; 4. incest; 5. the shedding of blood; 6. stealing; 7. the cutting of the flesh of a living animal for food. The above represents a rabbinic definition, formulated at the end of the second or beginning of the third centuries CE, of the basic minimum requirements for human society; in our terminology, humanism. It is essential to understand that from the rabbinic point of view, whoever keeps those seven "commandments" is worthy not only of Olam HaBa (the World to Come) but also of being taken seriously in this world. Moreover, when they live close to, or among, Jews, they have rights (and obligations) which must be respected by both sides.

This position is apparently accepted by Maimonides (twelfth century CE) as found in Hilchot Melachim 8:11: "One who accepts the 7 [Noachite] commandments and takes care to fulfill them, is to be counted among the Righteous of the Nations and is deserving of the World to Come." However, he continues with a very problematic caveat: "But if one observes them due to having arrived at this conclusion on the basis of human logic, he is neither to be considered a *ger toshav* [a non-Jew allowed to live among Jews as he is not an idol worshipper—a rabbinic redefinition of a biblical concept] nor one of the Righteous of the World, nor one of their wise men."

While one is obligated out of intellectual integrity to quote the last sentence of this Halakhah, one cannot agree with its premise if one is committed to the principle of true dialogue, which by definition would have to include both atheists and theists as active and invaluable partners.

Summary

We have drawn from the literature those sources that point to dialogue as well as mutual respect between Jews and non-Jews. Obviously, there are also texts that testify to the tendency toward separation and seclusion. I truly hope that there has been a change in the understanding of what man is and the expectations that are held of him/her from the twelfth century to the twenty-first century, and that we can all agree that understanding among people cannot be achieved on the basis of physical force or threat. But how can it be achieved? Through true dialogue, that is, discussion and deepened knowledge of the other, which will enable the creation of a common base of assumptions on which we can build and move forward, as provided by the seven Noachite Commandments in earlier times.

The subject of dialogue as discourse arose within a Jewish-Christian framework. Those of us already involved in this process who are truly committed to peace and acts leading to peace (*darchai shalom*) in order to achieve *tikkun olam* and bringing nigh the messianic hope or the coming of the Savior have to be reminded of a most significant fact: the dialogue between us is not reflective of a new Jewish yearning that arose in nineteenth-century Europe and eventually led to the modern post-Holocaust, mid-twentieth-century Christian response but of a strong tradition of mutuality, respect, and an awareness of what is held in common and what separates us, found in the ancient, inspirational-revelation-permeated Jewish sources.

As is said in the Alenu prayer, with which every Jewish public service concludes: "[Then] shall all the inhabitants of the world know and acknowledge that to You every knee must bend and every tongue pledge loyalty." It is that same "You" that directs us toward knowing one another, toward harmony, while preserving that which is unique to each and every human being. In this way we nourish the divine image found in each one of us, which can be brought to the surface and realized through dialogue and *hesed*, in speech and in action.

The Goal of the Ignatian Exercises and Soloveitchik's Halakhic Spirituality

Christian M. Rutishauser, S.J.

1. Remarks on Soloveitchik's Intellectual Biography

Christians are perhaps familiar with the life and spiritual thinking of Ignatius of Loyola, but only a few know Rabbi Joseph Dov Soloveitchik, the spiritual mentor of so-called modern Jewish Orthodoxy in the United States. Soloveitchik was born in Lithuania in 1903 and died in Boston, Massachusetts, in 1993. His biography reflects the intellectual history of the twentieth century and its struggle with religion, which had to find a new standpoint in a secular world. Furthermore, his life was spent between two poles: the rabbinic intellectual and European culture of his origin, on the one hand, and on the other, the modern and secular American culture, with its belief in science, in which he tried to establish an Orthodox rabbinic lifestyle. He is considered a transition figure in a double sense: he embodied the shift from European to American Jewry, and he tried to bridge the cultural change with which the twentieth century was impregnated.

Three cities with their intellectual character left their mark on Soloveitchik's life: Brisk, Berlin, and Boston.

Brisk: His grandfather was the founder of the Brisker Talmud School, with its highly rationalistic and formal hermeneutical method and its openness to Maimonides' Halakhic work *Mishneh Torah*. Being the heir of an intellectually trained rabbinic family, Soloveitchik had a disciplined, classical rabbinic upbringing. His mother, who was influenced by Russian authors, implanted an appreciation for literature in him.

Berlin: The Berlin of the Weimar Republic was the second decisive stage in his biography. He was a young, sensitive, and eager student when he came into contact with the intellectual world of the German metropolis in the 1920s. He became involved with the latest developments of scientific and cultural life. But above all, he took part in the revival of Jewish culture and tradition that seemed evident in those years. He majored in philosophy and received a doctorate for his dissertation on Hermann Cohen, "Das reine Denken und die Seinskonstituierung bei Hermann Cohen." The neo-Kantianism he got to know there would serve him later in interpreting the Halakhah as a system of categories and tools in order to structure the world according to God's will.

And finally, Boston: Soloveitchik would become the builder of bridges between science and rabbinic studies in the United States, where he lived from 1932 to the end of his life. His dialectical way of thinking, which he was trained in through the study of the Talmud, unfolded itself in connecting the different worlds he lived in. As professor of Talmud and philosophy at the Rabbi Isaac Elchanan Theological Seminary, which is affiliated with Yeshiva University in Manhattan, as well as rabbi and teacher in the field of adult education, he had only one goal: the implementation of a halakhic lifestyle in the different realms of modern secular and pluralistic society. At heart he was not just a scholar or a scientist but a charismatic figure who dedicated himself with all his vigor to establishing an Orthodox rabbinic community. The growing new Jewish-American community was to be deeply rooted in the genuine core of Judaism—the Halakhah—and at the same time be open and ready to participate in the life of American society, so quickly developing in his time. Soloveitchik perceived the contemporary successful growth of Liberal and Conservative Judaism as a "chumming up to the *zeitgeist* and a watering down of the true Jewish identity."[1]

This short summary of Soloveitchik's biography and the goals for which he lived may have a familiar ring to Christians formed in Ignatian spirituality. Building up a religious community in dialogue with the larger society and operating by establishing a well-organized way of life are strategies similar to those of the Society of Jesus. More by intuition than by study, I recognized an affinity between Soloveitchik's way of thinking and living and a Jesuit approach to reality. Then, by mere accident, I took his book *Halakhic Man* from the shelves of the Hecht Synagogue at the Hebrew University in Jerusalem and leafed through it on a boring summer afternoon. This short text was for me the beginning of an intensive research into his writings that strengthened my first impression more and more. Here I would like to present some observations and reflections on Soloveitchik's halakhic spirituality in comparison with an Ignatian spirituality that has its origin in Ignatius of Loyola and *Spiritual Exercises*.

2. *Halakhic Man* and the *Spiritual Exercises*: Structural Similarities

My main source for Soloveitchik's halakhic spirituality is his *Halakhic Man*, a classical essay that describes the lifestyle of modern Orthodox Judaism. This publication fits especially well with our purpose, for it is not a rabbinical commentary on parts of the Torah nor does it present a theologico-theoretical worldview. It outlines in its first part, however, the halakhic approach to reality by contrasting it with other ways of perceiving the world that surrounds us. In the second part, Soloveitchik paints a portrait of a halakhic person's life task, his vocation and creativity, which he has to realize in a more and more perfect form. He shows a way of personal development based on the Halakhah that Orthodox Jews should follow. The essay is a spiritual text in the strict sense of the word: a spirituality that designs the concrete practice of religious life and helps guide the individual to self-realization before God.

Of course, the genre of *Halakhic Man* is different from Ignatius's *Spiritual Exercises.* The latter is a manual containing a series of meditations to find one's own vocation, a book with actual, practical exercises. It enters more into the psychological inner world of the individual and offers tools to form it. *Halakhic Man*, by contrast, is an essay that describes the halakhic way to mold one's life. But both texts present a concrete spiritual path and both are based on a twofold structure. Whereas Soloveitchik presents the lifestyles of *Homo religiosus* and *Homo scienticus* in order to distinguish a life lived according to Halakhah, Ignatius guides the person doing the exercises in the first phase to inner freedom through liberating him from sinful and negative behavior: life should be structured according to the order of creation. Thus both works present a "negative image" to open a new way of life.

The second part of the *Spiritual Exercises* begins with a new perspective marked by a new "principle and fundament," the "Call of the King."[2] Now the goal is to find the personal form of following the historical Jesus and to imitate his way of life as authentically as possible, even if it should lead through suffering, as the book's section on the Cross teaches. Part two of Soloveitchik's essay also focuses on presenting a role model. He transforms Maimonides' ideal prophet into a model of a wise, pious, and creative personality living in accordance with the Halakhah; the reader is invited to an analogous self-creation. Hence both Soloveitchik and Ignatius first deliver a negative image and then follow it with a model of life the addressee should adopt.

3. Evaluating Religious Experiences

Halakhic Man opens with the following passage:

> Halakhic man reflects two opposing selves; two disparate images are embodied within his soul and spirit. On the one hand

he is as far removed from *homo religiosus* as east is from west and is identical, in many respects, to prosaic, cognitive man; on the other hand he is a man of God, possessor of an ontological approach that is devoted to God and of a world view saturated with the radiance of the Divine Presence. . . . Halakhic man is an anti-nomic type for a dual reason: (1) he bears within the deep recesses of his personality the soul of *homo religious*, that soul which, as was stated above, suffers from the pangs of self-contradiction and self-negation; (2) at the same time halakhic man's personality also embraces the soul of cognitive man, and this soul contradicts all of the desires and strivings of the religious soul. However, these opposing forces, which struggle together in the religious consciousness of halakhic man, are not of a destructive or disjunctive nature. Halakhic man is not some illegitimate, unstable hybrid. On the contrary, out of the contradictions and antinomies there emerges a radiant, holy personality whose soul has been purified in the furnace of struggle and the opposition and redeemed in the fires of the torments of spiritual disharmony to a degree unmatched by the universal *homo religious*. The deep split of the soul prior to its being united may, at times, raise a man to a rank of perfection, which for sheer brilliance and beauty is unequaled by any level attained by the simple, whole personality who has never been tried by the pangs of spiritual discord. "In accordance with the suffering is the reward" (*Avot* 5, 23) and in accordance with the split the union! This spiritual fusion that characterizes halakhic man is distinguished by its consummate splendor, for did not the split touch the very depths, the innermost core, of his being? . . . Our aim in this essay is to penetrate deep into the structure of halakhic man's consciousness and to determine the precise nature of this "strange, singular" being who reveals himself to the world from within his narrow, constricted "four cubits" (*Berakhot* 8a), his hands soiled by the gritty realia of practical Halakhah (see *Berakhot* 4a) . . . to comprehend the nature of halakhic man, the master of Talmudic dialectics.[3]

These opening sentences are simply an overture that casts a first glance at the spiritual growth of a halakhic existence. The central themes already appear. A way of life according to the Halakhah is perceived as the fruit of a means of purification and self-creation. It cannot be implemented in a person's life overnight but will end up as a religious ideal that develops out of strict self-control.

Soloveitchik delineates the common *Homo religiosus* to contrast him with the halakhic man. The *Homo religiosus* he has in mind is, on the one hand, the romantic believer, the idealistic (and Protestant) Christian individual standing in contrast and tension, if not in opposition, to the religious community and institutions, perceived as alienating the true religious core. Soloveitchik rejects this concept of the Christian believer that had been praised in nineteenth- and twentieth-century Germany and which has been popular in some European and North American circles up to the present. His religious self-understanding wants to be quite different. Soloveitchik is also opposed to mysticism. The *Homo mysticus*, with his tendency to flee the concrete reality of creation, with his hope of overcoming the world, and with the ultimate spiritual goal of illumination or mystical experience is Soloveitchik's antitype. Yet if we look closer at Soloveitchik's argumentation, we realize that he does not completely reject mystics or the natural religious striving for an experience of transcendence.

The experience of *Homo religiosus* is, however, relativized and integrated as a necessary phase in the growth of the halakhic personality. The experience of sublimity and grandeur or any other religious experience is not the aim of halakhic life. Its goal, rather, is the molding of concrete reality through practical Halakhah. Halakhic man is deeply touched by natural religious feeling and can find God's presence in it, as Soloveitchik illustrates by the experience of an overwhelming sunset.[4] But the ideal of the halakhic man is serving God by mitzvoth and not a sounding of the religious feelings. The experience becomes integrated in personal act, which is itself formed by the stream of tradition, by the Halakhah coming down to the present through the rabbinic chain. Subjective experience, personal behavior, and ethical prescription are welded together.

Let us now look at Ignatius of Loyola, who, after being deeply moved and touched by the beauty of the sky at night with its stars, did not confine himself to the religious feeling provoked by the sublimity and grandeur of the universe but asked how he could serve the Lord and the Creator. Ignatian spirituality has an ambivalent attitude similar to that of Soloveitchik toward spiritual and mystical experiences. On the one hand, the Christian should pray to obtain consolation, the experience of the divine Spirit, and to be strengthened by the real presence of God. On the other hand, this subjective and inner experience is strictly integrated into a way to follow Jesus. The mystical experience is linked to apostolic service in regard to the world. Christ, living for the Kingdom of Heaven on earth and for the redemption of the world, is the framework in which to mold a mystical experience.

Of course, Ignatius does not have to reject the romantic believer in the sixteenth century as Soloveitchik has to do at the beginning of the twentieth. And Ignatius is more open to mystical experiences and leads people on a mystical path, whereas Soloveitchik expresses a certain distrust of mysticism—although the religious and aesthetic experience radiates throughout his writings. But both of them, facing the subjective experience of God's grace or presence, immediately integrate it into an ethical framework, Ignatius into the *imitatio Christi* and Soloveitchik into the Halakhah. This reaction or answer on the ethical level does not derive immediately from the religious or mystical experience but is transmitted through an external factor, the revelation of God given to the whole religious community, the Gospel or the Torah respectively.

The transformation of the religious experience into religious ethics, rendered possible through the objective revelation, is a typical Jewish gesture, according to Soloveitchik. But it was also the gesture of Ignatius and the first Jesuits, as we have seen. A historical perspective could throw some light on this. The fact that the Jesuit way of life was developed in sixteenth-century Spain, where the Islamic spirit and the Jewish spirit were still present but in hiding because of Roman Catholic domination and persecution, can explain some structural similarities. The historical influence of structural elements from Judaism on the Jesuit order is especially significant.[5] Ignatius had a warm sympathy for Jews, and the Inquisition even suspected him of observing the Sabbath.[6] The second general superior of the order, Ignatius's successor Diego Laínez, was a *converso*, and in his converted family several halakhic prescriptions remained valid. Moreover, at the end of the sixteenth century one third of the Jesuits were of Jewish origin.

However these historical facts may be interpreted, we can observe similar structures in Ignatius's and Soloveitchik's approach to religious experience. For Ignatius, the transformation of the religious and aesthetic experience into ethics serves a soteriological aim, because every Christian should contribute through his life to the redemption of the world that Christ's coming expresses. In the spirituality of the *Spiritual Exercises*, each Christian should help to proclaim the good news through words and deeds so that faith and justice may flourish and the history of salvation be experienced as something present. According to Soloveitchik, an analogous transformation insures the participation in God's act of the ongoing creation. Halakhic man creates the world anew through observing mitzvoth. The religious and metaphysical motives are different, but both provide the human being with a great responsibility and give him an enormous dignity. In a typically modern gesture, man becomes, in cooperation with a redeeming God, the fulfiller of creation, and thus a religious humanism is established.

The identification of the *Homo religiosus* in *Halakhic Man* with the Christian believer, so often asserted by interpreters of Soloveitchik's writings, cannot be accepted any longer. It misunderstands Soloveitchik's halakhic justification. By not perceiving the real target of his argument, it contributes to an image of Soloveitchik being in opposition to Christians on all major theological questions. His evaluation of the religious and mystical experience, however, shows quite a number of structural similarities with Ignatian and so with Christian spirituality.

What is the fruit of this outlook on Soloveitchik for a Jesuit theology? First of all, this Jewish-Christian comparison makes one realize how similar is the approach to reality of both religious traditions and how both perceive the human being in his spiritual pilgrimage. Both link the subjective experience to factors that do not stem from spiritual conduct. By doing so, they connect the individual spiritual way closely with ethics. They also build a bridge between the individual and his religious community, with its task to take an active part in history. In the *Spiritual Exercises*, this dimension is stressed by the rules of charity, the rules of *sentire cum ecclesia*, the daily Eucharist, the imperative of the Church, and the representation by the spiritual director of the religious community.

According to the individualistic *Zeitgeist* that infuses the spiritual searching of our time, these dimensions are very often secondary, if not repressed. To discern the connection between the spiritual life of the individual and the religious community and to link it with an ethical dimension is even more important as the Ignatian spiritual way is compared with the spiritual ways of Eastern religions, such as Zen, yoga, or sadhana. Keeping in mind Soloveitchik's perception of religious experience formed by the Halakhah and put into the chain of rabbinic tradition, followers of Ignatius may be encouraged to put the spiritual way of the *Spiritual Exercises* again in the context of the general vocation of the Church and in the framework of the history of salvation.

4. Intellectuality as a Religious Ideal

We return to the *Homo scienticus*, the second type of being and approach to reality that Soloveitchik uses in order to describe the halakhic existence in his essay *Halakhic Man*. By this second demarcation Soloveitchik creates the space for his own vision of Jewish life. So he neither criticizes Jewish life modes, nor paints a negative image of Jewish existence, nor recalls sins in order to stimulate his reader to follow a halakhic way. *Teshuwa* (repentance), as it marks the first phase of the *Spiritual Exercises* of Ignatius, is indeed a topic dear to Soloveitchik too. But he does not start with a call for teshuwa in *Halakhic Man*. He prefers to describe the positive seductive modes of life that fascinate the modern religious Jew. Being aware of the power of mimesis in the act of learning, he first deconstructs the appeal of these life modes.

According to this pedagogic strategy, alongside the *Homo religiosus* he presents the modern scientist who advances by verifying his method of empiric research. The belief in science threatens modern man insofar as its way of life tends to replace religion. Although religion and empiric science are not only differentiated but very often in opposition or contradiction in modern societies, and although halakhic man is a deep religious personality, Soloveitchik sees a true affinity between the *Homo scienticus* and the halakhic man. Whereas the scientist is not afraid to approach any realm of reality with his instruments, his methodological concepts, and his critical thinking, the halakhic man approaches all reality with a rational attitude and with the Halakhah as a tool in his hand. Both submit reality and construe a coherent system, the first in order to optimize living conditions and the second in order to present reality according to God's will.

The parable of the *Homo scienticus* for a halakhic existence so dear to Soloveitchik was often commented on by showing the neo-Kantian presumptions it implies and by comparing it to other hermeneutical concepts.[7] In our context, it is the effects of this comparison for a halakhic existence that are of interest:

1. There is no fixed profane or sacred domain, but the halakhic man has the task to enter into all realms of reality in order to sanctify it through mitzvoth.
2. The Halakhah is perceived not only as a system of rules and laws but as a set of methods to approach the world.

3. Life has to be formed, organized, and based on the source of Halakhah so that it bears its imprint. The Orthodox Jew becomes God's copartner in the field of creation. The *imitatio Creatoris* contains the genuine characteristics Soloveitchik adds to the general concept of *imitatio Dei*.
4. The parable has a positive effect on the perception of modern science, above all on natural science. Halakhic man is very open to science for he sees in it the secular parallel to developing creation, for the natural and rational approach to reality is evaluated as the means the Halakhah uses for sanctifying reality.

The *Spiritual Exercises* of Ignatius do not themselves explicitly deal with science and education. But even in the earliest period of the Society of Jesus, Jesuits began to contribute to secular education and training. Science and intellectual training were always perceived in the history of the Jesuits as means to the greater glory of God or, in other words, for his sanctification. Ignatian spirituality offers in the *Spiritual Exercises* two major tools in order to deal with the autonomous laws of the different realms of reality as found in the Gospel. On the one hand, there is the text of the *principle and foundation*, and on the other hand, there are the rules for the discernment of the Spirits. Sent by the king, Christ, into all domains of reality, the *principle and foundation* teach the relationship of all reality by integrating it into the process of glorifying God in an ever more perfect form. The rules of discernment help one to act in ways that are not fixed in advance but open to discernment in any moment as to how this situation can be directed to God and be related to God. The *Spiritual Exercises* do not deliver first and foremost spiritual content. However, they offer a *modus procedendi*, a mode for going ahead into unknown fields. The rational approach and the will to shape life in all its aspects are common to Ignatian spiritual existence and to that of the halakhic man.

The intellectual aspect of the mode of life was strongly emphasized in the history of the Jesuits, above all in the nineteenth and early twentieth century. But in their foundation texts, especially in the *Spiritual*

Exercises, it is less explicit than in Soloveitchik's writings. Ignatian spirituality wants to form human beings on all levels of social competence, intellectual training, spiritual ability, and the like. Humble and modest behavior, moreover, should express a certain poverty and give a special tone to apostolic activities. The intellectual task is no more important than any other activity in Ignatian spirituality, but knowledge is necessary to act correctly.

However, Soloveitchik, due to his origin in an intellectually well-trained and anti-Hasidic family, stresses intellectual studies. So he follows, in the second part of *Halakhic Man*, Aristotle's and Maimonides' concept of actualizing the possibilities and capacities that lie hidden in the human being. The use of the intellect is the highest form of actualization and aims finally to be part of the divine intellect. Seen in a Jewish Orthodox framework, it means, on the one hand, that God's intellect is best expressed in his revelation, in the Halakhah. In consequence, the halakhicly trained and wise man is the real prophet and the ideal religious hero. Studying Talmud is the outstanding self-realization for a halakhic existence. On the other hand, the belief in science that Soloveitchik shares with his contemporaries and the cult of the ingenious personality of his time which influenced him led to a strong emphasis on the intellectual aspect of religious life. Both Soloveitchik and Ignatius paint a religious ideal, on the intellectual and on other levels of existence, which can be reached only by few. So it is no wonder that both concepts of religious life were labeled elitist and Soloveitchik was judged as the "poet of the Halakhic hero" (David Hartman).

Let us summarize our reflections: intellectual training in secular fields combined with deep understanding of one's own tradition of revelation is characteristic of both spiritualities. Whereas according to Soloveitchik the Orthodox Jew has to concretize this pretentious ideal in an ongoing process—often named by the formula *Torah va-Avodah* or *Torah im Derekh Eretz* by his interpreters—the Jesuit-trained Christian tries to carry out his secular activity and profession by his ethical and theological training. Just as halakhic man walks on the path of Halakhah as developed in the rabbinic tradition and thereby infiltrates all parts of society with its spirit, so Ignatian spirituality invites one to walk in the *imitatio Christi* and thus diffuses the spirit of his "Rabbi" in the modern world. The intellectual training, so praised in both traditions, is never an end in itself but is directed to concrete deeds and to taking responsibility for others. The realm of the Halakhah for Soloveitchik parallels that of the Kingdom of God for Ignatius: they are realms to be developed and unfolded.

5. The Human Being Facing God's Revelation

Joseph D. Soloveitchik and Ignatius of Loyola lived in different social and religious contexts that left their genuine imprint on both of them. The structural similarities between the religious ways of life they formulated, however, are obvious. The question arises: Where does this affinity come from? It is a fact that Soloveitchik worked on at least one project with the Jesuit-run Loyola University in Chicago. The cooperation, however, is late and limited and witnesses to nothing more than the common interests and strategies of Yeshiva and Loyola University.

Soloveitchik's adoption of non-Jewish European intellectual history in Berlin and later in North America brought him in contact with the spirit of the Romantic movement and the post-Kantian and neo-Kantian philosophies. His theological counterpart on the Christian side was the Lutheran and Protestant culture marked by thinkers such as Sören Kierkegaard, Karl Barth, and others. Of course, he studied the philosophical writings of Roman Catholics, such as Max Scheeler and Henri Bergson, for example. Both were Catholics of Jewish origin. So Soloveitchik encountered the Roman Catholic faith community in the United States as another religious minority that fought for its own stand in the secular and Anglican-dominated society. The influence of contemporary Jesuit theology on him is nowhere to be found. Thus the affinity between halakhic and Ignatian spirituality stems not from historical influence but above all from two main preconditions, an anthropological and a theological one.

Concerning anthropology, Soloveitchik developed his existential perspective during his lifetime. Although it seems to be sometimes overshadowed by idealistic thinking, his existential attitude always radiates through his writings. According to him, the original existential experience is not caused by confrontation with fear or death, with the absurdity of life or with loathing, but arises out of the awareness of loneliness.

> However, loneliness is not a physical fact, nor is it a most painful psychological condition. It is far more than that. Loneliness is a spiritual human situation. If I may say, it is an existential awareness or a metaphysical state, not only of the mind but of the soul as well. Loneliness reflects both the greatness of man as a unique metaphysical being, as well as his ontological insecurity as an incomplete being. . . . Metaphysical man finds himself in the throes of loneliness.[8]

Loneliness becomes reality and creates its own life conditions, and in Soloveitchik's eyes it has many aspects: self-alienation and not knowing one's own identity, dumbness and loss of language, living in anonymity even in intimate relationships where the partners do not know one another, being torn through dialectical impulses, social uprootedness, and so on. But the deepest reason for this human condition lies in the fact of being separated from God. Individuals in modern societies experience this exile deeper than any generation before, for the breakdown of religious traditions has deprived them of any social, intellectual, or spiritual homeland.

> Judaism says that not only the Jew is in exile, but that man as such, man in general, leads an exilic existence. As we said above, when we speak of exile in historical terms, the Jewish experience is unique. However, if we approach the idea of exile, of *galut*, from an existential, metaphysical viewpoint, then the *galut* experience is a universal one, shared by all men.[9]

Soloveitchik extends and transfers the notion of exile on an existential level and states then that homeless man must pray, for "through prayer he redeems himself from loneliness."[10] Teshuwa, prayer, and Talmud Torah are means to regain relationship with God. He describes the inner way of searching for redemption supported by God's help and initiative in his essay "*Uviqastem mischam*" (You will search me from there). The Halakhah will not be a pure tranquilizer and an easy solution to overcome loneliness and will not provide superficial harmony but it leads man into a dialectical synthesis of the different powers he is torn by. Above all, it deepens the original loneliness so that the halakhic man finds his vocation and mission as a "lonely man of faith": communion with God through the Halakhah and its religious community produces a split with others but provides a true identity.

Of course, one cannot call Ignatius an existentialist. Yet he starts his *Spiritual Exercises* with the assumption that every human being is deeply marked by sin. This does not mean only the false deeds a person performed. The original state of the human being is, rather, seen as disordered and under the influence of the "enemy of human nature." The first part of the spiritual way is nothing but becoming aware of the general disorder in history and in one's own biography in order to overcome this alienation and to gain an inner freedom that can finally be granted by God alone. The experience and awareness to be affected by original sin create the basic existential experience. Having experienced God's healing and forgiving mercy, man has to find his personal expression of thanksgiving through a life in the service of the Kingdom of God. One's own vocation has to be found in the light of Christ. Ignatian spirituality wants the individual to realize in the framework of the history of salvation what he has to contribute through his life.

Besides this similar approach to the *conditio humana*, Soloveitchik's halakhic spirituality and the way of the *Spiritual Exercises* share some common theological features. Both construct a radical theocentric worldview with a transcendent God. Creator and creatures are sharply differentiated. God is the God of revelation who descends out of free will as well as out of mercy. The concepts of revelation in both traditions are different and do not harmonize, indeed, but the structural analogy is obviously formed by the figure of the kenosis inviting man to participate in it. The form of participation results in the adjustment of the human will to the divine will through learning from its revelation.[11]

For Soloveitchik the divine will is realized first and foremost in the fact of the Torah given at Mount Sinai and in the human Talmud Torah, and only secondarily in prayer. His halakhic man, with his back turned toward God, looks into the world in the direction of the descending word of the revelation in order to mold reality. He is guided by a matter-of-factness beyond any numinous or charismatic gesture, but without losing the deep spiritual rootedness. God is related to the world by his will, which becomes visible in the performing of mitzvoth. The descending of God into the four cubits of the Halakhah brings the Orthodox Jew into all realms of social life and nature. A similar perspective is gained in Ignatian spirituality, which is based on the principle that every object and all constellations are limited worldly facts that have to be used to the greater honor of God.[12] The learning out of the revelation is here mediated through the person of Christ, for in his companionship man is sent into the world to work with Christ. The incarnation of God in the person of Jesus of Nazareth here takes the form of the kenosis expressed through a special meditation in the *Spiritual Exercises*.[13] It invites the Christian to take part in all kinds of social commitment to bring all parts of the world into right relation to God. The sanctification of reality is here also caused less by prayer or esthetical expression of faith than by apostolic deeds.

The classical contemplative and ascending spiritual figure of the Christian Middle Ages is replaced in Ignatian spirituality by a spirituality that invites men to participate in the descent of God into every realm of his creation. The bringing about of God's reality into this world finally depends, according to Ignatius, on finding God in everything. The final glorious meditation at the end of the *Spiritual Exercises* is dedicated to this mystical dimension of discovering God's presence in all things.[14] This meditation to attain love which expresses the final goal of the spiritual life according to Ignatius does not have a counterpart in Soloveitchik's halakhic spirituality. The only thing they have in common is the invocation of God as King, so omnipresent in Jewish prayers, for Ignatius not only sees God as the King of the universe who calls man through King Jesus to shape his life in accordance with God's will, but even in his mystical and culminating meditation, he perceives God's presence flowing out of his majesty.

6. Spirituality and Social Demarcation

The last characteristic of the halakhic existence I want to deal with lies on the religio-social level. It concerns the necessity of self-demarcation from non-halakhic lifestyles. The Halakhah is not a personal and internal practice but it regulates the social life of an individual and therefore creates a realm for a community that lives in contrast to the rest of the society. According to Soloveitchik, the public marking of difference is not only a sociological *conditio sine qua non* for the development of a halakhic community but also a constitutive element for Jewish existence with its own religious significance.

Halakhic existence is the vocation for an individual living as a member of a social minority. This community has a priestly vocation with the universal mission to represent God's creative power, both in creation as well as in its prolongation. The halakhic realm has to be revealed as governed by an ethical purpose. In addition the separation has to express above all God's otherness. Soloveitchik's vision of Jewish life according to the Halakhah not only brings him into contrast with the non-Jewish world but also lets him remain at a distance from other forms of Jewish life.[15]

Therefore Soloveitchik rejected a common cause with Liberal and Conservative Jews, reproaching them for adopting Christian patterns of religious thinking and behavior. They would betray the genuine paradigm of Judaism that has to construct itself according to the Halakhah. After a long period of hesitation he began, however, to support Zionism. He accepted the secular project of a modern democratic state insofar as it brought Jews to Eretz Israel, where the Halakhah could be practiced more completely. This strictly halakhic thinking, combined with the conviction that Jews need their own state to protect them, guided his religious Zionism. Any messianic interpretation of Zionism that became popular among religious Jews was refuted by him. This logic explains Soloveitchik's openness to other religious communities and to secular society in the United States; this openness led him to a cautious dialogue, although he was always careful not to undermine his own halakhic identity which had to be rooted and established in his time.

Does this attitude have any significance for Ignatian spirituality? Soloveitchik's coherent halakhic logic, even when he had to judge matters in the political and social realm, is impressive. It may encourage people to live in accordance with their own spiritual source without fearing they might find themselves in unnecessary contradiction of other concepts of life and without bowing his head before the short-lived booms. The Jesuit order also created in history its own signs of demarcation, its internal realm out of which its members were sent to their missions. This social difference that both rabbinic Judaism and the Society of Jesus erected in history may be one explanation of why an oppositional literature was developed against both communities, whose arguments are in large part analogous.

However, the *Spiritual Exercises* and Ignatian spirituality, which are somewhat broader than the Society of Jesus, do not by themselves create social demarcations. On the contrary, Ignatian spirituality is a Christian alternative to the monastic tradition, with its visible, social markers of difference. Whereas the monastic lifestyle structures social behavior through concrete rules, the spirit of the *Exercises* provides an attitude, an inner structure of life, a method with which to proceed. This should infuse all social domains and all cultures. Although Ignatian spirituality is not a mere inner habit but a way to act, it determines human behavior on a more intellectual level than does the halakhic spirituality, with its defined mitzvoth. In Ignatian spirituality this leads to less social difference, it opens up greater individual freedom concerning practical deeds, and it allows a spiritual way of life not as visible at first glance as halakhic-shaped life is.

The interreligious comparison between Rav Soloveitchik and Ignatius of Loyola that I develop in this chapter shows that each of these religious leaders set up a structural foundation for spiritual life that grew out of their respective traditions. In doing this, both were aware of the universal meaning of spiritual life. Written from a Christian perspective, this chapter aims neither to collect the halakhic way of life nor be an expression of crisis in Ignatian spirituality leading one to borrow from rabbinic Judaism. But these pages have the goal of demonstrating the kind of structural similarity that can exist in the concepts of a Jewish-rabbinic religious path and a Christian-Catholic religious path. With this insight, comparison of these paths makes conscious through a case study that Jewish-Christian closeness is not just a question of common origin but has its repercussions even in the concrete lifestyle of today. Moreover, for Ignatian spirituality this comparison ensures retaining the relation with the Jewish tradition that was discovered anew by the Second Vatican Council and has been recommended so often since then, and it can provide criteria for the direction that a dialogue might take in the future between the Ignatian way of life and spiritual paths of other religions.

An Ignatian Perspective on Contemporary Jewish Spirituality

Donald Moore, S.J.

On March 31, 1963, a crucial meeting was held in New York City. It was chaired by Abraham Joshua Heschel. Among those present were Augustin Cardinal Bea, head of the Vatican Secretariat for Promoting Christian Unity, his assistant, Monsignor (later Cardinal) Jan Willebrands, and a number of key Jewish scholars in the United States. They gathered to discuss the proposed Declaration on the Jews through which it was hoped that the Second Vatican Council would lead the Church to a new insight and attitude toward the Jewish people.

Some thirty-three years later, reflecting back to that meeting, Cardinal Willebrands wrote:

> I shall never forget this meeting, not only the setting and the historical happening, but especially the atmosphere, characterized by Cardinal Bea as "excellent and fraternal." . . . I felt a sense of awe for the presence of God among us. To me it was clear that we had broken new ground, that a new era had begun in the relations between the Church and the Jewish people. . . . If the Vatican Council fulfilled its intention concerning the

Declaration on the Jews, we would have a dialogue of a spiritual nature with the Jews.

Cardinal Willebrands went on to describe a later visit he had from Rabbi Marc Tannenbaum, who had convened the March meeting. It was a Saturday evening, and the rabbi wanted to involve the cardinal in his prayer. "For a moment I remained silent and embraced him. Our relationship was not only one of common study and interest, but it included our relationship to God. We wanted together to stay before God and to invoke His blessing, His grace."[1]

This "dialogue of a spiritual nature" carried over into Vatican II's *Nostra Aetate*, which urges all Christians, while witnessing to their own faith and way of life, to "acknowledge, preserve and encourage the spiritual and moral truths" found in other religions. This is especially true in the attitude of Christians toward Jews and Judaism, since, as *Nostra Aetate* reminds us, "Christians and Jews have such a common spiritual heritage"; there are unique spiritual ties "which link the people of the New Covenant to the stock of Abraham," for the Church continues to draw nourishment "from that good olive tree onto which the wild branches of the Gentiles have been grafted."[2]

It is this "dialogue of a spiritual nature" that I would like to develop further in this paper, limiting myself to certain aspects of Jewish spirituality expounded by two of the more prominent Jewish writers of the twentieth century, Martin Buber and Abraham Joshua Heschel, and showing the relevance and similarity of this spirituality to the *Spiritual Exercises* of St. Ignatius. Probably no other Jew had such a profound effect on the final version of Vatican II's *Nostra Aetate* as Abraham Heschel.

Early in 1962 Rabbi Heschel had submitted to Cardinal Bea an extraordinary thirteen-page memorandum entitled "On Improving Catholic-Jewish Relations." Heschel begins the memorandum: "With humility and in the spirit of commitment to the living message of the prophets of Israel, let us consider the grave problems that confront us all as the children of God." Both Judaism and Christianity, Heschel adds, share the certainty that humankind is in need of ultimate redemption, that God is involved in human history, that in relations between persons God is at stake. Our common task lies in history. "Openness to the historical, to the divine call and its demands" is what Heschel calls "the outstanding characteristic of the prophets."[3] God's demand for justice and righteousness can be satisfied only in our concrete historical living. It is only within the realm of history that we can carry out the mission given to us by God. Of the various proposals that Heschel submitted to Cardinal Bea, I mention two that have a particular bearing on a "dialogue of a spiritual nature."

In expressing his own distress at the failure of the Church to acknowledge the holiness of Jews who remain loyal to the Torah, Heschel writes:

> Through the centuries our people have paid such a high price in suffering and martyrdom for preserving the Covenant and the legacy of holiness in faith and devotion. To this day our people labor devotedly and with commitment to educate their children in the way of the Torah. Genuine love implies that Jews be accepted as Jews. Thus it is our sincere hope that the Ecumenical Council would acknowledge the integrity and permanent preciousness of Jews and Judaism.

Heschel also proposes that the council emphasize the need of Catholics "to seek mutual understanding of Jews and their traditions" because ignorance too easily breeds suspicion and prejudice. Catholics and Jews are called to love one another, but we cannot love those we do not know; knowledge and love are interrelated.[4] Heschel later stated categorically to Pope Paul VI that he would rather have gone to Auschwitz than give up his Jewish faith. And he described an evening conversation he once had with the renowned Father Gustave Weigel, S.J., in which he turned to Weigel and said:

> Is it really the will of God that there be no more Judaism in the world?

> Would it really be the triumph of God if the scrolls of the Torah would no more be taken out of the Ark and the Torah no more read in the synagogue, our ancient Hebrew prayers in which Jesus himself worshiped no more recited, . . . the law of Moses no more observed in our homes? Would it really be *ad majorem Dei gloriam* to have a world without Jews?[5]

These are words that Catholics, and we Jesuits in particular, must ponder. In *Nostra Aetate* as well as in numerous other statements in the past forty years, the Church has in so many ways heeded and responded to these pleas of Heschel.

To expand on these remarks of Heschel, I would like to focus primarily on what I consider a spiritual gem from the pen of Martin Buber, *The Way of Man: According to the Teachings of Hasidism*, with additional comments from Heschel taken for the most part from his monograph *Who Is Man?* I recognize the sharp criticism by Gershom Scholem and others concerning Buber's interpretation of Hasidism, that he was too subjective especially in his formulation of Hasidic tales. Scholem charges that Buber's presentation of Hasidism is based almost exclusively on the tales and aphorisms, ignoring the vast writings on the teachings of Hasidism. For Scholem the teachings present the most authentic and authoritative interpretation of Hasidism and precede the tales and aphorisms by half a century.[6]

Buber defended his understanding of the Hasidim by arguing that there are two ways of rescuing a religious tradition. One is through historical scholarship, by an objective analysis of its teachings and its role in the history of Judaism. The other is by communicating the vitality and power of the faith that underlies the tradition. The latter approach "derives from the desire to convey to our own time the force of a former life of faith and to help our age renew its ruptured bond with the Absolute." Certainly, knowledge of the spiritual and historical aspects of the tradition are required, but the transmission of the old faith to contemporary times requires above all "a selection of those manifestations in which its vital and vitalizing element was embodied." This is what Buber seeks to convey in the choice of those tales and aphorisms that for him embody Hasidism's living core, a selection based not on scholarship but on the "reliability of the man in the face of his special task." What is crucial is that one perform this task "with fidelity."[7]

The center of Hasidism's development, according to Buber, is not its theoretical teaching but the tales and anecdotes. Here we find the power and vitality of Hasidic faith. Buber wanted to capture the moment of lived encounter. The Hasidic relationship to God is so clearly an existentialist one that no theory can do it justice; only the anecdote or tale can capture this relationship. For Buber the tales came first, were transmitted orally, and only at a later date were written down. The teachings were preserved by those who originated them or by their disciples. The hallowing of all things, as emphasized in Buber's Hasidic writings, is prior in Hasidism to the spiritualizing tendencies that emphasize the negation of all things. I would agree ultimately with a comment made by Heschel; a group of students had asked how they should begin the study of Hasidism, and when the response was given: "We now have Scholem in English. Read him," Heschel intervened, "No, if you want to know Hasidism as it was, begin with Buber."[8] And so we will follow Heschel's advice.

The opening chapter of Buber's *Way of Man* deals with searching of the heart and could provide a helpful background to the First Week of the *Spiritual Exercises*. Rabbi Shneur Zalman, the rabbi of Northern White Russia, is languishing in jail in St. Petersburg and is asked by the chief of his Russian jailers: "How are we to understand that God, the all-knowing, said to Adam: 'Where art thou?'" It would seem that your God does not know all things. The rabbi nodded, yes, God did indeed stroll through the Garden asking "Adam, where art thou?" The rabbi then turned around the jailer's question. God asked the question, however, not for God's own knowledge; it was asked for Adam's knowledge:

> In every era God says to every person: "Where are you in your world? So many years and days of those allotted to you have

> passed, and how far have you gotten in your world?" God says something like this: "You have lived forty-six years. How far along are you?"

When the chief heard his age mentioned, he trembled. The question is aimed at us. "You yourself are Adam," the rabbi added, "you are the one whom God asks: 'Where art thou?'"

Buber then reminds us that Adam hides himself in order to avoid rendering an account, in order to escape responsibility for his way of life. Everyone hides for this purpose, for every person is Adam and finds him- or herself in Adam's situation. To escape responsibility for life, we turn existence into a series of hideouts. We do not not want to face that question: Where are you? "A new situation thus arises, which becomes more and more questionable with every day, with every new hideout. This situation can be precisely defined as follows: Man cannot escape the eye of God, but in trying to hide from God, he is hiding from himself." God's question is aimed at helping a person destroy this system of hideouts, to show him to what pass he has come and to awaken in him the determination to get out of it. The only valid response to God's question is the response of Adam: "Lord, I have been hiding." This, for Buber, is the beginning of our way. This type of critical heart-searching is "again and again the beginning of a human way."[9] This is a simple tale, but it helps us understand what Buber means when he says he wants to recapture that moment of lived encounter, his primary concern in his study of Hasidic writings.

There are two other key aspects of Hasidic thought that resonate throughout Buber's *Way of Man* and that have a close affinity to Ignatian spirituality: the Hasidic emphases on the uniqueness of each person and on the hallowing of all things. In chapter two of *The Way of Man*. Buber skillfully employs the use of Hasidic tales and aphorisms to stress a basic Hasidic teaching expressed by Rabbi Pinhas of Koretz: "In everyone there is something precious which is in no one else"[10] There is no single way of developing this preciousness. The Seer of Lublin remarked:

> It is impossible to tell men what way they should take. For one way to serve God is through learning, another through prayer, another through fasting, and still another through eating. Everyone should carefully observe what way his heart draws him to, and then choose this way with all his strength.[11]

We can learn from the great spiritual leaders within our traditions, we should study their achievements, but we should not try simply to imitate them lest we miss what we, and we alone, are called upon to do.

Heschel, who was reared in the Hasidic tradition, likewise stresses the uniqueness of each person. From without, he writes, I may seem to be quite average and ordinary, but from within, through self-reflection, I see myself as unique, precious, unprecedented; I am not to be exchanged for anything else. Beyond the distress and anxiety and busyness of life lies this most fundamental aspect of self-reflection: I am of great moment, I am an original, not a copy. Each person has something to say, to think, to do that is entirely unprecedented. Every human being is a disclosure, an example of exclusiveness, of uniqueness. And what I recognize of myself, I must also recognize of others: each person has a task to carry out, a task so great that "its fulfillment may epitomize the meaning of all humanity."[12] Thus there is no such creature as the typical or average person; this is the creation of the statisticians, the sociologists. In real life the average person is nonexistent unless one should allow oneself to be "drowned in indifference and commonness."[13] Such spiritual suicide is, unfortunately, within easy reach of us all, a perennial temptation for every person, a temptation that with each passing age seems to grow greater and greater.

That is why there is something so refreshing and healthily countercultural in Buber's exposition of Hasidic tales and aphorisms. For example, there is the wisdom of the aged Rabbi Bunham: "I should not like to change places with our father Abraham! What good would it do God if Abraham became like blind Bunham, and blind Bunham like Abraham? Rather than have this happen, I think I shall try to become a little more myself." In the same vein Rabbi Susya remarks:

"In the world to come I shall not be asked: 'Why were you not Moses?' I shall be asked: 'Why were you not Susya?'"[14] Each one of us is unique and unprecedented. No matter how trivial our achievements might seem in comparison to others, "they have their real value in that we bring them about in our own way and by our own efforts."[15] This is the insight expressed by Menahem Mendel of Kotzk (the Kotzker): "Everything in the world can be imitated except truth. For truth that is imitated is no longer truth."[16]

Buber expresses this Hasidic teaching:

> Every person born into this world represents something new, something that never existed before, something original and unique. . . . Every man's foremost task is the actualization of his unique, unprecedented and never-recurring potentialities, and not the repetition that another, and be it even the greatest, has already achieved.[17]

Each one of us is able to say: there has never been anyone like me in the world, for if there had been someone like me, there would be no reason for me to be. Heschel puts it very simply: "With every child born a new expectation enters the world."[18] There is, then, in everyone something precious that is found in no other. This preciousness is one's uniqueness. To live one's uniqueness is to respond to that personal vocation given to each of us by God in calling us into being.

This closely corresponds to that which is at the heart of the *Spiritual Exercises* of St. Ignatius Loyola, namely, the "Election," which can be understood either as the discernment of the state of life to which one is called by God (what is it that God expects of me?) or as the reformation within an already chosen state of life so that one gives oneself more completely to the demands of God on one's life. St. Ignatius refers to the exercises as "every way of preparing and disposing the soul to rid itself of all inordinate attachments and, after their removal, of seeking and finding the will of God in the disposition of my life for the salvation of my soul."[19]

Herbert Alphonso writes that the most profound and authentic meaning of Ignatius's "election" is the discernment of one's "truest and deepest 'self,'" and this truest and deepest self is one's "God-given *uniqueness*" or what he also calls one's "Personal Vocation"; in other words, at its deepest level, to find God's will in the disposition of my life is to find "my unrepeatable *uniqueness*."[20] This goal of the exercises, along with its method of Ignatius's discernment, finds its parallel in the wisdom of the Hasidim as summarized by Buber: we realize our uniqueness only through the knowledge of our own being, the knowledge of our essential qualities and inclinations. The precious something within us is revealed to us if we truly perceive our strongest feeling, our central wish, that in us that stirs our inmost being.

If we are aware of our uniqueness, then there is nothing in the world that of itself could turn us from God. According to the Hasidic saying, "God does not say: 'This way leads to me and that does not,' but he says: 'Whatever you do may be a way to me, provided you do it in such a manner that it leads to me.'"[21] Buber writes in *I and Thou*: "I know nothing of a 'world' and of 'worldly life' that can separate us from God. What is designated that way is . . . the life of experiencing and using. Whoever goes forth in truth to the world, goes forth to God."[22]

We develop our preciousness/uniqueness not ultimately for our own sake but for the world's sake. A Hasidic spirituality, both for Buber and Heschel, begins with self but does not end with self. There are two types of persons, says Rabbi Bunham, the proud, who, even in the most sublime form, think only of themselves, and the humble, who in all things think only of the world. There is the story of Rabbi Hayyim, who is so worried that he has not yet atoned that as a result his hair turns white. The advice of Rabbi Eliezer to him: stop wasting your energy on self-reproach and apply it instead to that active relationship with the world that is destined for you.[23] The conversion and repentance that are demanded of each of us mean breaking away from the web of selfishness in which we are entangled and finding our way to God, that is, to the accomplishment of God's goals in our world.

The atoner in this Hasidic tale is too concerned with his own personal salvation, a concern that is perhaps the most sublime form of that pride or self-centeredness mentioned by Rabbi Bunham.

Instead of excessive self-reproach, one should be concerned with what Heschel calls the fundamental question posed to the person of biblical faith: What is required of me? "Over and above personal problems, there is an objective challenge to overcome inequity, injustice, helplessness, suffering, carelessness, oppression. Over and above the din of desires, there is a calling, a demanding, a waiting, an expectation."[24] There is a cry for justice that only we can answer, a need for gentleness, for compassion, for community that only we can satisfy. The most crucial experience of human living is the recognition of this "mysterious waiting," an experience, ultimately, that God is waiting for us, that God is asking something of us.

Our being human, says Heschel, depends on our recognizing that something is asked of us. I am being inescapably challenged on every level of existence. It is precisely in my being challenged that I discover my authentic self in all its uniqueness and preciousness. And being challenged is another way of expressing what Heschel calls the fundamental indebtedness that is given with our very being. I cannot think of myself as a human person without being conscious of my indebtedness, of an experience of life as receiving and not merely as taking; it implies that I have a task to perform.

Indebtedness is a constitutive element of our being, because our being is not simply being, it is being created. Our being is a response to the biblical command "Let there be!" To be is to obey the command of creation; my being endures as a response to God's command. I am because I am commanded by God. God's word is at stake in my being. Thus there should be a given sense of indebtedness within us to which we reciprocate by living in a way, as Heschel states it, "compatible with the grandeur and mystery" of being human. Yet we live in a civilization that has strayed far from this ideal. "I am afraid," Heschel writes, "of people who are never embarrassed at their own pettiness, prejudices, envy and conceit, never embarrassed at the profanation of life. A world full of grandeur has been converted into a carnival."[25] Heschel calls us to be alive to the mystery of the moment, to the possibility of quiet exultation, to the marvel of being. No two moments are alike. Every moment is a new arrival, a new opportunity, a new gift calling forth from us a response of wonder, awe, reverence.

Buber emphasizes the same point with this Hasidic aphorism: "God says to everyone as he said to Moses: 'Put off thy shoes from off thy feet'—put off the habitual which encloses your foot and you will recognize that the place on which you happen to be standing at this moment is holy ground."[26] The fulfillment of our existence, of our unique role in the world, is to be found in only one place, the place where we are standing here and now.

Thus the Hasidic tale of Rabbi Eizik, son of Rabbi Yekel of Krakow. He had a recurring dream to go to Prague, where he would find a treasure under the bridge leading to the king's palace. Rabbi Eizik makes the long trek to Prague, and walks around and around the bridge, and finally the captain of the guard asks him what he is looking for. Eizik tells him of his dream, and the captain laughed and told of a dream of his own in which he was to go to Krakow and dig for a treasure under the hearth in the room of a Jew, Eizik, son of Yekel. "I can just imagine what it would be like, how I would have to try every house over there, where one half of the Jews are named Eizik and the other Yekel!" The captain laughed again. Eizik bowed, traveled home, and there, of course, was the treasure under the hearth in his room.

This is an old story, popular in a number of traditions, but the Hasidic treatment is quite clear: there is something that can be found only in one place, that great treasure known as the fulfillment of existence. It is found in the place where one stands here and now. We tend to search for this fulfillment in various provinces of the world or of the mind, but it can be found only here where we stand, where we have been set. Buber expresses it: "The environment which I feel to be the natural one, the situation which has been assigned to me as my fate, the things that claim me day after day—these contain my essential task and such fulfillment of existence as is open to me." If we had power over the ends of the earth, it would not give us that fulfillment of existence available through a quiet, devoted relationship to life at hand. If we perform with holy intent the tasks of our daily lives, we will realize indeed that "our treasure is hidden beneath the hearth of our own home."[27]

Everyone's task is "to affirm for God's sake" both the world and oneself, and by this means "to transform both."[28] If we can develop authentic relationships with and be present to the persons and things that belong to our world, then each encounter opens to a deeper, more spiritual significance. All things call out to us to liberate the divine spark found within them, and we do this by our relationships with them. One hallows all that one does by living with all things in a spirit of reverence. Each deed becomes redemptive according to the degree of presence with which one acts. Thus a disciple of Moshe of Kobryn was asked: "What was most important to your teacher?" The response: "Whatever he happened to be doing at the moment."[29] And Rabbi Pinhas of Koretz told his disciples that there are no actions that in themselves are useless, but one can make them useless by "doing them uselessly."[30]

What is key here is our relationship to the things and persons of our life. Heschel insists that if faith means *anything*, it must shape our attitude toward *everything*: this paper, this place, this person, this moment. One hallows the things of this world by a relationship of presence that is open to the transcendent. It is not primarily our knowledge or power or technology that forms the marrow of our human existence, but our relationships. "In the beginning is the relation," writes Buber in *I and Thou*; it is the personal that really counts.

For Buber, Hasidism emphasizes the living power of meeting and the living power of presence. A person is fully human, fully alive, when fully present. Buber believed that all Hasidic teaching could be summed up in one sentence: "God can be beheld in each thing and reached through each pure deed." And he continues:

> no thing can exist without a divine spark, and each person can uncover and redeem this spark at each time and through each pure action, even the most ordinary, if only he performs it in purity, wholly directed to God and concentrated in Him. Therefore, it will not do to serve God only in isolated hours and with set words and gestures. One must serve God with one's whole life, with the whole of the everyday, with the whole of reality.[31]

Hasidism challenges us to accept the task of hallowing all things, of entering into genuine relation with all things, to do all that one does with the whole of one's being. To paraphrase Buber's summary: we cannot approach God by reaching beyond the human; we can approach God only through becoming human; to become human is what we have been created for. "This, so it seems to me," writes Buber, "is the eternal core of Hasidic life and of Hasidic teaching."[32]

These Hasidic insights closely parallel the apex of Ignatian spirituality, and in a sense the apex of all Christian spirituality: the grace of finding God in all things. Father Jerome Nadal writes of Ignatius that: "in all things, in every action or conversation, he was aware of God's presence. . . . In a word he was *simul in actione contemplivus*—contemplative even while engaged in action, a habit that he was accustomed to explain while remarking: 'God must be found in all things.'"[33] For one formed in the *Spiritual Exercises*, long periods of formal prayer ought not be necessary; rather, one should find God in all that one does. Prayer or contemplation leads one to engage oneself in God's plan for the redemption of the world, and this engagement, carried out with "*devotio*—commitment—commitment of the whole person," leads one back again to God.[34]

Nadal is describing a radically new way of perceiving reality that is evocative of the Fourth Week of the Spiritual Exercises and the accompanying Contemplation on the Love of God. God is found in all objects, in all creatures, in all people. The world is revealed to be a sacred place. Hungarian Jesuit Janos Lukacs writes that through the *Spiritual Exercises* one's spiritual horizon embraces everyday activities and the entire created world so that one can return home:

> with a new way of perceiving reality and with a new freedom to act in response to God's action in the world. . . . A new form of life becomes possible as the Fourth Week dynamic is progressively embodied in a variety of everyday-life situations; this is how one becomes fully receptive to the grace of being contemplative even while being active.[35]

Similarly Father Peter-Hans Kolvenbach points out that:

> at the end of the *Spiritual Exercises* it is apparent that there is no other possibility of seeking and finding God, and of living His life, than to insert oneself fully, each in the place which, in the Election, he has found to be his own, in the ongoing history of the world . . . to seek and find God in all things, becoming one with them.[36]

There are many other fruitful comparisons to be made between the spiritual messages of the Hasidim and those of St. Ignatius. These, however, might be sufficient to indicate that both Buber and Heschel, by their interpretation and understanding of the wisdom of their own tradition, have much to offer us Christians as we strive to witness to the meaning of our humanness, our uniqueness, our own covenant of faith with God, as we strive to find God in all that we do. And it should be clear that we Christians do indeed continue, as *Nostra Aetate* reminded us, to draw great nourishment from "that good olive tree," from the rich spiritual traditions of Israel, onto which we have been grafted.

THE JEWISH THEOLOGY OF ABRAHAM JOSHUA HESCHEL AS A CHALLENGE FOR CATHOLIC THEOLOGY

Stanisław Obirek

I belong to the increasing group of Christians for whom Rabbi Abraham Joshua Heschel's life and thought have become a vivid light and an example for religious experience and social engagement. To read his writing is like coming back to the common Jewish and Christian heritage; to read Heschel means to allow his thoughts to penetrate the deepest recesses of your heart.

But before speaking about Heschel and his impact on me, I would like to return to one of our previous meetings in Krakow in 1999. Some of you might remember that I was asked to read an essay by Fr. Stanisław Musiał titled "Black is Black," which is concerned with the problem of anti-Semitism in Poland. Fr. Musiał unexpectedly passed away in March 2004, but his legacy in Poland is still very vivid (and perhaps after his death even more so), particularly among Polish Jews, however, not so much in the Catholic Church. According to his expressed wish—and probably for the first time in the history of Polish Jesuits—at his funeral the Jewish prayer Kadish was said by a Hasid, a descendent of the rabbi of Bobowa, a village not far from the place where Musiał was born.

Why am I reminding you of Musiał and his text? Because Jewish-Christian relations in Poland are not only a field of academic discussion but also a problem that involves and requires the whole of a man—his soul, his heart, his mind, and even his body. Stanisław Musiał in a way paid the highest price for his commitment to Jewish-Christian dialogue and mutual understanding. He was rejected by his own institution, including the Society of Jesus, but at the same time he was considered the greatest friend of the Jewish people and also of the State of Israel, as the current ambassador of Israel to Poland, David Peleg, recently said. These words might sound strange, but Fr. Musiał's involvement in the controversy concerning the presence of the Carmelite convent and the so-called "papal cross" at Auschwitz was perceived in Poland as a lack of obedience and respect toward the Church. However, the truth is that Musiał was asked by the archbishop of Krakow, Cardinal Franciszek Macharski, to take up this mission.

My own involvement in the field is also an emotional one. It is similar to the journey of Israeli writers coming to Poland. Here is how Shoshana Ronen describes it:

> A journey to Poland, in Israeli literature, is not a typical one. A person who decides to travel to Poland is not simply a tourist who wants to explore unknown places, climates, habits, works of art, etc. It is not a chance decision, as in the case when, for example, one hesitates whether to spend their time by the beach in Greece or visit museums in Paris.
>
> A journey to Poland in Israeli literature is a very loaded one. The narrator is not an ignorant traveler who is going to a place he does not know anything about, or to a place he has not seen before. The narrator who travels to Poland was there before, even if not physically, he was there psychologically. Even if he was born in Israel and has never been to Poland before, he comes to Poland full with knowledge, stories, stereotypes, prejudice, beliefs, pictures, smells, memories, nostalgia, pain and horror. In this respect, even for those who were not born in Poland, the journey to Poland is a return.[1]

So for myself, becoming acquainted with Jewish theology was a kind of new reading of my own theological studies, but with a completely different perspective. Until then the central figure for me was Jesus Christ—the promised Messiah—as the definitive fulfillment of the promises of the Hebrew Bible. However, in Jewish theology he was almost completely ignored. Therefore my question: Is it possible to reconcile both perspectives? Is it thinkable at all to pray together to the same God of Abraham, Isaac, and Jacob?

And speaking generally, is this not the situation of a Christian theologian who tries to read Jewish thinkers? James Carroll, describing his meeting with Abraham Joshua Heschel's thought, uses different concepts from those of Shoshana Ronen quoted above, but the idea is similar. This meeting is a transforming one: "To read Heschel was to step aboard the endangered but still seaworthy idea that the most transforming adventure of all can be intellectual. Heschel changed my notions not only of Judaism but of religion itself, and of God." And the author of *Constantine's Sword* continues:

> As is obvious by now, I had been raised with an anachronistic idea of Judaism: the Scribes and the Pharisees worship at the Temple, the stereotype of the vengeful Old Testament God. Catholics like me knew nothing of the living tradition of Jewish thought and observance, ignorance that reflected the Christian assertion that after Jesus, Israel had been superseded by the "new Israel," the Church. Heschel's vital theology, rooted in a biblical vision but informed by two millennia of rabbinical wisdom, was a stark rebuttal of this. The central thought of Judaism is a *living God*. . . . The craving for God has never subsided in the Jewish soul. Heschel put words on that craving as I experienced it, requiring me to revise entirely what I thought of Judaism. He did something similar for many Catholics.[2]

Carroll is treating Heschel as his own rabbi, and his perception of Heschel's thought is a very personal one. I would like to quote him again:

> When the priest at the consecration says, "This is the cup of the New Covenant," he is pronouncing the Old Covenant superfluous. Its job, after Jesus, is to leave the sanctuary. The Jew's job is to disappear. From the Christian point of view, just by continuing to exist, Jews dissent. Because of the threat it poses to the faith of the Church, that dissent can be defined by Christians as the core of Jewish belief, which of course continues the insult.[3]

It is easy to criticize Carroll by saying that his perspective is shaped by his very personal approach, which was influenced by his decision to leave the priesthood. Nevertheless, I think that his doubts have to be taken seriously. The same has to be said about many other former priests who left the priesthood for theological reasons. We can learn a lot from "exs." Let me mention only one more—Geza Vermes and his inspiring books *Jesus the Jew* and *The Changing Faces of Jesus.*

Let us come back now to Abraham Joshua Heschel and his theology. From among his many well-known books, I will concentrate my attention on two articles: "No Religion Is an Island" and "The God of Israel and Christian Renewal."

1. What Do We Have in Common?

Exactly forty years have passed since Heschel's inaugural lecture, "No Religion Is an Island," at the Union Theological Seminary in 1965. Still it is worthwhile to recall the opinion of John C. Bennett, the president of the Union at the time:

> In that lecture he gave two essential messages, one to Christians and one to Jews. He asked Christians not to seek to convert Jews to Christianity. His message to Jews, somewhat less expected by the audience, was: "It is our duty as Jews to remember that it was the Church that brought the knowledge of the God of Abraham to the Gentiles. It was the Church that made the Hebrew Scripture available to all mankind. This we Jews acknowledge with grateful hearts."[4]

These forty years have changed a lot in our mutual relationship, but some of the remarks made by Heschel are still valid and have not lost their relevance.

I would like to start with a Jesuitical accent in this text. The questions directed by Heschel to Gustav Weigel I hear, in a way, as questions directed to me:

> Gustav Weigel spent the last evening of his life in my study at the Jewish Theological Seminary. We opened our hearts to one another in prayer and contrition and spoke of our own deficiencies, failures, hopes. At one moment I posed the question: Is it really the will of God that there be no more Judaism in the world? Would it really be the triumph of God if the scrolls of the Torah were no longer taken out of the Ark and the Torah no longer read in the synagogue, our ancient Hebrew prayers in which Jesus himself worshipped no more recited, the Passover Seder no longer celebrated in our lives, the Law of Moses no longer observed in our homes? Would it really be *ad maiorem Dei gloriam* to have a world without Jews?[5]

Of course we can say that these are only rhetorical questions; it is obvious that God's will is to preserve Judaism with all its beauty and theological richness. But it is not so obvious when we read some of the Church's documents, including more recent ones. Several times I heard these questions from my Jewish friends, religious and agnostics: How can you believe in all that the Church and the priests are preaching, particularly in my Catholic Poland? Those questions are louder today than ever. It is useful to spend some time listening carefully to these questions, perhaps more important than quoting from several Church documents. I am tempted to repeat with Heschel: "Humility and contrition seem to be absent where most required—in theology. But humility is the beginning and end of religious thinking, the sacred of faith. There is not truth without humility, no certainty without contrition."[6]

But I want to emphasize the common elements in both our religions as they are presented by Heschel. He speaks in his opening lecture of a variety of common elements. The first is our common condition, being human. The second point which he underlines is the obvious reality: no religion is an island. And third, speaking about Jewish-Christian relations, Heschel mentions pathos. Of these three elements, he says:

> First and foremost, we meet as human beings who have much in common: a heart, a face, a voice, the presence of a soul, fears, hope, the ability to trust, a capacity for compassion and understanding, the kinship of being human. My first task in every encounter is to comprehend the personhood of the human being I face, to sense the kinship of being human, solidarity of being."[7]

It is obvious that Lévinas is coming to mind, with his passionate defense of otherness.

It is very touching to read the passage that shows how deeply Heschel was aware of the pluralistic reality of world religions:

> The religions of the world are no more isolated than individuals or nations. Energies, experiences, and ideas that come to life outside the boundaries of a particular religion or all religions continue to challenge and to affect every religion.
>
> Horizons are wider, dangers are greater. . . . *No religion is an island*. We are all involved with one another. Spiritual betrayal on the part of one of us affects the faith of all of us. Views adopted in one community have an impact on other communities. Today religious isolationism is a myth. For all the profound differences in perspective and substance, Judaism is sooner or later affected by the intellectual, moral, and spiritual events within the Christian society, and vice versa.[8]

And of the third important element for both religions—the divine pathos—which involves the core of each religion, Heschel says:

> The supreme issue is today not the *halacha* for the Jews or the Church for the Christian—but the promise underlying both religions, namely, whether there is a *pathos*, a divine reality concerned with the destiny of man which mysteriously impinges upon history: the supreme issue is whether we are alive or dead to the challenge of the expectation of the living God. The crisis engulfs all of us. The misery and fear of alienation from God make Jews and Christians cry together.[9]

Is this pathos still alive in both our religions? And what exactly does it mean? It is not easy to answer,[10] but I think that we can call it the seriousness of life as seen from human and divine perspectives.

Those three elements—awareness that we all are human, that we are connected, and that we have to take our life seriously—are the foundation for a real and honest dialogue. Heschel states:

> Dialogue must not degenerate into a dispute, into an effort on the part of each to get the upper hand. There is an unfortunate history of Christian-Jewish disputations, motivated by the desire to prove how blind the Jews are and carried on in a spirit of opposition, which eventually degenerated into enmity. Thus any conversation between Christian and Jews in which abandonment of the other partner's faith is a silent hope must be regarded as offensive of one's religious and human dignity[11]

Heschel's wish, which, by the way, is now being fulfilled by so many Jewish-Christian initiatives, is:

> Let there be an end to disputation and polemic, an end to disparagement. We honestly and profoundly disagree in matters of creed and dogma. Indeed, there is a deep chasm between Christian and Jews concerning, e.g., the divinity and messiahship of Jesus. But across the chasm we can extend our hand to one another.[12]

Allow me one last quotation from "No Religion Is an Island" that indicates the key to the complex question of all religions claiming the truth:

> Religion is a means, not an end. It becomes idolatrous when regarded as an end in itself. Over and above all beings stands the Creator and Lord of history, He who transcends all. To equate religion and God is idolatry. Does not the all-inclusiveness of God contradict the exclusiveness of any particular religion? The prospect of all men embracing one form of religion remains an eschatological hope. What about here and now? Is it not blasphemous to say: I alone have all the truth and the grace, and all those who differ live in darkness and are abandoned by the grace of God?[13]

This question is still an important one for Jews and perhaps particularly for Christians.

2. Differences as a Blessing

Two years after his opening lecture at the Union Theological Seminary in New York, Heschel was invited to take part in the Congress on the Theology of the Renewal of the Church Centenary of Canada, 1867–1967, where he spoke on "The God of Israel and Christian Renewal." Just the fact of having been invited by Catholic theologians was for Heschel a blessing: "Is it not a moment of blessing that this congress of illustrious Catholic theologians is willing to submit the great movement of Christian renewal to a confrontation with Jewish understanding of the meaning of the God of Israel?"[14]

Heschel is very honest and open in presenting his understanding of a possible and a real dialogue with Christianity. First of all, the condition sine qua non is mutual respect, or as he calls it "mutual reverence," which has just been achieved:

> I believe that one of the achievements of this age will be the realization that in our age religious pluralism is the will of God, that the relationship between Judaism and Christianity will be one of mutual reverence, that without denying profound divergences, Jews and Christians will seek to help each other in

understanding each one's respective commitment and in deepening appreciation of what God means.[15]

On this basis it is possible to formulate the difficulty in understanding the fundamental Christian concept of God and the role of Jesus Christ: "With your permission, I should like to say that it is difficult for a Jew to understand when Christians worship Jesus as the Lord, and this Lordship takes the place of the Lordship of God the Creator. It is difficult for a Jew to understand when theology becomes reduced to Christology."[16] I have to say that the most recent Christological discussions among Christian theologians do not help me to answer Heschel's question. And it is obvious that this question lies at the core of interreligious dialogue and its understanding by Catholic theology.

The next important difference between Judaism and Christianity is their respective understanding of redemption. For Christians the only and universal Redeemer is Jesus Christ. For Jews the problem is formulated differently. As Heschel puts it:

> The world is unredeemed and deficient, and God is in need of man to be a partner in completing, in aiding, in redeeming. Of all the forms of living, doing is the most patent way of aiding. Action is truth. The deed is elucidation of existence, expressing thirst for God with body and soul. The Jewish *mitzvah* is a prayer in the form of a deed. The *mitzvot* are the Jewish sacraments, sacraments that may be performed in common deeds of kindness. The nature is intelligible if seen in the light of God's care for man. The good act, ritual as well as moral, is a *mitzvah*, a divine offer, a divine representative.
>
> Ultimate issues confront us in immediate situations. What is urgent for the Jew is not the acceptance of salvation but the preparing of redemption, the preparing *for* redemption.[17]

Heschel concludes his passionate deliberation on the essence of redemption in Judaism with a call to reveal God's love in His name:

> The urgent issue is not personal salvation, but the prevention of mankind's surrender to the demoniac. The sanctuary has not

> walls; the opportunity to praise or to aid has not limits. When God is silent, man must speak in His place. When God is hiding His compassion, man must reveal His love in this name.[18]

This quotation helps us to understand Heschel's approach to human activity, which is as an effective collaboration with God in the redemption of the present world. On the practical level, Christian understanding is very similar (particularly the Protestant one), but on the level of theological reflection, we need a major clarification. This approach is also very appealing to many agnostics.

The final part of Abraham Joshua Heschel's essay is dedicated to his recent visit to Israel, where he discovered "a new radiance, a new awe." It seems to me that the importance of the existence of the State of Israel for modern Jewish thought and for Abraham J. Heschel has to be discovered and evaluated for Jewish-Christian relations.

I would like to finish my paper by recalling a very moving experience in one of the Reform synagogues in St. Louis, where I was invited by Rabbi Sylvia Talve to deliver a kind of sermon in November 2004. Let me recall some fragments of my talk, which I entitled "Common Destiny."

To welcome Sabbath, religious Jews used to sing: "*Lecha dodi, likrat kalah, p'nei Sabbath nekablah*" (Come my Beloved to greet the bride—the Sabbath presence let us welcome!). This wonderful song was composed by Rabbi Shlomo Halvey Alkabetz (1505–1584), one of the Kabbalists of Safed. The name of the Friday evening service is *kabbalat Sabbath*, which according to Rabbi Abraham Joshua Heschel helps to understand the importance of the Sabbath, "which means to accept the sovereignty as well as to welcome the presence of the day. The Sabbath is a queen as well as a bride."[19]

When non-Jews welcome Sabbath, they are sharing with their Jewish friends the joy of this particular moment. And when I was invited by the rabbi to say few words, I was embarrassed and confused in doing so, particularly as a Christian, a Catholic priest, who comes from Poland. There are many reasons for this uneasiness.

But we started the prayer of Sabbath together. So we were in a sacred time. And when we are in a sacred time and sacred space, then the difficulties could and should be transformed and become the sources of sabbatical joy!

I would like to share with you my experience of Jewish-Christian dialogue in Poland, the country where I was born and where I grew up. My small town—Narol—is remembered in Jewish history for two reasons. In 1648 Chmielnicki's Cossacks killed all inhabitants, including twelve thousand Jews. And during World War II, not far from Narol, Germans perpetrated the darkest deed in our history—the death camp Belzec, where in less than one year (from February to November 1942) almost six hundred thousand Jews perished. But this part of the history of my town was long unknown to me. My awareness of the Holocaust was affected by a calculated amnesia that permeated Polish society, especially the postwar generation. The founders of "the best system" took care that Polish young people would remember only the martyrdom of the Polish nation, with a strictly limited remembrance of Jews and others. Thus, although I was born in 1956, I heard about the Holocaust for the first time when I was eighteen. I have to add that the same perspective was presented by the Polish Catholic Church, in which only Catholic martyrology was presented.

In late 1999, the first international congress of Jesuits working in the field of Jewish-Christian relations was held in Krakow. Our focus as Jesuits at this meeting was not on guilt but on shared responsibility. I think it is fair to say that we recommitted ourselves to the commandment Elie Wiesel quotes once again in his latest memoir, *And the Sea Is Never Full*: "Thou shalt not stand idly by." As Jesuits, we committed ourselves unknowingly to violate that biblical injunction.[20]

Let us come back to the beginning of Christianity, to the time of Jesus of Nazareth. What happened after his death? Some of the Jews recognized in him the Messiah, but most of them did not. It was not the first and not the last time in Jewish history that someone was considered to be the Messiah. First of all, Judaism is a religion that is waiting for the Messiah, so it is no wonder that messiahs keep coming.

The problem is that till now none of them has been successful, including Jesus of Nazareth. As Rabbi Irving Greenberg said, he was a failed Messiah, because he was crucified as a criminal, and did not bring any political changes. But his religion has been successful. And this is a problem for both Jews and for Christians. The Jews wondered why this group of Jews and many Gentiles recognized in this failed messiah the Final Messiah. The Christians (former Jews and former Gentiles) were amazed that not all Jews became Christian.[21] This amazement we know all too well—and also the consequences.

And now, in the beginning of the twenty-first century, we are two different religions. We have a lot in common, but we are focused in our daily life on differences. Honestly we have to say that we ignore our respective traditions, we do not remember how much our prayers, our feasts have similar roots or, more precisely, how deeply Christianity is rooted in Judaism. But there are exceptions. The most eminent figures of our time are very much involved in mutual understanding, and we observe a growing interest in tradition and history among the younger generation. What we have to understand is that we have the right to have different memories of the past, but we cannot remain in the prison of this past. We have to remember history in order to transform our future.

Abraham Joshua Heschel became one of the most eminent Jewish thinkers of the twentieth century. He died in the United States in 1972, having produced works that greatly influenced the Second Vatican Council, particularly its declaration *Nostra Aetate*. I am proud that Abraham Joshua Heschel, a great Jewish thinker, and a real prophet of our time, was born in my country. I am less proud of the reception of the teaching of the first Polish pope in his own country, particularly of his teaching concerning Jewish-Christian relations. But this problem I would prefer to leave for further discussion.

The Genius and the Wisdom of Harold Bloom

Peter Du Brul, S.J.

1. An Elastic Title

By way of introduction to this subject, to this contemporary Jewish thinker and his relevance for us, I ask you to write the name of one of the best novels or poems you have ever read on the paper that I will distribute to you. Another way of finding the best may be to ask you to search for the strongest experience you have had in such reading, or the one book you would most want to recommend to another person in need of it. After you have written that title, turn the paper over and write the name of the best film you have ever seen. The time we are taking here is the time it takes to form a little "canon" of books and movies that are valuable to us. And the idea of a canon is essential if we are to enter into the thought of Harold Bloom. After the papers are collected, we shall list the titles on a board for all to see. No more will be made of this, since the point of the exercise is simply to quicken in us a sense of looking for and communicating titles of personal value. No more, no less.

Yet "canons" and struggles to get into canons are a very important part of what life is all about. The world awareness of the matches and prizes of the Olympic Games, the Eurovision Song Contest, the Oscars, Golden Palms, Golden Bears of the international film industry, the Nobel Prizes for research and discovery in physics, chemistry, biology, literature, and peace, the Prince of Asturias Awards! The more cynical recognitions of the most treacherous floods, earthquakes, famines, child-abuse scandals, murders, terrorist attacks! The *Guinness Book of World Records* has become a sort of secular substitute for the books/accounts to be opened on Judgment Day. The planet is as if surrounded by spheres of competition and recognition for excellence and/or depravity. Our very small canon of books and films here this morning is but a chirp in the cacophony of the invisible Internet.

Yet this has not taken us away from our subject. For the full and more exact title of this talk would be: "The Canon, the Genius, and the Wisdom of Harold Bloom." I feared that such a baroque title would not attract many listeners, but in fact these words refer to three books that Bloom has written: *The Western Canon* in 1994, *Genius* in 2002, and *Where Can Wisdom Be Found?* in 2004. The most exact title of the talk would be even longer but finally complete if I were to add the word *blessing*: "The Blessing of Harold Bloom." For the whole point of his work on canon, genius, and wisdom is to reach the "blessing." And the blessing is the experience of reading such sublime literature that the act of reading participates in the transcendence of the writing, such that the experience of reading and writing is one shared experience.

Elsewhere in our discussions someone used the word "anagogic," which is the fourth and highest level of classical meanings, after the literal, the allegorical, and the moral levels. Anagogic refers to the "end" or goal of meaning, at which point one has reached not only the end but the origin of the communication. It is the moment I remember in *Wuthering Heights* when Catherine Earnshaw cries out: "I *am* Heathcliff"; when in the Gospel Jesus took the bread and blessed it and said: "This *is* my body." The "blessing" for Bloom is "more life: time without boundaries." It is the "*olam*." what Christians and Jesus himself refer to as "eternal life." For Bloom, there is a reading experience that can be called by such a name, though he himself is not a believer. He is a "knower," or, as he likes to say about himself, he is a Gnostic sect of one. No normative Jew is he, but rather a Gnostic before Judaism, Christianity, or Islam ever was. One can take him or leave him. The joy is in taking him, and taking him on.

For he is a teacher, an entertainer, a serious, funny, outrageous sort of prophet; a wise and foolish old man: Lear and his Fool combined—a sort of Charles Laughton–like character actor who takes himself much less seriously than that toward which he is pointing, and he is pointing to a wonderland of literature that is a sort of kingdom, which contains a special kind of crown. Need I situate him in his field of "literary criticism"? Need I say that his greatest tribute is to the man he considers the greatest literary critic: Samuel Johnson? Need I say how he cannot praise Giambattista Vico enough for having seen the relation between rhetorical tropes and psychological defenses and for having grasped the four ages of the cycle of world history: from the religious to the aristocratic to the democratic to the chaotic? And back/on to the religious once again. Need I add that he considers Kenneth Burke the truest son of Vico? Need I mention the other critics who rise and fall in his texts like accompanying dolphins: Auerbach, Curtius, Northrop Frye? Need I add that Bloom never has a footnote, never gives a page reference to his cited authors, and sometimes does not even mention the title of the book of an author he quotes? Perhaps I need to say all those things and much more, but it is essential to say that I have not read all of Bloom's writings nor all that he writes about.

I write simply to communicate something of the blessing and the joy of crossing the path of Harold Bloom, and I draw him to your attention at this conference on contemporary Jewish thinkers because I think his presence and his concerns give us a much-needed balance. For the Jewish-Christian dialogue is a dialogue not just about religion but about life. And it may be that we come closer to one another and articulate our differences in more vital ways when we get off the subject of religion and pick up more so-called "secular" subjects, such as atomic physics, politics, medical ethics, or literature, and get into it together so we can get on with it. So we can reach the blessing. And avoid the curse.

One point I must add: Bloom is not an imperialist. His canon, his geniuses, his wise men are *his* writers. He knows very well that others have their favorites, as we ourselves listed our favorite books and films. But to search out our best and to communicate them, to share them with others, to defend them, to criticize them, is the human task of recognizing the blessing, of knowing what we know, and of valuing it. It is Bloom's enthusiasm that I want to share. If I have some critical remarks to make about him, it is in the nature of his own enterprise, which I wholeheartedly share. And so we can move to the next point.

2. Stolen Time and Time Redeemed

It is very important for me to align this presentation of Harold Bloom with my purpose. For my purpose is to keep at the work of unbedding, of unearthing our canon, our prophets, our wisdom, so that the blessing can flow on. Literature and indeed all of the arts require an element of freedom to their appreciation that we sometimes have to steal. I present a few examples of times I have stolen a glance at other people's books or interests.

1. I heard the story of a theology student who had finished his studies and went to see Karl Rahner before leaving the theologate to ask for some final advice about how he was to continue his studies afterwards. Rahner is supposed to have told him something like this: "Now, read contemporary literature. Study and try to appreciate contemporary art, drama, exhibitions. Theology can only take you so far. The arts will take you farther into the world in which we live, and the world we have to make."
2. When I was studying philosophy at Weston College in Massachusetts, Bernard Lonergan came to visit. I made an appointment to talk with him in his room about the philosophy paper I

was doing on his *Verbum* articles. He was called to the phone, and while waiting for him to return, my eyes scouted the room. On a corner of his desk I saw a copy of Elizabeth Bowen's *Death of the Heart*.

Many years later, I met him when he was at Harvard Divinity School. Again I made an appointment, for I was working on my philosophical approach to the symbolism in the Apocalypse of John. I asked if I could read the typescript of his *Method in Theology*, which was not yet published. He had some teaching to do and gave me the key to his Harvard office, and I sat there patiently reading the pages of *Method*. Tired, I once again scouted over the almost empty shelves, but my eyes fell on a volume of the *Collected Poems* of Constantine Cavafy—a modern Greek poet I knew only from the occasional references to him in Lawrence Durrell's *Alexandria Quartet*.

3. Moise Mouton, French Jesuit biblical theologian, tells the story of his meeting Paul Beauchamp very early in his formation—perhaps just after the Novitiate. When Beauchamp learned that Moise was interested in biblical studies, he could not have been happier than to encourage him to begin by reading Proust's *À la recherche du temps perdu*, nothing less than a seven-volume novel that tells a story taking a few thousand pages for the plot to bring all the characters round to a single party and celebration of their age and their ages.

If I mention these stories about Rahner, Lonergan, and Beauchamp, it is only to show how they had "other" sides to them. And indeed they were many-sided. But it was the literature they read that fascinated me and encouraged me not to feel guilty about the time I so often stole from my duties of required work, but rather, eventually, to realize—as did the protagonist of Proust's novel—that everything comes round: that Swann's Way eventually meets the Way to the Guermantes. Those two roads that went in opposite directions before the child's house finally came round to join in the very composition of the character of the grown man.

Is this so far from Paul's exclamation in Romans 8 that for those who love God everything works toward what is good? Or from the exclamation found in Psalm 23: Goodness and mercy will follow me all the days of my life?

It is a confirmation of this discovery that I found in Bloom and that took me on further discoveries that are still not ended. Let me tell you about him.

3. Bloom's Enterprise or Recherche

I will first tell briefly how Bloom crossed my path and swept me away. Then I will take a look at Bloom's works, presenting a hypothetical periodization of his work (a periodization that he would abhor, as a really strong piece of literature transcends its period, and contextualizing criticism is a waste of precious time).

A. Crossing Bloom's Path My Way

I had come across some critical reviews of Bloom's *Book of J*, in which he claimed that the Yahwist tradition of the Torah or Pentateuch was written by a woman shortly after the reign of Solomon and that it was nothing less than the most ironic, vital, engaging and enraging and enrapturing portrait of "God" that can be found in world literature. I did not read the *Book of J* at that time, but Bloom's name was on my screen.

I took a leap into Bloom himself on the advice of an older friend, a diocesan priest from Vermont who had spent his life as a military chaplain in various places around the world with an experience of American soldiers and others that was diverse and deep. He advised me to read Bloom's *The American Religion*, which he said was a kind of maverick book but it was on to something. The Southern Baptists, Mormons, Christian Scientists, Pentecostals, and New Agers had formed a sort of skein, mentality, vision that was not just expressing an American faith or religiosity but forming it. And anyone inside the

American whale or influenced by it had better catch on to what is making it swim, devour, and live as it does.

And then, after years of teaching the humanities, the great books, some philosophy, and Scripture at Bethlehem University, I heard of Bloom's *The Great Canon*. I obtained a copy of it and in American fashion I devoured it . . . only to find that I had swallowed Jonah himself, Harold Bloom, who was on a mission of his own. Converted, I realized that I did not have to "follow him" . . . rather, I had been more or less on the same track all along! Encouraged, awakened, I could only be grateful. Among other discoveries, he gave me Whitman. Do you know the difference between years of occasionally reading Whitman and being somewhat bored by him, and finding a critic who leads you into the inner streams of Whitman—the Me, the Me Myself, and the Real Me—the three dimensions of Whitman, and how he needs those aspects of himself to open to the world? It was not a tight New Critical approach but the open road of Bloom, who repeated himself, took leaps, offended his enemies, and moved on. No wonder that he invariably appreciates Chesterton.

The *Canon* then led to other works, and finally to his collection of the best poems of the English language: a canon, of course, but with the poems themselves and his usually brief and vibrant introductions. Enraptured, and with a request of my own, I wrote to him, and I will later tell you about our brief correspondence. No wonder that when Tom Michel asked me to participate in this conference on Jewish–Christian dialogue, I agreed to go. When asked if I wished to present any contemporary Jewish thinker of importance, I scouted about for a Jewish writer. At first I most wanted to take up Hannah Arendt. But on learning that Jim Bernauer was going to present her at the conference, I wondered whether it would be better for me to demur from any presentation. But there I was, on a bus from Boston (Soloveitchik's home) to Cincinnati (one of Heschel's first teaching positions in the United States was at Hebrew Union College), reading Bloom's *Where Can Wisdom Be Found?* for the pure pleasure of it, when I suddenly wised up, and said to myself: Why not present Bloom, you fool!

And so Tom Michel admitted me into the program, an amateur Bloom-reader, pushing him onto the stage with Abraham Heschel and Dov Soloveitchik and Hannah Arendt! And I push him on shamelessly, all the more shamelessly, after finally—under the stress of needing to "prepare a talk"—reading the two books of his that I could find in our Bethlehem University Library: *The Anxiety of Influence* and *Poetry and Repression*. For these, with only slight foreknowledge on my part, took me into Bloom's theory and practice of "antithetical criticism" based loosely but deeply on the Kabbalah of Isaac Luria. Somehow I had circled back/on into more Judaism than I could imagine.

Wonder of wonders, other books of his began to make more sense. But this brief presentation of how I crossed the path of Harold Bloom may also show how certain authors, certain works of literature, parallel our lives, are following us like our shadow, which only appears where there is light and an object, wall, pavement, surface it can fall upon. Yet even when it has no surface to fall upon, it seems to be there all the time, an invisible "other" or "doppelganger." I think of my life with Rilke, which began by reading a poem of his on Mary in the Novitiate in a volume of poetry on Mary. His poem was unlike any other. Later, in the Juniorate I read further poems; but in Philosophy I finally fell into the *Duino Elegies* and did my first reading of *The Notebooks of Malte Laurids Brigge*. Then Paul de Man's criticism wiped him off the map, only for him to reemerge in a new translation of the *Sonnets to Orpheus*. His letters, and especially those to and from Lou Andreas-Salomé, opened other vistas. During my ordination retreat at the Jesuit Retreat House at Annecy, I found an old copy of *Malte* once again and slipped into it effortlessly, and I read Malte's own retreat notes as I made my own retreat.

We all have such writers in our lives: painters, musicians, films, philosophers, theologians, Scriptures! Rituals! Friends and enemies. And they grow stronger! That is one of Bloom's points, indeed, the central point. *Read to enjoy!* Everything else is ideology. It is the enjoyment of beauty that is the central human experience that links other experiences to one another. It is *tiferet*—beauty—that lies at the navel of the body of Kabbalah: that joins victory and praise as well as power and mercy, that lies in alignment with the crown of wisdom and intelligence, with the genital foundation and the basic kingdom.

A brief presentation of these ten *sefirot* assumed in Lurianic Kabbalah will follow later in this talk, as they are essential and practical in Bloom's "antithetical criticism." Indeed, this may be the place, indeed is the place, to say that Bloom finds that the dialectic of Lurianic Kabbalah is the most adequate approach to bring to strong Romantic literature. And let there be no mistake: Romantic literature is post-Enlightenment literature. Modern and postmodern literature is nothing more nor less than further cascades of the river of Romantic literature: a river of no return.

And the various schools of criticism, be they New Critical, formalist, structuralist, semiotic, feminist, antiracist, anti-imperialist, and so on, tend to be ideologies, feeding on resentment. The School of Resentment, Bloom calls them. And with his sword of "antithetical criticism" (compounded out of the Kabbalah, Vico, Freud, and Valentinian Gnosticism—as we will see in *Poetry and Repression*), he defends the canon, genius, and wisdom. He defends not himself, but the experiences he has had with the greatest writers: defending the more difficult pleasures, but above all, pleasure—and, I would say, the joy of being human in the heart of all its tragedy, irony, comedy, and romance. In the face of death, life. In the face of the curse, the blessing. The blessing: more life, time without boundaries. An experience to be had in time but not of it. And so we come to Bloom himself.

B. Bloom's Way

I would like to find some hypothetical order in the works of Bloom, the better to appreciate *The Canon*, *Genius*, and *Where Can Wisdom Be Found?*

As for his life, I glean from his writing that he was born in New York on July 11, 1930, and that he began reading Blake at the age of six and Hart Crane by the age of ten. Precocious reader, at least. He did his undergraduate studies in English literature at Cornell and he is still alive!

His works are said to number some twenty-eight volumes, and he is billed as having written some five hundred brief but substantial introductions to student editions of various classics, everything from a fine introduction to *King Lear* to a disappointing introduction to *The Revelation of St. John the Divine* (these are my own evaluations). One of my favorite introductions is the one he did for the prestigious Millennium Series English translation of Proust's *In Search of Lost Time*. In the appendix to this article you will find a list of Bloom's works, minus the five hundred introductions.

I would add here that Bloom is only interested in what he calls strong poems, dramas, stories, and novels. Among such "poems" he includes the works of Freud and Nietzsche for he believes that long after psychoanalysis has proved to be—as Karl Krauss quipped—the disease it is trying to cure, Freud will prove to be one of the greatest of Romantic writers. And Nietzsche has not had to wait so long for such recognition; he is already canonized as such.

It may be useful to divide Bloom's own works into four overlapping periods, separated by two books of passage:

1. The early works (1959–1972) on particular poets such as Shelley and Blake and then into series of poets of the Romantic Age.
2. His more theoretical works (1973–1988) develop his form of antithetical criticism, based on the Kabbalah and other sources, in opposition to increasing attacks on and erosion of the canon of great, if difficult, literature. This theory arises from his practice and returns to it. His book on Wallace Stevens is proof that the particular studies of his first period are not abandoned.

   Books of Passage: I think *The Book of J* (1990) and *The American Religion* (1992) represent two extremes of his criticism, for on the one hand he presents the writer of the most complex and impish portrait of God in the Yahwist tradition, and on the other hand he presents the American Gnosticism in which he lives. Since Bloom considers himself a Gnostic sect of one, we might see that he is eminently suited to prowl through the Gnosticism of his age, but he finds little reason for hope. He indeed calls himself a Gnostic without hope.

Yet the sheer vitality of his writing, empowered and enthused by the reading experiences he has had and more than fifty years of embattled experience in the classroom, points elsewhere, as if into a hidden landscape in the darkness off the side of the road. His eyes on the road, he is driving into eternity: into a time without boundaries, without belief! Or is it rather "within belief," just as we are all within God, according to Spinoza? Bloom's pantheism nevertheless is mediated by the Word, by words, by their images, tropes, and defenses, as we indicate below.

3. The extravagant works begin with the twenty-six authors in *The Western Canon* (1994), extend through the hundred portraits of *Genius* (2002), and may end with the ten authors in *Where Can Wisdom Be Found?*

   The reader should know that this trope of considering these three works to form a sort of trilogy is my own responsibility. I see the *Canon* as a Torah, *Genius* as the Prophets, and *Wisdom* as the Wisdom Books. Similarly I see the Hebrew Bible or Tanach, the Talmud, and Kabbalah as a further representation of this threefold dynamic. But to return to our subject of the three works of Bloom, it is no mere chance that Shakespeare and Cervantes, Montaigne, Goethe, Samuel Johnson, and Proust are found in all three. All the more reason to recognize their vitality and freshness, indeed, the blessing to be found in them.

4. The anthologies form a further expansion of Bloom's genres: *Stories and Poems for Extremely Intelligent Children of All Ages* (2001), and *The Best Poems of the English Language* (2004). By this time he seems to have become the grandfather

> teacher of an entire English reading public. Settled in his positions, he ranges over the field of works like some old farmer who knows each pasture, each fence, each nest. His very company is an education. But his work on *Shakespeare: The Invention of the Human* (1998) and on *Hamlet: Poem Unlimited* shows that his early concern with particular poets and particular poems has hardly ceased but only deepened.

With this we come to his theory, or rather the theoretical presentation of the antithetical criticism he practices. And here my own knowledge is so limited that I can do little more than point to what I am still trying to understand. I base myself largely on the Ratios of Revisionism, as presented in the pattern of terms found at the beginning of *Poetry and Repression.* "Revisionism" is the name of Bloom's "school," so to speak, and antithetical criticism is his approach. By "revisionism" he does not mean the sort of falsifying adaptation of thought from one ideology to another, but rather a revision, a re-envisioning, a re-seeing. Here we find that basic position of Bloom that a close reading of a great or strong poem is a great and strong experience; the reading participates in the strength of the writing. There is one poetic act that one shares, the reader with the writer and the writer with the reader. Indeed, the very poem is a re-vision, in a relation to a previous poet, whose influence causes an anxiety in the following poet. The poem represents a repression. A poem is born of that anxiety and communicates it. But repression is only one of the defenses involved. We cannot be expected to comment on the "Ratios of Revisionism" in detail, but the reader will be well repaid if she takes time to meditate on the terms and relations of the ratios presented here.

To begin with, the ratios combine at least four authors or sources: the stages and images of the Lurianic Kabbalah, the rhetorical tropes of Vico, the psychic defenses of Freud, and the vocabulary of the Valentinian Gnostics. Each of these sources is developed, parallel to one another, in six successive stages.

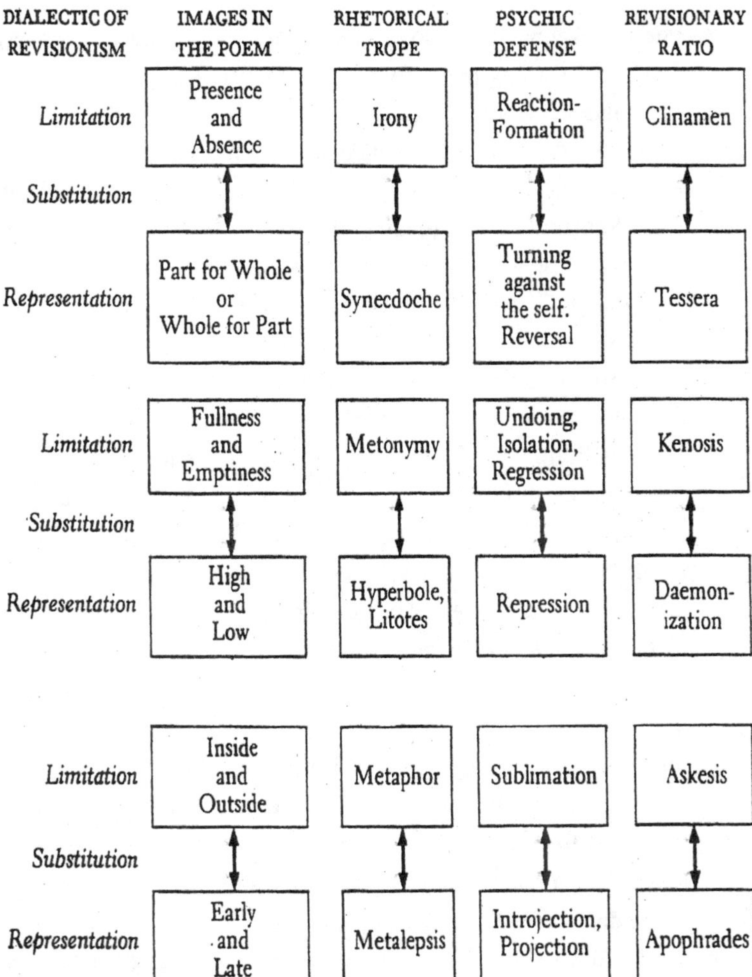

1. The first source of Lurianic Kabbalah is presented in three terms or stages: the Limitation (*tzim tzum*), the Substitution or Breaking of the Vessels (*shavret qellim*), and the Representation or Reconciliation (*tikkun*). These stages are repeated twice. Only the first and third stages are parallel to stages of the other sources, as we shall see.

2. Lurianic Kabbalah is also the source of the six images. Thus the images in a strong poem follow the pattern of pairs. First, Presence and Absence pair dialectically with Part for Whole and Whole for Part. Presence and Absence comprise the Limitation, while Part and Whole comprise the Representation. The central term, Substitution or Breaking of the Vessels, occurs in the passage from one to the other. The Limitation is an immense contraction of God into himself before the act of creation. The Breaking of the Vessels is the event that occurs on creative release from that contraction. The Representation is the act of reassembling and restoring the pieces. In the second pair of images, Fullness and Emptiness are dialectically paired with High and Low. In the third pair, Inside and Outside are paired with Early and Late. In each of those pairs, the first pair is a Limitation and the last is a Representation, consequent on a Breaking of the Vessels. Thus the first row of a triple repetition of the Lurianic stages corresponds to images that are no less Lurianic.

3. and 4. The third and fourth sources are related as language is related to psychology or, to put it more specifically, as rhetorical tropes are related to terms of Freudian psychoanalysis. The rhetorical trope of Irony corresponds to the psychic defense of Reaction-Formation, and the trope of Synecdoche corresponds to the defense of Turning against the Self. In the vertical developmental direction, just as Irony is in a dialectical relation to Synecdoche, so Reaction-Formation is in a dialectical relation to Turning against the Self, or Reversal. Horizontally, Irony expresses Reaction-Formation, as Synecdoche expresses a Reversal or Turning against the Self.

   So it is with the other pairs. In regard to the second pair, the dialectical relation between the tropes of Metonymy and Hyperbole/Litotes corresponds to the dialectical relation between the defenses of Undoing-Isolation-Regression and Repression.

Likewise in regard to the third pair, the dialectical relation between the tropes of Metaphor and Metalepsis corresponds to the dialectical relation between the defenses of Sublimation and Introspection/Projection. These terms and relations and their dialectical relations and correspondences are indeed mind-boggling and well beyond my own grasp of their full meanings. But when I start to talk about their "full" meanings and my emptiness, my "partial" "presence" to what Bloom is talking about, I begin to find in my own expressions the very terms he is using.

It is fascinating and at least partially and increasingly satisfying to see how Bloom in his book *Poetry and Repression* finds these stages in the strong poems of the Romantic Age, from Blake's *Tyger* to Wordsworth's *Tintern Abbey*, from Whitman's *Song of Myself* to Wallace Stevens. For Bloom's thesis is that a strong poem *is* strong because it moves anxiously through these six stages of imagery, with their tropes and defenses. And he maintains that no critical system is more practically adequate to the task and joy of reading strong Romantic literature than the antithetical criticism he practices, which is largely based on the Lurianic Kabbalah.

5. Bloom appears to use the strangest terms for the stages of the fifth source: Clinamen (swerving away) and Tessera (mosaic), Kenosis (emptying) and Daemonization, Askesis (asceticism) and Apophrades (returning from the dead). The terms are taken from various sources: from Valentinian Gnosticism, but also from Epicurus, Coleridge, Mallarmé, Lacan, St. Paul, Walter Pater, and an Athenian custom of emptying the house each year so that the dead can return. Bloom's well-known book on *The Anxiety of Influence* (1973) presents the six stages according to these apparently arcane terms. In his later book *Poetry and Repression* (1976), he situates these six Gnostic terms in the larger context of nothing less than the Lurianic Kabbalah, the rhetorical tropes, and Freud's psychic defenses—following Vico's insight into the relation between rhetoric and defenses! A heady

mix indeed. And a tangle of ropes that at first looks rather impractical.

But Bloom, like a literary Quasimodo, knows how to leap on the ropes and ring the bells, and he makes a music that keeps its promises and expands horizons. All you can do is take my word for it. I took Bloom's word, and I do not regret it, even if I have to admit that I can barely keep up with my guide. If Bloom did not have a sense of humor as well as a sense of cultural and critical urgency, I would not have tried to keep up with him. And with no more than this brief presentation, I must leave Bloom where he stands. His books are listed below, and they await your venture into them.

Some readers might want to know more about Lurianic Kabbalah. Isaac Luria was born in Jerusalem in 1534 and died in the Galilean mountain town of Safed in 1572. His teachings are said to constitute the basis of a concentrated effort to hasten the coming of the Messianic Age. I can say no more here in this context. But other readers may want to know how the ten *sefirot*, numbers, letters, and regions of the body connect with the three stages of Lurianic Kabbalah. The mere affirmation that the *sefirot* or attributes of God correspond to various parts of the human body can only hint at the use that Bloom makes of them.

With my limited (cf. Limitation!) knowledge of Bloom, I can only guess at how his *Wisdom* corresponds to the *sefer* or attribute of Wisdom (Hokhma), at how *Genius* corresponds to all ten *sefirot* as well as to the fourth Gnostic term of "daemonization." His *Canon* would also seem to be a complete figure of the *sefirot*, but presented according to the four ages of history established by Vico. Canonical works are those that most strongly work through their anxiety and repression by articulating in various orders the six terms of the three pairs of Imagery. This said, I move on to some final criticism.

4. Some Remarks on Antithetical Criticism

Although this is hardly an academic work, I will number my remarks by way of keeping the reader from thinking that I am merely ranting mindlessly.

1. By "antithetical criticism" Bloom means a form a criticism of the strong works of literature, and especially Romantic literature, from a "revisionist" viewpoint—a viewpoint that is free from canonical criticism which tends to eulogize and idealize the great works. Only the Kabbalah, joined to Vico and Freud, with a strong dose of Valentinian Gnosticism, can provide the dialectic that frees canonical works from a canonical criticism that is not equal to them. Bloom prides his antithetical criticism on the strength of its dialectic and claims that—by using Karl Popper's test of true dialectic—while the dialectics of both Hegel and Marx fall short of that test, the Kabbalah does not.

I would point out, however, that there is a stage even deeper than dialectic, and it is illustrated in Bernard Lonergan's *Method in Theology*; it is no more and no less than a transformation or "conversion" that takes place at the level of the heart, or spirit, or that place where the Myself, the Me Myself and the Real Me (to use Whitman's terms) are one. A loose, wild, free, yet quiet "one, as free and at peace" as the man who had been possessed by a "Legion" of demons but who was exorcised by Jesus in the Gospel of Mark. By a simple command, a word, Jesus freed him from the demons that haunted him and sent them into the pigs that fled to their deaths in the sea. Thus this first remark would point at something beyond the dialectic of antithetical criticism. For want of a name, let us call it the Naked Method, or No-Method. Neither anti- nor pro- but just there, in a relationship that some would call "anagogic," that others would call the state of "being in love."

2. Bloom describes himself as "a Gnostic without hope." He also claims that he is not a believer. That may be. But what is certain is that he is a lover—of literature, of strong literature, and of those who want to learn ways of getting into it.

3. Bloom appears to me as more of a pantheist than an atheist, more of a prophet and visionary of the word than a lawgiver, less a fool than a wise man, an imp created in the image of Yahweh.

4. Due to the limits of my own knowledge of Bloom, I can only express temporary dissatisfaction with the way that the ten *sefirot* are

used to classify the one hundred authors in *Genius*. If the categories of the Kabbalah—both the *sefirot* and the three Lurianic stages—and the categories of Vico are used as mere tropes, one might ask what psychic defenses are at work. Since his whole work constitutes a sort of gigantic poem, we must assume that Repression is at work and that Bloom himself is anxious with regard to his master, Samuel Johnson! Not to speak of the authors with whom he has shared moments of the Sublime, their resurrection from the dead. If the use of such categories has led to such a work as the books he has put into our hands, then they probably interconnect with one another more effectively than I have yet understood, and I would give the benefit of the doubt to Bloom.

5. As for the Ratios of Revision, I have been most helped by the three pairs of six Images: from Presence and Absence to Part and Whole; from Fullness and Emptiness to High and Low; from Inside and Outside to Early and Late. I miss, however, an Image of suffering to correspond to acting. I also miss references to the social, economic, political, and military situations that are implied in the present age. For Bloom no longer considers our age an Age of Chaos but an Age of Terror, leading back or round again to an Age of Religion and religious coercion. He was once nostalgic over the erosion of the School of the Ages and the disintegration of the university. In their place came the School of Resentment and the multiversity of multiculturalism. He does more than strike a pose, fiddling on the classics as Rome burns. He, too, is putting out the fires, and building fire walls, and training firefighters. To "read" and to experience the Sublime that is found there is to receive the Blessing and thereby to be freed from a fundamentalism that breeds terror. The Sublime breeds civility, but it is pressed by the Limitation that leads to the Breaking of the Vessels. It is not clear to me how the violence of that Breaking is to be distinguished from the Chaos that he laments and the Terror that he experiences.

6. Bloom claims that he wanted to include Jesus in his Mosaic of Creative Minds and indeed seems to have written something on him. But his editor advised him not to print it. In view of the several references to Jesus (as opposed to the way Christians have abused him) and especially to the deserved canonicity of the Gospel of Mark (which

was also a favorite of Auerbach, as witnessed by its analysis in *Mimesis*), I wish that Bloom had succeeded in opposing his editor and published his portrait of Jesus. As he will say below, every book is a compromise. More the pity.

7. Here I would add that I am almost always stimulated when Bloom makes some sharp, and to me offensive, remark about Christianity, Catholicism or Protestantism. The offense awakens me, and I often find that I move my barricades of defense back somewhat, or to the side. When he speaks of the "so-called New Testament," or describes the New Testament as the Belated Testament and the Hebrew Bible as the Early Testament, or when he strips Shakespeare and Melville of their Christianity, or fails to recognize the Catholicism of Flannery O'Connor (one of his favorites), or when he underlines the Jewishness of Proust, Freud, and Montaigne, he makes me uneasy. It may be that some hidden anti-Semitic self in me twists, as if Bloom were doing me some injustice. But it is a salvific twisting, a salubrious wind a-blowing. Like alcohol on a cut, it burns but it is somehow right, and I am somehow freer.

I dislike the way he seems to feel obliged to mention T. S. Eliot's anti-Semitism just about every time he mentions Eliot. But these men have scores to settle, and I am not completely outside the match that involves them. I chuckle to read his remark on Eliot's High Church criticism and Northrop Frye's Low Church approach; and I think that Eliot and Frye would chuckle too. Bloom cuts his swath through the fields like Levin out reaping in the great scene of the harvest in *Anna Karenina*, and I rejoice in his going at it. But I still want to jump out of the way of his swinging blades and join him in the reaping. And sometimes I too swing widely and not well. This too is Jewish-Christian dialogue! Taking it when you deserve it and fighting back when the issue calls for it. Being willing to make a mistake, and being willing to be corrected, and being willing to correct, too. If there is time. For we are living in an Age of Chaos, even Terror.

8. It is in this context of the Age of Terror, of the battles waged between a presumed imperialism and a presumed fundamentalism,

that I would quote a brief correspondence that I had with Bloom. Insofar as it is a letter from a Christian to a Jew requesting that he write about Islam, we might claim that we are not far from the heart of Jewish-Christian "dialogue." But we are also somewhere else: we are teachers who are still students of something so much bigger and more important than ourselves. In that spirit, and with Bloom's permission, I print our brief correspondence here.

September 1, 2004

Dear Dr. Harold Bloom,

Many times in the course of my reading of *The Western Canon* and your recent *Best Poems of the English Language* I have wanted to write to you simply to thank you. I say to myself, Before he dies you ought to let him know what joy and incandescence he has added to your own life by what he has to say! Even when you find him outrageous, opinionated, and wrong.

I mean: How could he forget to include Dylan Thomas among the best poets in the English language? And how could he fail to see that T. S. Eliot was right: too many free-thinking Jews in a "Christian society" (as Mr. Eliot conceived it) would be unwelcome? I might add that too many free-thinking Christians in a "Jewish society" as Mr. Sharon conceives it would be equally unwelcome. And didn't James Merrill deserve to be included among the poets who have reached the sublime, with inevitability, cognitive power, splendid figurative language, and allusiveness? So be it.

But I write not only to offer you my great thanks for your work and your uninhibited style and your exercise of the right to express unpopular opinions, but to ask you to consider undertaking a further task. Could you possibly take it upon yourself to write a (short) book or essay on the Quran? Do for the Quran what you have done for the Book of J? Perhaps this thought has been stirring you previously. If so, I would like to boost it over the edge to your appreciative and critical reading and writing.

Although I am convinced that much of the religious power of the book comes through the rhetoric and especially through the rhyming variety and repetition of the names of God (like warp to woof), you may find the translation that will serve your purposes. Being an amateur reader of the Quran, in Arabic, I would not be able to recommend the English translation you may need.

With this request, I repeat my gratitude for your writing and wish you good health to accomplish the work that is of most value to you and to the world as it is, and as it might be, despite its seeming determination to go down like the Pequod. I labor in the other direction. May I add how happy I was to see Melville among your poets.

All the best.

Peter Du Brul, S.J.
Dept. of Religious Studies
Bethlehem University

With this letter I sent a postcard of one of the fourteenth-century Apocalypse tapestries exhibited at Angers in France. I chose a card of a ship being swallowed into the lip-like waves of a bloody sea, and made some remark on our apocalyptic age and the dangers that we face, as if we were on the *Pequod*—the doomed ship and its crew as depicted in Melville's great novel, *Moby Dick*. I also added that I much appreciated Melville's long poem, *Clarel*, which relates the story of a group of pilgrims traveling from Jerusalem to the Dead Sea, the monastery of Mar Saba, Bethlehem, and back to Jerusalem. Bloom will refer to both the *Pequod* and *Clarel* in his response and take them one step further, as he does with just about every subject I raised in the letter.

New Haven, Conn.
September 24, 2004

Dear Father Peter Du Brul,

Thank you for your kind note. I already am an amateur reader of the Holy Quran, relying on the Aramaic and Hebrew I have known since childhood, and on some study of Arabic. I tend to rely though on the eloquent translation by Ahmed Ali (Princeton University Press) and I *have* written a brief essay on the Quran, to be found in my rather outsize book called *Genius*, which I assume can be found in the Hebrew University Library.

Nor do I differ from your esteem for Dylan Thomas and my late friend James Merrill. If you look again at the preface to my *Best Poems of the English Language*, you will find that I explicitly exclude all poets born in the 20th century, and thus end with Hart Crane, born in 1899. Since the publisher demanded a limit of a thousand pages, 300 of them to be my prose commentaries, I decided on the time limit. All commercial anthologies (and books) have to be compromises, one way or another.

General Sharon is no particular favorite of mine, and I fear that the U.S.A. is fast becoming a land where free-thinkers of any kind will scarcely be tolerated. My countrywomen and men are mindlessly going to keep our vicious regime in power, and four more years of this *could* turn the cosmos into the Pequod. As for Eliot's quite nasty anti-Semitism, I cannot believe that you condone it, any more than I condone Sharon.

All that said, I *am* moved by your generosity in writing me. I have a large readership, national and international, but am all too aware that I am rather a maverick, and doubtless too expressionistic. One is condemned to be what God made one. And *Clarel* is one of my favorite poems.

With all good wishes—

Harold Bloom

As you can guess, I then went in search of *Genius: A Mosaic of One Hundred Creative Minds*. There I found, in the *sefirot* of Hokhma, together with J (the Yahwist), Socrates, Plato, and St. Paul, the prophet Muhammad. It was an interesting but somewhat disappointing presentation as it did not take up the Holy Quran as such, that is, as I had asked Bloom to do. But who was I to badger the old man further, after he had been so generous in his magnificent "Mosaic" of those creative minds, and even more generous to me? His answer was a way of saying to me: Go on and do it yourself. Which is what I intend to do, and am engaged in doing, encouraged by what I have learned from him, his antithetical method, his willingness to make mistakes.

With this correspondence my few remarks come to an end. It is a long way from Bethlehem to New Haven. It is a longer way from a Greyhound bus on the road from Boston to Cincinnati to a Jesuit conference hall here in Bad Schönbrunn, Switzerland. But it is a very short way from person to person when they have shared an experience of the Sublime! And that is what this talk of mine has been about. Such shared moments are to be found, not just in literature, but in life, in relationships, in dialogue, even in debate, in difference, wherever Limitation leads to the Breaking of the Vessels and *tikkun*. "Grace under pressure." Flight from that pressure may indeed lead round and release the pressure in unsuspected forms. This talk is one of those releases. Our journey into the Canon, the Genius, the Wisdom and the Blessing of Harold Bloom is over. Fittingly, I will end with a fantasy that slightly modifies the historical facts. But it points to a truth that is truer than history. If it did not take place, it should have.

Coda

Several times in the course of this conference some speakers have compared their authors—be he Heschel or Soloveitchik—to Ignatius of Loyola, finding some point of relevance. I too could point to the four stages of history of Vico and remind you that Vico was once a student in the Jesuit college of Naples and that his stages could well parallel the four weeks of the *Spiritual Exercises*. I could also compare the brief prayer at the beginning of each spiritual exercise to the three stages of the Lurianic Kabbalah; for the retreatant asks that his intention, action, and operation be purely ordered to the praise, reverence, and service of God; and I am more than ready to compare the intention to the *tzim tzum* contraction, the action to the Breaking of the Vessels, and the operation to the *tikkun*. Likewise I could compare the concern with the "canon" to the recapitulatory collection of high or strong points of the meditations, so that they take on a cumulative force leading to a total self-offering to the will of God. And Bloom's insistence on the joy of reading is comparable to the discernment of those places in a meditation where one has experienced the profoundest pleasure or the deepest sorrow. But rather than develop such comparisons, I prefer the poorer option of recalling an episode in Ignatius's own life.

Jesuits and other readers of the *Autobiography* of St. Ignatius know that a seminal turning point in his life took place during his long convalescence in his castle home at Loyola. Having time on his hands he asked for a copy of the adventures of *Amadis de Gaul*, a popular Portuguese prose epic translated into Spanish. The knightly military adventures of Amadis were undertaken in view of his wooing the Princess Oriana, and he ultimately won both her and the kingdom. Such readings were not to be found in the castle, but a life of Christ and a volume of lives of the saints were brought to his bedside, and this led to a close reading and an even closer discernment of his feelings while reading. We know that this led him to imitate Jesus and to commit himself to combat for the kingdom that Jesus sketched out and died for.

However, about a year after this discernment, while living in Manresa, a long stopover on his pilgrimage to Jerusalem, Ignatius had an experience while sitting above the Cardoner River that was the greatest single grace of his life, as he recounted it in his own words. It was an insight into the underlying "spiritual" value of everything: not just of theological matters, on the one hand, and profane matters, on the other, but of the spiritual dimension, on the one hand, and both theological and profane matters, on the other. The common denominator of all things was this spiritual dimension. And it was only after this insight that he had the foresight to see that a previously consoling and enchanting vision that he sometimes saw was really the devil himself.

So I wonder if Ignatius could have been so strengthened and heartened by that insight into the spiritual dimension of things that he once again picked up the adventures of *Amadis de Gaul*? I would like to imagine that when Fr. Polanco, his beloved secretary, came back to Ignatius in the room where he had been dying, came back with the blessing from the pope that he had run off to procure, he found Ignatius well asleep—indeed, dead—and on his chest a copy of *Amadis de Gaul*, the pages held slightly open by his inserted crucifix. One hand on the adventures, the other hand on the Cross like the crisscrossed hands of Jacob on his grandsons. May Ignatius's grandsons grasp and live more fully with the blessing they have received—not merely in this fantasy on Ignatius's deathbed reading, but in fact. And the blessing is this: Live. Give more life. "Magis." Time without boundaries. This journey toward the blessing of Harold Bloom is over. Our journey toward a further blessing is far from over.

Now this may sound like and may even be a banal way to end what I would wish to be a strong statement. And it is no mere rhetorical trope or overcoming of a psychic defense to say what I am now going to say, namely, that the Society of Jesus is dying, if not entirely, at least in certain societies, in certain parts of the world. It may be that this is the Breaking of our Vessels, a necessary breakdown or breaking apart before we can be assembled. Are we able to hear this? Are we able to "overhear" ourselves when we come out with the old formulas of the "magis"?

Bloom claims that the "invention of the human" to be found in Shakespeare and in Cervantes is the capacity to get an existential distance from ourselves: in the soliloquies of Hamlet, in the conversations between Don Quixote and Sancho Panza, a deeper light or word emerges, makes space for us, brings us readers to a more complete humanity. Can it be that our very distractions are what will save us, as they bring us to a deeper level of ourselves and to that from which we were distracted? Indeed, attracted. Do we trust our attractions?! For there is not only the blessing, but the curse. The stage of "daemonization," so necessary to reach and be reached by the Sublime, is a sort of necessary—or even better, a free—transgression, or passage. Not all the "daemons" are in hell. There are angels, messengers, in heaven as in hell. And our task is the discerning, the hearing, the re-vision. In other words, can we read our own "poem"? Or have we lost it? Are we, dis-tracting, coming round again? Here Bloom stands, and he may help us more than we can imagine.

Jim Bernauer quotes some words of Hannah Arendt when she was met by Jesuits and other Christians who were too eager to find correspondences between her thought and theirs. They had not passed through what she was passing through. She told them—as I recall—that they should beware of making it too easy for themselves. She could not and would not be so easily recuperated into their thought. So we, too, might beware of taking even Bloom, especially Bloom, for granted. With this in mind, with the possibility of a curse in mind, we might continue our journey toward the blessing. But the one who stays behind, because he is reading a book that he cannot put down, may be on the righter road, may already have passed through the narrower gate, may indeed have found the kingdom we were searching for.

Appendix: The Works of Harold Bloom

Hypothetically separated into five periods: early studies of particular poets, more theoretical work, two works of passage, the more extravagant works, anthologies and recapitulations.

1959 *Shelley's Mythmaking*
1961 *The Visionary Company*
1963 *Blake's Apocalypse*
1965 Commentary on David V. Erdman's edition of *The Poetry and Prose of William Blake*
1970 *The Ringers in the Tower: Studies in Romantic Tradition*

1973 *The Anxiety of Influence*
1975 *A Map of Misreading Kabbalah and Criticism*

1976 *Poetry and Repression*, Revisionism from Blake to Stevens (He uses his Ratios of Revision—six stages of poetic development, based on imagery, rhetorical tropes, psychic defenses, and Valentinian Gnosticism, following the three moments of Lurianic Kabbalah—to show their presence and usefulness in better understanding the strongest works of Blake, Wordsworth, Shelley, Keats, Tennyson, Browning, Yeats, Emerson, Whitman, and Stevens.)

1976 *Figures of Capable Imagination*

1977 *Wallace Stevens: The Poems of Our Climate*

1979 *The Flight to Lucifer: A Gnostic Fantasy*

1982 *The Breaking of the Vessels*

1982 *Agon: Towards a Theory of Revisionism*

1987 *The Strong Light of the Canonical*

1988 *Poetics of Influence*

1989 *Ruin the Sacred Truths*

1990 *The Book of J*

1992 *The American Religion*

1994 *The Western Canon*

(He presents twenty-six canonical authors, following the order of the four ages of history according to Vico:

1. The Theocratic Age [not considered in this book]
2. The Aristocratic Age: Shakespeare, Dante, Chaucer, Cervantes, Montaigne and Molière, Milton, Samuel Johnson, Goethe
3. The Democratic Age: Wordsworth and Jane Austen, Walt Whitman, Emily Dickinson, Dickens and George Eliot, Tolstoy, Ibsen
4. The Chaotic Age: Freud, Proust, Joyce, Woolf, Kafka, Borges and Neruda and Pessoa, Beckett)

1996 *Omens of Millennium*

1998 *Shakespeare: The Invention of the Human*

2000 *How to Read and Why*

1. Short Stories: Turgenev, Chekhov, de Maupassant, Hemingway, Flannery O'Connor, Nabokov, Borges, Landolfi, Calvino
2. Poems: Houseman, Blake, Landor, Tennyson, Browning, Whitman, Dickinson, Brontë, Shakespeare, Milton, Wordsworth, Coleridge, Shelley, Keats
3. Novels I: Cervantes, Stendhal, Austen, Dickens, Dostoyevsky, James, Proust, Mann
4. Plays: Shakespeare, Ibsen, Wilde
5. Novels II: Melville, Faulkner, Nathanael West, Thomas Pynchon, Cormac McCarthy, Ralph Ellison, Toni Morrison

2001 *Stories and Poems for Extremely Intelligent Children of All Ages*

2002 *Genius: A Mosaic of One Hundred Exemplary Creative Minds* (one hundred authors listed according to the ten *sefirot* of the Kabbalah)

2003 *Hamlet: Poem Unlimited*

2004 *The Best Poems of the English Language*

2004 *Where Shall Wisdom Be Found?*

I. The Power of Wisdom
   1. The Hebrews: Job and Ecclesiastes
   2. The Greeks: Plato's Contest with Homer
   3. Cervantes and Shakespeare

II. The Greatest Ideas Are the Greatest Events
   4. Montaigne and Francis Bacon
   5. Samuel Johnson and Goethe
   6. Emerson and Nietzsche
   7. Freud and Proust

III. Christian Wisdom
   8. The Gospel of Thomas
   9. Saint Augustine and Reading
   Coda: Nemesis and Wisdom

From Midrash to Rashi to Contemporary Narrative Exegesis (R. Alter, M. Sternberg, et al.): Continuity in Jewish Biblical Reading

Jean-Pierre Sonnet, S.J.

> It is this extraordinary presence of the [biblical] characters, this ethical fullness and the mysterious possibilities of exegesis that originally meant transcendence to me.[1]
>
> —E. Lévinas

In 1968 an article was published in the Israeli periodical *Ha-Sifrut* by two young scholars from Tel Aviv University, Menakhem Perry and Meir Sternberg, which stirred up a hornet's nest of protest and nevertheless engaged biblical exegesis in a new chapter of its history.[2] The article's title is "The King through Ironic Eyes: Biblical Narrative and the Literary Reading Process."[3] It is a verse-by-verse analysis of 2 Samuel 11–12, the story of David and Bathsheba, demonstrating that an elaborate system of gaps between what is told and what must be inferred places the reader before (at least) two possible interpretations, both of them compatible with the narrative's data. According to the first interpretation, Uriah, Bathsheba's husband, was far from knowing that King David had committed adultery with his wife, whereas according to the second, he was well aware of it. Each one of the two mutually exclusive hypotheses entails a set of secondary hypotheses concerning the motives and states of knowledge of the principal characters (Uriah, David, and Bathsheba).

According to Perry and Sternberg, a structural analogy exists between the story told in 2 Samuel and Henry James's deliberate ambiguity in *The Turn of the Screw*: it is possible to uphold both that James's young heroes really see phantoms and that they are victims of an hallucination.

The most recurrent critique addressed to Perry and Sternberg was that they were analyzing a biblical narrative that was religious, moral, and didactic in intention and that it was therefore out of place to see in it any affinity whatsoever with the multiple forms of irony that we moderns so love. Perry and Sternberg responded with a rejoinder entitled "Caution: A Literary Text!" arguing that they did not apply to the (Hebrew) Bible contemporary literary criteria but that they had meticulously identified the general norms of biblical narrative—norms that the episode of David and Bathsheba illustrates in a particular way. The first of these biblical techniques is the narrative gap: it is the narrator's skill to involve the reader in the construing of the sense of the narrative by deliberately skipping some elements of the chronological and causal chain, starting with the motives and states of mind of the characters.[4]

The inquiry on the process of reading of 2 Samuel 11–12 is now a chapter of *The Poetics of Biblical Narrative*, Sternberg's masterwork published in 1985.[5] Unacceptable to some minds, the essay on David and Bathsheba turned out to have been seminal for others since its initial publication as an article in 1968. Robert Alter, professor of comparative and Hebrew literature at the University of California, recognizes that he owes his involvement in the study of the literary art of the Bible to the stimulation given by Perry and Sternberg's pathbreaking article. Alter's intellectual engagement led to the two classics of biblical literary scholarship, *The Art of Biblical Narrative* (1981) and *The Art of Biblical Poetry* (1985).[6] Alongside Sternberg and Alter, a pioneering generation—Moshe Greenberg, Shemaryahu Talmon, Jacob Licht, Adele Berlin, Shimon Bar Efrat, Uriel Simon, Moshe Garsiel, Yair Zakovitch, and Frank Polak, to name but the major figures—got down to work.

Mapping out anew the biblical landscape, these scholars took into account the intuitions already expressed by two precursors, Martin Buber and Franz Rosenzweig, particularly sensitive to the Bible's *Leitwortstil*—the way the biblical narrative associates a set of catchwords to the unfolding of the plot.[7] In this reading venture, the Jewish exegetes found partners in the Christian world, such as Luis Alonso-Schökel, Jan Fokkelman, James Ackerman, and Robert Polzin. In their dialogue, both groups referred to the first chapter of *Mimesis*, the essay by Erich Auerbach (originally published in 1946), in which the antithetical modes of representing reality in Genesis and the *Odyssey* are compared at length.[8] Upstream of this dialogue, it is the Jewish moment of the contemporary "narrative" revolution that I would like to scrutinize, in both a retrospective and a prospective view.

I use the term of "revolution" because the contribution of the scholars in question took place against the background of what Hans W. Frei has called *The Eclipse of Biblical Narrative*.[9] During the eighteenth and nineteenth centuries, the "history" contemplated in scholarship was never the story told by the narrative but redactional history or factual history: "The realistic or history-like quality of biblical narrative, acknowledged by all, instead of being examined for the bearing it had in its own right on meaning and interpretation, was immediately transposed into the quite different issue of whether or not the realistic narrative was historical."[10] On such premises, how is it possible to explain the recent comeback of the issue of narrative? The factors are evidently multiple. In an essay entitled "La 'Nouvelle Critique' et l'exégèse anglo-saxonne," Jean-Louis Ska has suggestively linked this exegetical turn with the recent history of Anglo-Saxon literary criticism (the Jewish scholars mentioned above all live in the Anglo-Saxon cultural area, whether in North America or in Israel).[11]

No doubt, the New Criticism (which developed between the last century's thirties and fifties), with its apprehension of literary works as autonomous artifacts, thus freeing them from reliance upon the author's intention, as well as from history, sociology, or psychology, played a significant role in the revolution in question. It is also probable that the "literary" exegetes drew inspiration from the so-called Reader-Response Criticism, one of the offsprings of New Criticism, which stressed the involvement of the reader in the construing of the meaning of a literary work. One has, however, to recognize that few references to I. A. Richards, R. Wellek, or R. Warren—figureheads of New Criticism—are found in their writings. Other filiations are often more prominent, notably the relationship to Russian Formalism and therefore to Aristotle's *Poetics*.

Nonetheless, generally speaking Sternberg, Alter, and their emulators call for a narrative poetics sui generis, distinct from the received models. Sternberg contends that "Scripture emerges as the most interesting as well the greatest work in narrative tradition," and thinks that Scripture has more to teach literary criticism in general than to learn from it.[12] There is, however, an intellectual tradition that our authors do not repudiate: the Jewish exegetical tradition, to which they explicitly refer. I take as witness the last part of Sternberg's foreword in his *Poetics of Biblical Narrative*:

> I want to end where my schooling began and my affection still lingers: with a tribute to the great tradition of Jewish exegesis, originating and to me culminating in the ancient rabbis. My admiration for their interpretive genius—and I do not use such terms lightly—is only equaled by my variance from their premises and licences. At a level higher than method, deeper than the ready-made opposition of the scholarly to the creative, their way with biblical language remains exhilarating and liberating.[13]

It is therefore interesting to explore the ways of continuity and of discontinuity between the ancient Jewish interpretative tradition and the invention of contemporary biblical narrative poetics.

Midrashic Preparations

In a particular way, it was the midrashic tradition that prepared the contemporary Jewish scholars to the "close reading" involved in the literary and narrative approaches. Alter makes this obvious in the first pages of his *Art of Biblical Narrative*, where he specifies that the views he develops about Genesis 38 were anticipated by the Midrash. The question is to make sense of the presence of the chapter in question, telling the saga of Judah and Tamar, his daughter-in-law, within the story of Joseph and his brothers (which opens in Genesis 37). In his Genesis volume in the Anchor Bible series, E. A. Speiser sees Genesis 38 as "a completely independent unit" having "no connection with the drama of Joseph, which it interrupts at the conclusion of Act I."[14] In a closer reading, Alter shows that the micronarrative of Judah and Tamar actually echoes the macronarrative of Joseph. In Genesis 37, after having conspired against Joseph and eventually having sold him into slavery, Judah and his brothers dip his cherished tunic in goat's blood and show it to their father; in Genesis 38, it is Judah who is confronted with personal belongings.

Analogies of situation of this kind, meant to arrest the reader's attention, play a structural role in the biblical narrative. Tamar's behavior vis-à-vis Judah actually prepares the reader to understand Joseph's strategy toward his brothers. Tamar induces Judah to recognize his misdeed *himself* ("She is more in the right than I!"); in a similar fashion, Joseph will lead his brothers to the recognition of their crime without accusing them directly. As for Judah, he is the brother who will bring about the resolution of the drama (notably in his speech in

Genesis 37:31–32	**Genesis 38:25–26**
They had the ornamented tunic brought to their father, and they said: "this have we found. Please recognize (*hakēr-nā'*), is it your son's tunic or not?" He recognized it (*wayyakîrāh*), and he said: "My son's tunic! An evil beast has devoured him; Joseph has fallen prey."	As she was being taken out, she sent word to her father-in-law, "By the man to whom these belong, by him am I with child." And she added, "Please recognize (*hakēr-nā'*), to whom do these belong, this seal and cord and staff? Judah recognized (*wayyakēr*) them and he said, "She is more in the right than I!"

Gen. 44), having apparently learned the lesson given by Tamar. Pausing in this superb exercise of close (and long-range) reading, Alter makes the following comment:

> It is instructive that the two verbal cues indicating the connection between the story of the selling of Joseph and the story of Tamar and Judah were duly noted more than 1500 years ago in the Midrash: "The Holy One Praised be He said to Judah, 'You deceived your father with a kid. By your life, Tamar will deceive you with a kid.' . . . The Holy One Praised be He said to Judah, 'You said to your father, *haker-na.* By your life, Tamar will say to you, *haker-na*'" (*Bereshit Rabba* 84:11,12).
>
> This instance may suggest that in many cases a literary student of the Bible has more to learn from the traditional commentaries than from modern scholarship. The difference between the two is ultimately the difference between assuming that the text is an intricately interconnected unit, as the midrashic exegetes did, and assuming it is a patchwork of frequently disparate documents, as most modern scholars have supposed. With their assumption of interconnectedness, the makers of the Midrash were often as exquisitely attuned to small verbal signals of continuity and to significant lexical nuances as any "close reader" of our own age.[15]

The masters of the Midrash indeed endeavored to identify and make sense of the analogies that span, at small or bigger scale, the biblical narrative. Scrutinizing the text, they brought to light intra-episodic or supra-episodic plots associated with the recurrence of catchwords. Educated in the analogical imagination of the Midrash, Jewish scholars of all ages have been exposed to the organic unity of Scripture and in our age immunized, so to speak, against the atomistic reflex of historical-critical exegesis.

Besides this attention to analogous language, there is an attitude in Midrash that anticipates and prepares the narrative inquiry as it is conceived by contemporary scholars. In an article entitled "Midrash and the Language of Exegesis," David Stern stresses that it is characteristic of Midrash to see "the interpretation of Torah as process and activity rather than as fully grasped understanding of the world.[16] The midrashic collections that juxtapose concurrent interpretative hypotheses on given biblical verses are a witness thereof. The midrashic heuristics is actually a response to the Bible's "built-in" indeterminacy, which a narrative reading has equally to face. As Alter writes:

> An essential aim of the innovative technique of fiction worked out by the ancient Hebrew writers was to produce a certain indeterminacy of meaning, especially in regard to motive, moral character, and psychology. . . . Meaning, perhaps for the first time in narrative literature, was conceived as a *process*, requiring continual revision—both in the ordinary sense and in the etymological sense of seeing-again—continual suspension of judgment, weighing of multiple possibilities, brooding over gaps in the information provided.[17]

The "brooding" in question is at the heart of the midrashic creativity, which can be described as the art of gap-filling, the art of filling in the "blanks" of the text. Commenting upon the book of Jonah, *Pirkei de Rabbi Eliezer* opens with the question "Why did [Jonah] run away?"—a question raised by the ellipsis wittingly inscribed by the narrator in his tale.[18] The narrator could have spelled out the answer to this "why" (by convention, he is omniscient); he refrained from doing so, in order to engage the reader in a play of hypotheses, up to the end of the book, where Jonah declares: "That is why I made haste to flee to Tarshish" (Jon. 4:2). In both the midrashic interpretation and the narrative approach, a similar interpretative play thus takes place as an answer to the solicitations of the text.

Midrashic Obstacles

Nevertheless, significant discontinuities between the two reading attitudes, old and new, are to be taken into account. In some of its aspects, the Midrash turns out to be an obstacle to a properly narrative approach. One of the principles of midrashic interpretation is read in Talmud *Pesachim* 6b: "There is no earlier and later in Torah." The axiom does not contradict the rules of narration if it means that the Torah (or biblical narrative in general) occasionally tells things in disorder (without following their chronological sequence);[19] in every narrative enterprise, the narrator is free to tell things in order or in disorder, so as to create an appropriate effect.[20] But if the principle means that every point in the Torah (each *parashah*, each verse or word) can throw light on every other point, whether it comes earlier or later in the text, this is more problematic. It is essential to a narrative approach that there be an earlier and a later in a story, that is, in its order of presentation.

As Perry states in the title of a thoughtful article, the "order of a text creates its meanings"; it is according to the temporality of reading that the reader progressively, in both a prospective and a retrospective dynamism, makes sense of a narrative.[21] "Although the Midrashists did assume the unity of the text," Alter writes:

> they had little sense of it as a real narrative continuum, as a coherent unfolding story in which the meaning of earlier data is progressively, even systematically, revealed or enriched by the addition of subsequent data.
>
> What this means practically is that the Midrash provides exegesis of specific phrases or narrated actions but not continuous *readings* of the biblical narratives: small pieces of the text become the foundations of elaborate homiletical structures that have only an intermittent relation to the integral story told by the text.[22]

What Sternberg calls the "universals" of narrative—suspense (the prospective interrogation by the reader), curiosity (the reader's progressive and retrospective reconstitution of the elements already told), and surprise (the way the narrative outsmarts the reader's prospective and retrospective hypotheses)—are all three, and for good reason, intimately linked to the narrative progression from earlier to later.[23] Acquainted with the midrashic "panoramism," Jewish literary exegetes had thus to adopt new interpretative reflexes in line with the temporality of continuous reading.[24]

Another presupposition of the Midrash did not contribute to the intelligence of the Hebrew Bible's narrative model. The presupposition is here a form of theological shortcut, implying that the character whose vocation or prophetic journey is told in a narrative should automatically be the narrator and the author of that narrative. Collapsing the personae of prophetic hero, narrator, and author, this principle casts Moses as the author of the five books of the Torah and the narrator of the (hi)story they unfold (and Joshua as the author and narrator of the book of Joshua, Samuel as the author and narrator of the book called after him, etc.).[25] With clear-mindedness, the Midrash recognizes that this can create problems, notably in the final verses of Deuteronomy, where Moses' death is told:

> Eight verses in the Torah were written by Joshua, as it has been taught: "And Moses the servant of the Lord died there." Now, is it possible that Moses being dead could have written the words, "Moses died there"? The truth is, however, that up to this point Moses wrote, from this point on Joshua wrote. This is the opinion of R. Judah or, according to others, of R. Nehemiah. Said R. Simeon to him: Can the scroll of the Law be short of one word, and is it not written, "Take this book of the Law"? No; what we must say is that up to this point the Holy One, blessed be he, dictated and Moses repeated and wrote, and from this point on God dictated and Moses wrote with tears.[26]

In its way to remedy a particular problem, the talmudic answer actually jeopardizes the ensemble, as Sternberg writes:

> Apparently a simple patch, this in fact opens holes in all that has gone before—and what comes after—for by its logic the reference to human canons of probability becomes not only gratuitous but invalid. Given divine inspiration, Moses could compose the rest of the Bible as well as the Pentateuch to the last letter.[27]

The theological and literary shortcuts of the tradition call for the elaboration of another model taking into account the essential role of the omniscient narrator capable of reporting the process of the creation, unattended by any human witness, and of telling of Moses' death and his burial by God in a tomb that no one "knows . . . up to this day" (Deut. 34:6).

In his *Poetics of Biblical Narrative*, Sternberg describes at length the privileges and duties of the narrator, whose credentials are not empirical (the narrator never pretends to be the witness of the events he reports) but prophetic (he rather shares, as by inspiration, God's "science"). His disincarnated yet inspired voice endows the narrative with reliability and authority beyond human measure.

The narrative model inherited from tradition had thus to be reformed by the reinsertion of the mediation of the narrating voice between the characters and the author(s). A dialogue was engaged to this end with contemporary narratology (W. Booth and G. Genette are regularly referred to). Yet the model of omniscient narration extant in literary theory also required adjustments: in the biblical narrative the first to be omniscient is the one God, a character in the story, and this creates a unique narrative situation. Between the transcendent God and the prophetic narrator, a determinate relationship exists, irreducible to the models of omniscient narration usually proposed by literary theory.[28] Thus in different ways, the narrative approach implied a reshaping of the traditional frame; as the thriving contemporary scholarship demonstrates, the new parameters did not mean the extinction of the interpretative spirit inherited from the ancient rabbis.

Rashi: The Turn toward Contextual Exegesis

A decisive turn, and a transition between midrashic and contemporary narrative reading, took place during the Middle Ages with the contribution of Rashi of Troyes (1040–1105) and of the school that followed him. Writing after the period of classical Midrash, Rashi engaged the

Jewish tradition in a new interpretative venture. Explaining Genesis 3:8, Rashi writes, in one of his rare methodological comments:

> There are many *midrashei 'aggadah* [on this verse], and our Rabbis have already arranged them according to their place [of appearance in Scripture] in *Genesis Rabba* and other Midrash collections. I have come only for the plain meaning (*peshat*) of the biblical text and for the *'aggadah* that sets the wording of Scripture on its proper bearings. Hayyim Dov Schevel, *Perushei Rashi al ha-Torah* (Jerusalem: Mossad Harav Kook, 1982), ad loc. [my translation].)

When he writes that he did not come except for the plain sense of Scripture, Rashi actually echoes a Talmudic principle: "*'ein miqra' yotsei miydei peshuto*—There is no text in Scripture that departs from its plain meaning (*peshat*)."[29] While Scripture can mean many things—like "the hammer shattering the rock" (Jer. 23:29) and splitting it into several sparks—it cannot repudiate what it says explicitly in its text and context. Quoting Psalms 62:12—"God has spoken once, twice have we heard"—in the foreword to his commentary on Song of Songs, Rashi notes: "A text of Scripture has more than one sense, but there is no text in Scripture that departs from its plain meaning."

When Rashi adds that he came "for the [Midrash] *'aggadah* that sets the wording of Scripture on its proper bearings," he reveals that his exposition of *peshat* will paradoxically borrow from Midrash by singling out and adopting those midrashic interpretations that settle the scriptural words in their contextual setting. This is the case, for instance, in Rashi's comment on Genesis 27:1, "And it came to pass that Isaac was old and his eyes were too dim to see": "*His eyes were too dim* because of the smoke of these [women]. Other interpretation: in order that Jacob may receive the benedictions." Extracted from midrashic sources (respectively *Tanhuma*, *Toledot* 8, and *Bere'shit Rabba*, 65:8), these two developments "midrashically" exploit the potentialities of the text without compromising its meaning in context.

The reference to the women derives from the verse that immediately precedes: "When Esau was forty years old, he took to wife Judith the daughter of Beeri the Hittite, and Basemath the daughter of Eylon the Hittite" (Gen. 26:34). These two women, the biblical narrator goes on, "made life bitter for Isaac and Rebekah" (Gen. 26:35). Idolatric incense-burning by Esau's pagan wives, the Midrash contends, provides a fitting rationale for Isaac's sight problems—and a fitting transition between Genesis 26 and 27, Rashi adds.

The teleological argument of the second interpretation ("in order that Jacob may receive the benedictions") does not depart either from contextual developments; on the contrary, it anticipates the narrative's central motif: Jacob's blessing by Isaac, made possible by the blurred vision of the latter. Produced by Rashi, "in an abbreviated and restructured form,"[30] the two midrashic comments effectively settle the elliptic report of Genesis 27:1 in its narrative context.

In their commitment to the plain sense of Scripture, Rashi and the Pashtanim (the *peshat* commentators who followed Rashi)[31] are an essential link in the chain that goes from the Midrash to the contemporary narrative approach. In the preface to his book *Reading Prophetical Stories*, Uriel Simon writes, "My reading has been nurtured by two exegetical schools—the medieval Jewish tradition of contextual exegesis, and the international biblical scholarship of the modern era. The combination of these two is natural for me as a contemporary Jewish student of the Bible."[32] In many aspects, the Pashtanim anticipate the "close reading" practiced nowadays. In a recent essay on Genesis 22, André Wénin shows that God's initial order to Abraham can be construed in two ways and that the entire plot is built on Abraham's journey from one sense of God's demand to the other.[33] God's injunction *veha'alehu sham le'olah* [*veha'lehu sham le'olah*], "bring him up there for a burnt offering" (Gen. 22:2), can translate a request formulated to Abraham to "bring up" Isaac as a burnt offering or a demand to bring Isaac up the mountain to offer with him a burnt offering. Is it surprising? This double reading is anticipated by two

Pashtanim, Joseph Bekhor Shor and Levi Ben Gershom.[34] Here is the comment of the latter:

> This word can be understood [as requiring] that he sacrifice him and make him a burnt offering, or [as demanding] that he bring him up there to offer a burnt offering so as to educate Isaac in the service of the Name—be he exalted! And the Name—be he exalted!—put him to trial: Would it be hard in his eyes to do whatever the Name command him, until he understands this word in another way that he had first understood it, that is, he had to bring up there another burnt offering, and not sacrifice his son?[35]

The sharpness of the medieval masters is often stupendous, and in some regards the contemporary narrative readings are just a way to update Rashi's and his successors' contextual exegesis.

The Ethics of Reading

Heirs of midrashic close reading and of medieval contextual exegesis, contemporary Jewish readers have also, as I have indicated, developed a dialogue with modern literary theory and with biblical scholarship at large. In their exposition of Scripture, however, they have shown a specific sensitivity to biblical narrative consistent with their tradition. Facing the aestheticism of the New Critics, the intellectualism of modern narratology, and some reflexes of Christian exegesis, Jewish scholars are most often driven by the ethical aspect of narrative issues. In Alter's view, the biblical narrative is a laboratory of theological ethics. Israel's ethical and monotheistic revolution is not confined to the Ten Words, the legal codes and the injunctions of the prophets; it actually takes place in each one of the literary genres promoted by the Bible, and particularly in the narrative:

> The oft-quoted rabbinical dictum *dibra torah kilshon benei 'adam*, "The Torah spoke in human language," must be applied

> not merely to the idioms of Scripture but to the adoption by the biblical writers of an elaborate set of literary instruments for the articulation—perhaps, indeed, for the discovery—of their religious vision. Ethical monotheism was delivered to the world not as a series of abstract principles but in cunningly wrought narratives, poetry, parables, and orations, in an intricate patterning of symbolic language and rhetoric that extends even to the genealogical tables and the laws. We will scarcely feel the forceful modulations with which the texts address us unless we somehow attend to the literary forms of the address.[36]

In this perspective, the act of reading is not only a cognitive or an aesthetic exercise, it is also an activity pertaining to our faculty of judgment. Far from providing characters with transparent morality (in good or evil), biblical narrative confronts the reader with dramatis personae for a part unpredictable, driven by complex motivations, and themselves confronted with God's ethical demands. If the narrator occasionally gives us a key of moral evaluation—"And what [Onan] did was displeasing in the sight of the Lord" (Gen. 38:10); "But the thing that David had done displeased the Lord" (2 Sam. 11:27)—he keeps silent most of the time and lets the reader, in what Sternberg calls "the drama of reading," untangle the web of hypotheses and moral appraisals.

The givens can be complex and challenge our first or spontaneous reactions (often mirrored in the narrative itself). All of the narrator's art is required to tip the balance and let us envision things in another way. In the last two chapters of his *Poetics*, Sternberg examines biblical narratives of this type—the story of Dinah's rape by Shechem in Genesis 34, which ends with mass massacre in retaliation by Simeon and Levi, and the story of the rejection of Saul by the Lord in 1 Samuel 13–15. Both narratives require moral evaluation (of relations between humans in the first case, of relations between God and man in the second) in complex and even provocative situations, implying the narrator's *grand jeu*.[37] We are far from critical aestheticism or intellectualism; we are in the laboratory of Israel's ethical monotheism.

In Alter's view, this type of reading is a way to recover the sharpness of the Hebrew Bible, blunted by centuries of dominant Christian exegesis. This is at least his contention in an article entitled "Northrop Frye, between Archetype and Typology."[38] There, Alter dissociates himself from the literary and theological perspectives developed by the Canadian literary critic in his *The Great Code*.[39] *The Great Code*, of course, does not sum up the whole of Christian exegetical tradition but it projects a paradigm of it on the wide screen of literature.

The immense metaphorical and typological system unfolded by Frye between the Old and the New Testaments is certainly fascinating; nevertheless, it overshadows, Alter contends, the ethical drama that takes place in the biblical story and the analogous drama that happens in the act of its reading. Alter takes the example of the scene in 2 Samuel 6 where Michal, David's first wife, gazes at her husband from the window and despises the king dancing in the presence of the Ark. "All such fascinating psychological and political complexities of this remarkable story vanish when the confrontation between husband and wife is explained as a type of the humiliated king"[40]—this is indeed Frye's construing of the episode in a double reference to a so-called Babylonian annual ritual of the king's humiliation and to the humiliation of the King of Kings in the Gospel. "The compelling interest of individual lives played out in the theater of politics in the David story disappears in a fog of archetypes."[41]

Alter concludes:

> Through centuries of Christian supersessionism, Hebrew Scripture was systematically detached from the shifting complications of its densely particular realizations so that it could be seen as a flickering adumbration of the Gospels that were understood to fulfill it. This is hardly a reading practice we want to revive, either for the Bible or for secular literature.[42]

Conclusion

These pages try to emphasize the continuity of Jewish reading. Something of the genius of the Midrash and of medieval Jewish exegesis is perpetuated in the narrative approach of contemporary Jewish scholars. Today, as yesterday, the questioning is refined, again and again, within the precinct of the scriptural text. "Turn it and turn it," as Ben Bag-Bag says in the Mishnaic *Teachings of the Fathers*, "For everything is in it."[43]

This questioning, at once literary and religious, has a distinctive ethical dimension. When the Midrash *Sifré* comments on the obligation of the future king of Israel to read in the book of the Torah "every day of his life" (Deut. 17:19), it specifies: "The reading of Scripture leads to Targum; the Targum to Mishna; the Mishna to Talmud and the Talmud to action."[44] The finality of traditional Jewish reading is ethical, as Emmanuel Lévinas has emphasized.[45] And this finality still underlies the contemporary Jewish exploration of biblical narrative poetics. Biblical narrative, for sure, ignores the didactic turn of the Midrash;[46] preferring the virtues of imagination and the play of dramatic representation, it is nevertheless interfused with the same sense of spiritual urgency: "The biblical tale might usefully be regarded as a narrative experiment in the possibilities of moral, spiritual, and historical knowledge," Alter writes.[47] In the interrelation of plot, characters, dialogue, and point of view, a map of human possibilities comes to light—a map of extreme possibilities, of men and women confronted with the living God. "The biblical writers," Alter adds, "fashion their personages with a complicated, sometimes alluring, often fiercely insistent individuality because it is in the stubbornness of human individuality that each man and woman encounters God or ignores Him, responds to or resists Him."[48]

In recent years, biblical narrative has been an exciting experimental ground where Jewish and Christian scholars have fruitfully met. In these pages, I want to pay tribute to the contribution of the former and open perspectives for the latter. Without repudiating anything that constitutes the Christian reading of Scriptures—and in particular the perspective of accomplishment (which is the ground of typological exegesis)—I believe that Christian readers have much to learn from the contemporary heirs of Rabbi Ishmael, Rashi, and Rashbam. This is true even in the field of the New Testament. The founding text of the New Testament is a narrative, and typology is not the primary objective of the literary genre adopted. The Gospel narrative rather aims at creating around the dramatic character of the Messiah a biblical "drama of reading." In the tradition of Jerome, who consulted the rabbis, and of the Victorines, inquiring about Rashi's interpretations, new "schools" have come into being.

Acknowledgments

I want to thank Elliott Rabin for his precious help in the translation of this essay, which was originally written in French and published in the *Nouvelle Revue Théologique* 129 (2007):17–34.

Inscribe the New in the Old: Inner-Biblical Exegesis (M. Fishbane) and the Hermeneutics of Innovation (B. Levinson)

Jean-Pierre Sonnet, S.J.

In memory of Timo Veijola (1947–2005)

Modern exegesis is the place of a paradox of measure: it works on a text that was produced in every detail within a particular tradition—the tradition of the Jewish people—and it applies procedures and models that have been developed in other intellectual traditions, whether that developed in Protestant Germany in the nineteenth century, with its romantic fascination with origins, or that of the United States of W. F. Albright and his archaeological empiricism, or that of the postmodern West, which, in its culture of crisis, spontaneously gives preference to the crisis experienced by biblical Israel at the turning point in its history, the Exile. Without a doubt, this transcultural dialogue is fascinating but it also has its limitations, and therefore one should be even more attentive to the approach developed within the tradition inaugurated about twenty years ago by M. Fishbane, at that time professor at Brandeis University and today professor at the University of Chicago. For the first time, in a reflective manner, a critical exegetical model was developed within the intellectual tradition of Judaism.

Briefly it can be said that Fishbane showed that a hermeneutical principle underlies the process of the growth of the biblical text. Furthermore, this principle anticipates what will develop in midrashic thought (Targum and Talmud included). Thus whilst an exegetical tradition strove to keep the biblical world at a distance from the subsequent rabbinic tradition, Fishbane showed the intellectual continuity that led from the Bible to the Midrash. Doing this, he opens hermeneutical perspectives that cannot but interest Christian exegesis.

Fishbane's decisive work on this subject was published in 1985 under the title *Biblical Interpretation in Ancient Israel*.[1] The American exegete did, of course, have precursors, and he himself pays a tribute to the pioneering work of R. Bloch, who in 1954 published a study entitled *Écriture et tradition dans le Judaïsme. Aperçus sur l'origine du midrash* (Writing and tradition in Judaism: Notes on the origin of Midrash).[2] Interest in the inner-biblical forms of reinterpretation was also illustrated at that same time by A. Robert, who spoke of an "anthological process," as well as by A. Gélin, who introduced the term "relectures" (rereadings)—whether one thinks of Deutero-Isaiah rereading Exodus or the Chronicler revisiting the book of Kings.[3] Fishbane introduces an unprecedented critical dimension to these perspectives by treating this phenomenon not only as a rereading but also as the rewriting of a previously given datum—and he brings to light the hermeneutical ways and means as well as the techniques of this rewriting.

Fishbane characterizes this phenomenon as *inner-biblical exegesis*. Long before becoming extrabiblical and influencing from the exterior the canonical Scripture, exegesis was already practiced within the canon. The growth of the scriptural corpus and first and foremost the legal corpus of the Bible, was motivated by the successive rewritings within a dynamic of *Fortschreibung*, which was conservative and innovative at the same time. The hermeneutics of the scribes, inscribing the new in the old, was practiced within the Bible so repeatedly and so pointedly that one might say, echoing B. Levinson, an enlightened disciple of Fishbane, that the Hebrew Bible puts us in the presence of the birth of the critical spirit, within the very womb of a religious tradition.

The Formula of the Canon

We speak of the "canon" of Scriptures, referring to its final state.[4] The "canonical" dimension is not, however, linked only to the ultimate stage of the growth of biblical texts. It concerns also the initial phase and each of the intermediate phases in the development in question. At a particular moment in time, a scriptural corpus was received as the "canonical" Word of God by ancient Israel and became authoritative in this quality. The Code of the Covenant (in Exod. 21–23) thus represented for a time the authorized legal corpus in Israel, normative, in its own way, for the life of the people. It is the starting point for the legal tradition of Israel.

A sign of the antiquity of the "canonical thinking" can be read in the so-called "canon formula" documented in Mesopotamian and biblical literature. The *Epic of Erra*, an Akkadian text of the ninth century BCE, ends thus with praise for the scribe who received it as a revelation and committed it to writing: "he did not leave out a single line, nor did he add to it."[5] The same formula appears in the Hebrew Bible on the lips of Moses: "You must diligently observe everything that I command you; *do not add to it or take anything from it*" (Deut. 13:1; see also Deut. 5:22). A canonical text is thus a closed text; it is forbidden to change anything in it by abbreviating or lengthening it. It has the authority of the Word of God, and no one is permitted to retouch what God has said through his prophet, "once and for all."

Canon and Innovation

However, if the text is frozen, how can it respond to the changing needs of the successive generations? These new generations have to face new realities and new challenges, whether they involve material, political, intellectual, ethical, or religious life. How can one ensure that the ancient Word of God does not become antiquated and useless? How can one "save" the relevance of this Word by giving it, again and again, renewed pertinence for the life of the people?

When legal decisions are not received as revealed laws but rather as human dispositions, the change of law does not pose much of a problem. In 1906 a corpus of laws, containing about two hundred paragraphs found in several copies dating from different epochs, was unearthed in Boghazköy, the capital of the Hittite empire (which developed in Anatolia between 1700 and 1200 BCE). These laws, which have neither a prologue (like those of the Code of Hammurabi) nor a narrative framework (like those in the biblical legal corpus) are enunciated impersonally. An interesting note appears in paragraph 7: If anyone blinds a free person or knocks his teeth out, *formerly* (*karû*) they would pay 40 shekels of silver, *but now* (*kinuna*) one pays 20 shekels of silver.[6] The paragraph thus explicitly underlines the difference between what one did "formerly" and what one does "now."

Other changes are introduced in a similar manner from one version of the Hittite code to the other (new distinctions between penalties, new cases involving slaves, etc.). Might one imagine similar procedures and parallel ways of speaking in Israel, where the legal decisions originate with God himself? In the biblical narrative, one does find one (and only one) parallel, with a similar formula. The text of Ruth 4 tells of a juridical debate between Boaz and his relatives. In Ruth 4:7, the narrator suspends the narrative and introduces a historical note. He explains to his reader that the symbolic gesture that is about to be described is a juridical custom dating from ancient times: "Now this was the custom in former times [*lepânîm*] in Israel concerning redeeming and exchanging: to confirm a transaction, one took off a sandal and gave it to the other." In other words, this is describing a practice that had fallen into disuse in the law of Israel. This practice, however—and this is the important point—is a custom that does not derive from the "revealed law" of Sinai.

A law of divine origin, in fact, cannot be declared obsolete (except by God himself). In order to legitimize legal amendments in divine law, the biblical authors had to develop specific strategies and editorial techniques that permitted them to introduce new issues and perspectives *at the very heart* of revelation and *as* revelation. They did, indeed, "add" or "take away" but they did so by outsmarting the canon: by stretching the "cover" of the canonical text up to them. Inscribing the new *within* the old, they practiced "the hermeneutics of innovation,"[7] as B. Levinson has termed it.

An Example: The Law about the Altar in the Books of Exodus and Deuteronomy

The law regarding the centralization of the cult with which the Deuteronomic code (Deuteronomy 12–26) begins illustrates the stakes and the methods of this hermeneutics. Deuteronomy is linked to a vast plan of reform taking the form of a centralization of the cult through restriction to the one unique sacrificial altar.[8] Until that time, practice followed what had been stipulated in the Code of the Covenant:

> You need make for me only an altar of earth and sacrifice [*wezavaḫta*] on it your burnt offerings of well being, your sheep and your oxen; in every place [*bekhol-hammaqom*] where I cause my name to be remembered I will come to you and bless you. (Exod. 20:24)

God guarantees his presence ("I will come to you") and his blessing ("and bless you") whenever any sacrifice is offered on an earthen altar *bekhol-hammaqom*, "in every place." The divine law thus legitimates a plurality of altars throughout the country. This practice was justified most notably by the fact that these altars also served as local butcheries. "You need make for me only an altar of earth and sacrifice [*wezavaḫta*] on it your burnt offerings of well being, *your sheep and your oxen*." The "village altar" allowed not only for the offering of sacrifice of certain animals to the divinity (this being the first meaning of the verb *zabaḫ*), but also for the ritual slaughtering (the second meaning of *zabaḫ*) of animals destined for local consumption.[9] Both activities, united by a single word, are equally "sacred": they are carried out on the altar.

The institution of the local altar, one has every right to think, has undermined the fidelity of the people: in the countryside and at cultic centers, certain manifestations of syncretism appeared, associating the "local" altars of YHWH with the "local" divinity of Canaan. The book of Kings introduces two royal reformers, Hezekiah (see 2 Kings 18:1–20:21) and Josiah (see 2 Kings 22–23), who destroyed the "high places" as well as all the other altars except for the one in Jerusalem. Josiah initiated his reforms, both in Judah and in Israel, in conformity with a certain "book of the Law" that had been found in the temple (see 2 Kings 22). This occurred in 622 (see 2 Kings 22:3), a few decades before the Exile (the deportations took place between 598 and 587/6). Exegetes, very early on, proposed an equivalence between this "discovered book" and Deuteronomy,[10] which, in its legal section, began with the order to tear down the altars of the foreign gods (Deut. 12:2–3) and institute the centralization of the cult (Deut. 12:4–28):[11]

> Take care that you do not offer your burnt offerings at any place [*bekhol-maqom*] you happen to see. But only at the place [*bam-maqom*] that the Lord will choose in one of your tribes—there you will offer your burnt offerings and there you shall do everything I command you. (Deut. 12:13–14)

Who proclaims such an injunction? It is Moses, teaching the people what God had revealed to him at Horeb. Could it be that YHWH has contradicted himself, for there he prescribed multiple altars and here he insists on one unique altar? Or might it be Moses who is putting God in contradiction with himself? Here it is important to scrutinize each letter of the text in order to identify the "hermeneutics of innovation" that is being put into practice by the authors of Deuteronomy.

The Code of the Covenant attributes a particularly open-ended spatial determination to sacrifices and ritual slaughtering: "in every place" (Exod. 20:24). The Hebrew text uses the expression *bekhol-hammaqom*, which should be translated "in the whole place." The more correct formulation for "in every place" is, in fact, *bekhol-maqom*, without the definite article (*ha-*). Although it is not an error (it is attested to elsewhere; see Gen. 20:13 and Deut. 11:24), the expression used in Exod. 20:24 (with the article) is nonetheless exceptional. The Code of the Covenant presents an undefined (or a surplus) meaning that the authors of Deuteronomy put to good use. In their eyes, the canonical expression, relatively ambiguous, called for and even justified a double reading. The expression used carries within it two spatial definitions:

> In *bekhol-hammaqom*, one can understand "in every place," *bekhol-maqom*, in a distributive sense;
> or on the other hand, if one focuses on the article, the expression of the Code of the Covenant can be understood as referring to a single place: "in the place," *bammaqom*.

On the basis of this distinction, Deuteronomy 12:13–14 carried out a redistribution of the data. On the one hand, sacrifice was forbidden where it had formerly been permitted: "Take care that you do not offer your burnt offerings at any place [*bekhol-maqom*] you happen to see" (Deut. 12:13). On the other hand, it was now required that the sacrifice be offered at the place chosen by YHWH: "But only at the place [*bammaqom*] that YHWH will choose in one of your tribes—there you will offer your burnt offerings" (Deut. 12:14). Those addressed by the law thus reformulated were not condemned, however, to go to Jerusalem every time they wanted to slaughter their ox or goat. The centralization of the cult came along with another, no less important reform linked to slaughtering: slaughtering of animals destined for consumption was no longer tied to slaughtering "on the altar":

> Yet *according to/in every* [*bekhol-*] desire of your heart you may slaughter [*tizbah*] and eat meat *within all* [*bekhol-*] of your towns, according to the blessing that the Lord God has given you. . . . The blood however you must not eat: you shall pour it out on the ground like water. (Deut. 12:15–16)

The authors of Deuteronomy thus specialized the meaning of the verb *zabah* (which in Exod. 20:24 signified both slaughter for sacrifice and slaughter for consumption). The verb and the corresponding activity were now disconnected from the link to the altar and took on a "profane" quality. Slaughtering for consumption could consequently be practiced in any place and took on the distributive meaning that had formerly been attached to the sacrificial altar: "*according to/in every* [*bekhol*-] desire of your heart," "*within all* [*bekhol*-] of your towns."

This creative hermeneutics of the scribes, "bringing out the new from the old," was placed upon the lips of Moses. Far from introducing a contradiction into the Word of God, Moses appeared as the truthful interpreter of what God had originally meant. The literal sense of the first law (in Exod. 20:24) was discovered to have a providential "surplus" of meaning, which permitted the insertion of the letter and of the spirit in the second law, that of Deuteronomy. In other words, in the letter of the Code of the Covenant, there was already place for the reform of Deuteronomy. Many of the laws of the Deuteronomic Code are similar reformulations of the "canonical" laws of the Code of the Covenant. The latter were reinterpreted and rewritten in Deuteronomy in terms of centralization (except for the laws of compensation and the laws of bodily injuries in Exod. 21:18–22:14; these two series were not affected by the centralization).[12]

In his study *Biblical Interpretation in Ancient Israel*, Fishbane uncovers the ways and means of this "interpretive rewriting," especially within the legal domain. Thus he describes the phenomenon of restriction of a previous law, using the words *'akh* ("but") or *raq* ("only") (see Deut. 20:16.20), or the phenomenon of expansion through the use of *'ô* ("or") and *khol* ("all") as well as by using the formulae *ka'asher . . . ken* ("because this . . . like that"; see Deut. 22:26) and *ken ta'aseh* ("you shall do that same"; see Deut. 22:1–3 rewriting Exod. 23:4; Deut. 15:17 reinterpreting Exod. 21:2–11). Most of the reinterpretations, however, are carried out under cover without explicit formulae, thanks to phenomena of conflation, recontextualization, and semantic specialization. When it comes to legal material, the art of the scribes surpasses itself. What is at stake in "the pen of a ready scribe" (Ps.

45:2) is no less than the actuality and the pertinence of divine legal revelation—Israel's life in relationship with YHWH.

Concordant and Discordant Inner-Biblical Exegesis

In a certain number of cases, the *Fortschreibung* is dependent on a "concordist" or harmonizing hermeneutics, seeking to reduce or hide altogether the tensions within the legal corpus. This is the case with regard to the laws of the Paschal lamb.

Whereas Exodus excludes any cooking of the lamb in water, Deuteronomy, going back to a different tradition,[13] commands cooking in water. This time the interpretative rewriting is the work of the Chronicler, who merges together in a rather unique fashion the two key terms used in the legal definitions that for him constitute canonical writ. Fishbane comments:

> The logic of this ritual statement is absurd since one does not boil meat *in* fire. . . . Evidently, the Chronicler knew the two distinct sets of ritual norms, and, regarding both as authoritative traditions, preserved them by an artificial exegetical harmonization. This is tendentiously called "the [ancient] law."[14]

Exodus 12:9	**Deuteronomy 16:7**	**2 Chronicles 35:13**
Do not eat any of it raw or boiled in water [*bāshēl mevushāl bammāyim*], but roasted over the fire [*tseli-'ēsh*].	You shall cook [= boil] it [*ubishaltā*] and eat it at the place that YHWH your God will choose.	They cooked [= boiled] the Paschal lamb in fire, according to the ordinance [*wayebashlu happesah̲ bā'ēsh kamishpāt̲*] . . . in pots, in caldrons and in pans.

In other cases, rewriting creates new tensions. An example of this is read in the laws of manumission (dealing with the freeing of slaves). In this case, the matrix of the law is also provided by the Code of the

Covenant. It opens with the words: "When you buy a male Hebrew slave [*'ebed 'ibri*]" (Exod. 21:2). The major innovation of Deuteronomy's rewriting is the inclusion of the fate of the female slave in the law, which now stipulates "*'ibrî 'ô 'ibriyyah*"—a male Hebrew or a female Hebrew (Deut. 15:12).

One of the techniques of expansion identified by Fishbane is involved here: the preposition *'ô*, "or," permits the inclusion of an element not specified in the matrix of the law *as if* it had been implicitly present all along. A second rewriting of the same law is documented in the Holiness Code in Leviticus 25. This time, the surprise is the negation applied three times to the root *'âbad*, "work as a slave," in the formulation of the law: as to the ruined brother who sells his services, "you shall not make him serve in a service of slave [*lo'ta'abod bo 'abodat 'ebed*]" (Lev. 25:39). On the contrary, "he shall remain with you as hired [*sakhir*] or resident [*toshab*]" (Lev. 25:40). The Holiness Code excludes the possibility that this service might resemble in any way a form of slavery. The use of the word *'ebed* is a contradiction in terms: Israelites face each other as free men without anyone but God as their master. However, what is the fate of the word *'ebed*, which is indeed present in the matrix? In the rewriting, the word is endowed with a new meaning. According to the Holiness Code, there is only one context that allows for the use of the word *'ebed* with regard to the Israelites: that is the context of their relationship with God. In Leviticus 25:42, YHWH thus declares: "For they are my servants/slaves [*'abâday*] whom I brought out of the Land of Egypt." The Israelites have found their master once and for all; they are no longer for sale: "they shall not be sold as slaves are sold" (Lev. 25:42).

When a Rewritten Law Says the Opposite of What the Original Once Said

The rewriting of a law might even go so far as to turn around the meaning of a law, making it say the opposite of what it once said.

Levinson shows this in a superb piece of research into texts that develop the theme of transgenerational punishment.[15] I will restrict myself here to presenting the sequence of the two biblical texts that mark the beginning and the end of a series of rewritings, underlining the contrast between them. (Levinson takes into account the basic intermediate texts, which are Lam. 5:7 and Ezek. 18:1–4.)

Deuteronomy takes up a key term of the original text, "those who reject me" (Exod. 20:5); however, the rewriting defines this expression so that it revokes the affirmation found in Exodus.[16] The scribes put the words in the mouth of the Moses of Deuteronomy in such a way that he strategically erases the references to the transgenerational consequences of sin ("upon the third and the fourth generation of *those who reject me*" [Exod. 20:5]) and supports the existence of an immediate punishment for the sinner: "who requites *those who reject him*—to their face, by destroying them. He does not delay with anyone who rejects him—to his face he requites him" (Deut. 7:10). This is obtained by using the expression *'el panayw*, "to his face," which can be translated "in his own person"[17] and which the medieval commentator Rashi correctly explains as meaning *beḥayyāyw*, "during his life."

These annotations redefine divine punishment and restrain it so that it no longer extends over the generations. On the contrary, it is applied only to the guilty party, "in his own person." Descendants are no

Exodus 20:5–6	**Deuteronomy 7:9–10**
For I, YHWH your God, am an impassioned God, visiting the iniquity of the fathers upon the children, upon the third and the fourth generation of those who reject me, but showing kindness to the thousandth generation of those who love me and keep my commandments.	Know, therefore, that only YHWH your God is God, the steadfast God who keeps his gracious covenant to the thousandth generation of those who love him and keep his commandments, but who requites those who reject him—to their face, by destroying them. He does not delay with anyone who rejects him—to his face he requites him.

longer mentioned and are thus no longer liable for divine punishment. The "key terms [of the original statement] are adroitly redeployed so as to abrogate trans-generational punishment and mandate individual retribution. . . . The paraphrase of the source thus abrogates the source, which now propounds the doctrine of individual responsibility."[18]

All this the scribes of Deuteronomy do by hiding their voice behind that of Moses so as to literarily and theologically authorize their reformulation of the Ten Commandments. The risk of discontinuity with the tradition is thus paradoxically avoided by attributing the revision of the doctrine of the Ten Commandments to the very speaker—Moses—who promulgated the doctrine in the first place. In a further step of his inquiry, Levinson shows how this hermeneutics of innovation, in this case, of revocation extends beyond the scriptural canon, most notably in the Targum Onqelos (between 200 and 640 CE). In other words, what inner-biblical exegesis had begun is carried on in extra- and postbiblical developments.

Conclusion

The perspective opened by Fishbane, his disciples, and his peers[19] is in my view the most stimulating in the field of historical-critical research. The intelligence of the biblical redactors is both respected and honored by the sophistication of this critical research. It is not surprising that non-Jewish exegetes (N. Lohfink, E. Otto, T. Veijola, to name only a few) have joined forces with this "school" in a particularly fruitful dialogue. Far from being restricted to the legal data of the biblical tradition, the inquiry covers the entire scriptural domain.

The organization of Fishbane's own work is instructive in this regard. It surveys legal exegesis, "aggadic" exegesis (in a narrative context) and "mantologic" exegesis (in an oracular context). Pioneering studies, like those of N. Sarna on Psalm 89, showing how the latter interprets the royal oracle in 2 Samuel 7 within the framework of an historical crisis,[20] or of L. Eslinger, analyzing the manner in which the prophet Hosea reuses traditions linked to Jacob in Genesis,[21] have demonstrated the pertinence of this approach in literary contexts other than the legal tradition. If this legal context has been privileged in these pages, it is because the phenomenon of legal rewriting is without a doubt the most decisive (seeing this rewriting has, so to say, "the force of law").

In his celebrated essay on Jewish messianism, G. Scholem analyzed the religious tradition of Judaism not as a heritage passively received from the past but rather as a selective and creative construction of this past.[22] The study of inner-biblical exegesis radicalizes this perspective and endows it with literary credentials. They reveal the "scribal" dimension of this hermeneutics, both traditional and innovative, in a give-and-take with the received text. All this occurs within a context of revelation—a prolonged revelation, which is reactivated in the crucible of the rewritings. Levinson writes, "From the perspective of ancient Israel, revelation is not prior to or external to the text; revelation is in the text and of the text."[23] Such a proposition does not lack for echoes in the New Testament. Levinson is the first to admit that "similar issues apply to the citation of the Hebrew Bible in the New Testament and at Qumran."[24] We must never forget that Jesus in the Gospel of Matthew praised the scribe who out of his treasure brings "what is new and what is old" (Matt. 13:52). The hermeneutics of innovation—this art of inscribing the new within the old—has found in Jesus one of its masters. Paul is another.[25]

One particularly important dimension of the phenomenon of inner-biblical exegesis has been emphasized by Levinson: in the constitution of the Hebrew scriptural corpus through *Fortschreibung*, from intermediary canon to intermediary canon, the critical spirit (and the imagination which is specifically linked to it) has emerged. "Citation," writes Levinson, "does not entail passive deference to the ostensibly authoritative—canonical—source but rather critical engagement with it."[26] That a religious tradition might be the sanctuary of the critical spirit is a statement quite unfamiliar to contemporary theory. In contemporary culture, "the biblical text, in particular, is regarded as a parade example of an unredeemed text that encodes and perpetuates concepts of power, hierarchy, domination, privilege, xenophobia, patriarchy, and colonialism. The truth is much more complex."[27] Throughout the long period of the formation of the biblical corpus, the (intermediate) canon has contributed to the emergence of a critical imagination: "It invites innovation, it demands interpretation, it challenges piety, it questions priority, it sanctifies subversion, it warrants difference, and it embeds critique."[28] Without doubt this critical faculty was primarily exercised by the scribes, putting the ancient texts back on the writing block, but this was not done without a link to the perception and evolution of the people's faith. Being heirs of the Bible, in a Jewish or a Christian context, also means being called to honor this critical tradition.

The perspective opened by Fishbane and Levinson gives hope that the living traditions of Judaism and of Christianity will carry on their hermeneutics of innovation or, as Thomas Mann called it in a different context, "*zitathaftes Leben*,"[29] "the life in the citation"—where the ancient letter is the matrix of creativity. When innovation is carried out conceptually, dispensing with the *textus receptus* of the Word of God, the latter becomes antiquated—and God's fidelity turns less perceptible.

Contemporary tradition might rather be inspired by the scriptural imagination of the biblical scribes, the masters of the Midrash and the redactors of the New Testament. "Therefore every scribe who has been trained for the kingdom of heaven is like the master of the household who brings out of his treasure what is new and what is old" (Matt.13:52).

Acknowledgments

I want to thank David Neuhaus for his precious help in the translation of this essay, which was originally written in French and published in the *Nouvelle Revue Théologique* 128 (2006):5–17.

A Catholic Conversation with Hannah Arendt

James Bernauer, S.J.

Hannah Arendt (1906–1975) would seem a less-than-ideal candidate for a contribution to a conference with our theme. Her biting critique of Christianity was braided with controversial analyses of modern Jewish thought and the State of Israel's twentieth-century practice. Indeed, was not her philosophy both a shrill lament over the ultimate unworldliness of Jewish and Christian religious communities as well as an effort to recapture for today the secular experience of Greece and Rome? Such a perspective would overlook Arendt's theological preoccupations which remained with her from her earliest university studies, when she decided to become a theology major after attending the lectures of Romano Guardini at the University of Berlin. Even as a philosophy student, Arendt would follow the theology courses of Bultmann and Tillich, study Kierkegaard, and write a dissertation on Augustine.[1]

While I would maintain that this theological concern survives at the core of her conceptual system, it is interesting to note that even George Kateb, who takes Arendt as "adamantly untheological," goes on to note that the "wonder and gratitude for being" which pervades her work and which is in opposition to totalitarianism's "contempt for the given" is "religious in quality."[2]

This paper draws out some implications of this religious interest. Section one, "The Worldly Faith of Hannah Arendt," delineates the common ground that she puts forward for human cooperation and solidarity. Scholars are still in the early stages of their examination of how influential America and its religious atmosphere were for Arendt's thought. She may never have read John Dewey but, like him, she fashioned a nondogmatic "common faith" for Christians and Jews, not to replace their own religious traditions but to supplement them and also to warn them of the dangers those traditions pose to political life.[3] This common faith establishes a plateau on which religious people of different communities may converse about the world and history without confining that conversation to strictly secular analysis or to a specific religious faith's categories. Section two treats her critique of Christianity, which was fundamental for her own articulation of worldly faith. Finally, the conclusion discusses the relevance of her notion of forgiveness to Jewish-Catholic relations in general and to Jewish-Jesuit reconciliation in particular.

1. The Worldly Faith of Hannah Arendt

"Amor Mundi" was the title that Arendt originally wanted to give to the book that was published as *The Human Condition* and is the best expression of her faith. While love for the world exhibits itself through action, this love for the world is also a faith that attempts to salvage for contemporary culture central religious experiences of the Hebraic-Christian tradition. Arendt's recourse to religious thinkers and experiences was more than a matter of mere theological background. They are intrinsic to the way that she herself experienced the crisis of our times.

As a result of their own modern assumptions, Arendt's commentators have generally failed to appreciate how her thought is not a criticism enunciated from within a modernist framework but actually breaks with that paradigm and becomes a radical postmodernism, a series of rejections of basic truths and assumptions structuring modern thought and practice: the sense of discontinuity with the past, which was once so important a part of modern self-awareness and has been betrayed by modernity's refusal to acknowledge the unprecedented rupture that totalitarianism represents; her analysis of alienation in terms of estrangement from the world rather than the self; her repudiation of the modern philosophy of history which conceives of itself as a process that we make and its replacement by a philosophy of politics in which the central category is action and not making; her refusal of utilitarianism, which she saw to be the twin of totalitarianism: "with populations and homelessness everywhere on the increase, masses of people are continuously rendered superfluous if we continue to think of our world in utilitarian terms. Political, social and economic events everywhere are in a silent conspiracy with totalitarian instruments devised for making people superfluous."[4]

Arendt's attempt to unify Nazism and Communism within the one concept of totalitarianism has been justly criticized. Although she came to modify that position, she held onto the more general point she had attempted to make, namely, that the fundamental *political* division is not between theories of the left or the right. Both share common assumptions about the character of history, the role of the economy, the nature of the person. Her thought's renewal of politics has as little to do with the conceptual democracy of western liberalism as it does with a conceptual democratic socialism. Both of these rest their cases on the continuing viability of an absolute morality for the direction of political life. It is this hope that Arendt perceived as groundless in the wake of modern history and the twentieth century's unprecedented disaster for our normal ethical conceptions. Her thought passed beyond modern attitudes because their recourse to morality actually betrayed a despair for politics itself. While this transcendence did not entail a conversion to a premodern theology, her own faith was articulated through its web of experiences and concepts.

Arendt realized that among the forces most needed for a renewal of the political realm were two that were not present in the ancient world: faith and hope, those two essential characteristics of human existence that Greek antiquity ignored altogether, discounting the keeping of faith as a very uncommon and not-too-important virtue and counting hope among the evils of illusion in Pandora's box. This faith in and hope for the world Arendt believes found perhaps their most glorious and most succinct expression in the few words with which the Gospels announced their "glad tidings": "A child has been born unto us."[5]

Arendt was convinced that institutional religion was in a state of crisis. There had taken place in modern times an indisputable loss of belief in religious dogmas, and she felt it was "sheer foolishness" to hope that religion would be able to dictate a code of conduct acceptable to the majority.[6] This institutional crisis was not a matter of indifference for her, however, because it nurtured the seeds of a more profound disaster. While loss of religious belief need not entail the forfeiture of faith itself, this was precisely the danger: "But who can deny that faith too, for so many centuries securely protected by religion, its beliefs and its dogmas, has been gravely endangered through what is actually only a crisis of institutional religion?"[7] *Amor mundi* was the faith she proposed as the way of overcoming this danger.

This project imitated that of her teacher, Rudolf Bultmann, whose theology sought to rescue an authentic Christian faith from the loss of credibility that many of its accompanying premodern beliefs had suffered. In its integration of religious experience, Arendt's *amor mundi* became a discourse of ultimacy, a faith not in God but in creation. This faith was articulated as an alternative to the appeal that ideology exercises once faith is displaced. Arendt understood, as had Dostoyevsky before her, that without faith a person will become a "flunkey of his ideas" and will believe anything, especially an ideology's total explanation and its promise to the masses of a "man-made fabrication of the Paradise they had longed for and of the Hell they had feared."[8]

A strictly secular form of thought is inadequate to this level of ultimacy and hence incapable of meeting the danger of loss of faith or the appeal exercised by ideology. Although her interpretations were political, Arendt appreciated how religious perspectives had been abused in the period of totalitarianism and in the struggle of the Cold War.[9] Her articulation of faith did not become ideology, for she incorporated into it the essential feature of the religious imagination as opposed to the gnostic. While the latter delights in the infinite, the endless, and the unworldly, the religious imagination dwells with the finite, the definite, and the worldly. Arendt's thought fashions a story out of religious images, which reveal meaning and ultimately inspire faith.

The continuing appeal of *The Origins of Totalitarianism* is due not primarily to its general historical analyses, which professional historians have so roundly criticized, but to its organization of that history within a particular religious horizon of meaning that enables the reader to confront and comprehend the horror of what is described.[10] The focus of her portrayal is not the wicked deeds perpetrated by individual men but rather a fallen state, a sinful condition, which is a feature of our age or, as the book's original English title had it, the burden of our time. This fallen condition is described as an "absolute evil," by which she means that it is not comprehensible in terms of wicked motives of "self-interest, greed, covetousness, resentment, lust for power, and cowardice." It is the person's rebellion against the human condition itself, the determination to create a new man according to a technology justified by ideological claims to absolute knowledge of the laws of life and history. Cecil Rhodes's wish—"I would annex the planets if I could"—expresses the love of excess and expansion that is the cry of our epoch.[11] Through the book is a sense of universal responsibility for crime which has often been misinterpreted as a moral condemnation not only of victimizers but also of victims.[12] In fact, she is describing a fallen state that makes revolt against the human condition a universal temptation. She later pays tribute to the American Revolution's Christian realism, which prevented its leaders from sharing the "absurd hope" that man "might still be revealed to be an angel." She praises this realism in a number of other contexts, a praise that conflicts with her tendency to see images of unworldly innocence as having their source in Christianity. For Christian theology, of course, it is only Jesus who is without sin.[13] This realism is beyond the horizon of the secular mind, which is committed to a universal innocence that is lost only by the evil actions of specific individuals. Totalitarian evil operated on a different terrain, and Arendt has recourse to a religious geography in order to capture it. For her, concentration camps represent "basic Western conceptions of life after death":

> Purgatory is represented by the Soviet Union's labor camps, where neglect is combined with chaotic forced labor. Hell in the most literal sense was embodied by those types of camp perfected by the Nazis, in which the whole of life was thoroughly and systematically organized with a view to the greatest possible torment.[14]

In attempting to symbolize the effect of this sin of totalitarianism, Arendt frequently employs a term rich with religious resonances, "wilderness." It entered her philosophical vocabulary with the dissertation on Augustine and comes to mean for her the dangers of a world laid waste by ideology and terror. Etymologically, it is a place of wild beasts, where humans are not at home and thus where they are subject to violent feelings of bewitchment and isolation. As Arendt's meditation on Joseph Conrad's *Heart of Darkness* indicates, wilderness possesses the same meaning for her that it had for the biblical writers.[15] It is a place of temptation where people are thrown back upon themselves and can come to believe anything. Separated from the stability of a shared world, the violence of interior emotions breaks forth like the vegetation; in Kurtz there is the "mystery of a soul that knew no restraint, no faith and no fear"; the "spell of the wilderness" had beguiled his "unlawful soul beyond the bounds of permitted aspirations," and there was, therefore, "no earthly reason for any kind of scruple." There was "nothing on earth to prevent him killing whom he jolly well pleased." Kurtz "had kicked himself loose of the earth. Confound the man! he had kicked the very earth to pieces."[16]

Conrad's opposition of the stabilizing earth and the lawless wilderness is mirrored in Arendt's own conception of the world as a refuge from the wilderness of totalitarianism. Her *amor mundi* is presented as a deliverance from the savage dark times that shadowed the earth in the twentieth century. As it was for the Bible, the wilderness is also for Arendt a place to be saved from, whether it be through religious covenant or through the American settlers' constitution of themselves as political units "in fear of the new continent's uncharted wilderness and frightened by the chartless darkness of the human heart." The wilderness, even that of our age, need not prevent exodus to a promised land of action.[17]

The passage to it requires a paradoxical asceticism. The heart of this asceticism is self-renunciation before the world. Concern with the self or the soul is subordinated to care of the world. The lack of such care cannot be disguised by a commitment to mere economic engagement within the world. Max Weber's study of inner-worldly asceticism demonstrated to Arendt that an "enormous, strictly mundane activity is possible without any care for or enjoyment of the world whatever, an activity whose deepest motivation, on the contrary, is worry and care about the self."[18] It is interesting to note that Arendt's denunciation of labor, of the slavery imposed in a society of consumers, and of the evils of the wealthy in our age echoes biblical perspectives and much of Christian teaching up to the modern period and frequently until today.

Arendt's asceticism is a paradoxical one, however, for the subordination of care of the self that she counsels must avoid becoming the "selflessness" that she saw as so characteristic a feature of the revolutionary, who holds that the "value of a man may be judged by the extent to which he acts against his own interest and against his own will." Such selflessness becomes the soil of totalitarian success, in which the instinct for self-preservation is lost and one can willingly accept one's condemnation, even "help in his own prosecution and frame his own death sentence" if the movement demands such.[19] This is where the asceticism of the self that Arendt counseled imitates the religious care of the self she seemed to reject. The religious care of the self entails a renunciation of the self before the Otherness of God and the needs of the human community. This renunciation brings a heightened sense of individuality to the self and a greater awareness of its place in the world. Although she displaces the accent of religious asceticism, she imitates the model in proposing a subordination of the self to the otherness of the world, a subordination that leads to the possibility of achieving a greater individual distinctiveness.

The religious aura of Arendt's conceptual schema is exhibited best in her analysis of action. The delineation of that realm allows her to introduce two powers that she sees as essential both to the character of the actor and to the preservation of the realm itself. These are the powers to forgive and to promise.[20] Both are put forward as specifically worldly acts. For Arendt, forgiving is a necessarily interpersonal act, and she contrasts it to the moral standards for ruling that were developed by Plato from the private experience of the self. Promising is put in opposition to the "darkness of the human heart" which symbolizes the unreliability of the human being, who is always capable of change from day to day. Forgiving and promising shelter the realm of action, for they remedy the two predicaments intrinsic to action. Forgiving is a "redemption" from the predicament of action's irreversibility, the fact that once an action is done, it cannot be undone.[21]

What allows the actor to recover from deeds that were performed but are regretted is the forgiveness received from others. Without such forgiveness, without release from the consequences of our acts, we would be confined to the first mistaken deed for which we are responsible. Forgiveness allows the continuance of a public life, which always carries the risk of unanticipated, regrettable consequences. Promising is a liberation from the predicament of the actor's chaotic unpredictability. When people come together and pledge themselves to a course of action, they make a mutual freedom and a common political achievement possible. The superiority of those capable of promising over those who are "unbound by any promises and unkept by any purpose" is that they have the capacity to "dispose of the future as though it were the present, that is, the enormous and truly miraculous enlargement of the very dimension in which power can be effective."[22] Deprived of the ability to make promises, we would be without a stable individuality and would lack the ability to join with others in contributing to the world an achievement worthy of future remembrance.

Arendt's tribute to forgiveness and promising enables her to introduce into political experience two of the most potent religious acts. Promising is the politicalization of the biblical covenant, and Arendt's utilization of it allows her conception of politics to bask in the light of the experience of salvation and of the establishment of a people's identity.[23] Arendt claims that Jesus of Nazareth was the "discoverer of the role of forgiveness in the realm of human affairs" and interprets his teaching to mean that forgiveness "must be mobilized by men toward each other before they can hope to be forgiven by God also."[24] While forgiving is eminently personal, where "what was done is forgiven for the sake of who did it," this capacity need not be rooted in an unworldly love but in the respect owed to others by their very existence.[25] Whether her distinction between love and respect ultimately holds up, Arendt nevertheless manages to incorporate the power and appeal of forgiveness into her model of politics. Such a power is crucial for a historical experience that has been conceptualized as sinful.

Arendt is at her boldest in absorbing the experience of Jesus into her model of political life. She regards his insights into the faculty of action to be as original and unprecedented as were Socrates' experiences of thought. Her esteem for Jesus is based on the conviction that his "faith was closely related to action" and that the New Testament's portrayals of him have philosophical implications. The most significant of these is that freedom is presented as the "power of performing miracles": "The only activity Jesus of Nazareth recommends in his preaching is action, and the only human capacity he stresses is the capacity 'to perform miracles.'"[26] The appeal of this form of freedom for her is that it directly confronts the modern fascination with history as a natural process: "the work of faith, actually its product, is what the gospels called 'miracles'" which are "interruptions of some natural series of events, of some automatic process, in whose context they constitute the wholly unexpected." As Arendt points out, this power to perform miracles is not rooted in will or thought but in faith.[27] Faith's most essential effect is the personal acceptance of natality. Specifically differentiated from the classical emphasis on human mortality is the experience of the promise that one's beginning possesses for the world. For her, the very purpose of being is to begin, and she never tired of citing Augustine's definition, "that there is a beginning; man was created, before whom nobody was." "Initium . . . ergo ut esset, creatus est homo, ante quem nullus fuit."[28] Natality is the "miracle that saves the world," and its source is faith's discernment, against the background of natural processes, of the "infinite improbability" that every new beginning represents.[29] Although the historical Jesus was central to her faith, Arendt certainly never accepted any orthodox claims regarding his divinity. For her, there was a chasm between the Jesus of the Gospels and the Christ of the Pauline texts. "I don't feel any loyalty to Christ. I may feel a loyalty to Jesus, because that is indeed an example, what Jesus did, and his whole life, the *logoi*, and all the stories, this can indeed become an example."[30]

Various interpretations may be given to the role that religious-theological categories play in Arendt's thought. Some will see in it merely the continuing survival of religious culture in the thoughts and attitudes of all modern thinkers, a testimony to the inability to think outside our Western heritage and to the power of language, for in it the "past is contained ineradicably, thwarting all attempts to get rid of it once and for all."[31] Others will acknowledge what seems evident in her texts: Arendt's deliberate effort to preserve and reinterpret religious experiences for an audience bereft of the modern conviction in historical progress. Thus her utilization of Jesus' life is comparable to what she thought the Church as an institution had done with it, namely, transformed it into a "worldly event" that could become a durable foundation as an example of action.[32] As I have indicated, her thought's incorporation of religious elements could be understood, then, as an antidote to both totalitarian and secular misappropriations of those elements. This is the level I believe Philip Rieff correctly grasped when he claimed that it was precisely Arendt's "covert theology" that made her "attractive to an antitheological intelligentsia."[33]

I would like to put forward yet a third interpretation which, while compatible with the other two, does the greatest justice to Arendt's thought. There is in fact a religious experience that permeates her thought and that seeks expression in the theological categories it uses. Her belief in God manifests itself in the specific acceptance of each human being as a gift to the world, in which each has a proper dwelling place. This conviction corresponds to the theological reality of a providential creation and is the fruit of a faith that overthrows two of the most appalling truths of modern experience: the conviction in and actual manifestation of superfluousness among human beings; in addition, the will to expansion and rootlessness that has wreaked such havoc and that nevertheless maintains its appeal.[34]

Arendt's *amor mundi* and her invitation to worldly action expressed and were nurtured by a religious faith in the intrinsic value of every human being and in love as the fitting response to each person's appearance. Despite her glorification of human action and the potential greatness and immortality to which it could lead, she recognized that the "specifically human quality of greatness" was "being greater than anything done." Although her political concern elevated respect as a virtue over an unworldly love, her religious faith affirmed that it was "only love, mutual love" which can give the "supreme confirmation of one's existence."[35] Arendt's commitment to a love of the world actually mirrors the biblical faith of a creative God who established creation and found it to be good. Despite her critique of religion in general and of Christianity in particular, Arendt's own personal faith led her to transmit religious models and experiences that showed that, like truth, they still have the promise of forming the "ground on which we stand and the sky that stretches above us."[36]

2. *Amor Mundi* and the Criticism of Christianity

My purpose in pursuing Arendt's covert theology is not to reduce her thought to a system that is foreign to it but rather to exhibit the fundamental vision underlying her project. In her perspective, we live in the twilight of a destroyed modernity and of an ever-declining Christianity. Her faith, *amor mundi*, is put forward as a replacement for the publicly evident spiritual weakness they left behind, a weakness that is a continuing invitation for the entry of ideologies. In place of the doubt toward the world generated by modern thought and practice, she constitutes a realm of meaningful attitudes for a contemporary worldly faith. In her analysis of worldlessness, she is careful to point out that modern knowledge "neither abolishes nor removes nor even shifts the unknown that is the region of faith." Although Kant misinterprets his own discovery, his grasp of the limits of knowledge secures a place for the meanings with which both reason and faith are concerned.[37]

Arendt also attempts to rescue this region of faith from the modern crisis of religious belief. She recognizes that Pascal and Kierkegaard carried modern suspicion and doubt into the very center of religion and that this doubting led the religiously motivated, like their secular counterparts, to seek an interior certainty of knowledge, a certainty that is forever a stranger to faith. Kierkegaard's leap is a descent into the self and undermines the "general mood of Christianity which resides in the importance of faith." It "may be that the leap into belief has done more to undermine authentic faith than the usually trite arguments of professional enlighteners or the vulgar arguments of professional atheists."[38]

In confronting this double assault on faith, Arendt fashions a "faith state," to use the expression of William James, or to employ that of Michael Polanyi, a "fiduciary program." It is a project of ultimate meanings and commitments intended to inspire a confidence in the promise both of one's natality and of the worth of assuming collective responsibility for the world; it is as well the foundation for a worldly questioning of experience, the "faith seeking understanding" that Augustine would have recognized.[39]

She intended this worldly faith to have an appeal that was potentially universal and thus sharply distinguished from specific religious commitments. It can be argued, however, that *amor mundi* also shows the directions by which a religious faith, especially Christianity, may nurture its worldliness and properly express its engagement in the political realm. Such an engagement would be guided by Arendt's central perspectives on politics: the role of forgiveness and public covenants; the essential virtue of opinion rather than truth claims in the public realm; the specific character of political action in contrast to efforts motivated strictly by the desire to improve economic conditions; a regard for the world and the freedom created within it that is irreducible to the role of the world in the salvation of souls. The particular form of engagement that Arendt's *amor mundi* promotes would offer a third model for participation in public affairs among the religiously committed, one that avoids both the intolerance of religious fundamentalism and the economic reductionism of movements inspired by Marxist analyses.

We know from Arendt's critique of religion, however, that she would find such a religious utilization of her model inadmissible and contradictory to its fundamental assumptions. In contrast to many other religions that have been identified with the protection of specific communities or peoples, Christianity displays a particularly intense form of otherworldliness.[40] In Arendt's examination, this unworldliness, with its intrinsic hostility to the public domain, derives from Christianity's glorification of the self and its individual destiny. As she puts it in "Collective Responsibility": "With the rise of Christianity, the emphasis shifted entirely from care for the world and the duties connected with it to care for the soul and its salvation."[41] This shift echoes throughout the proclamation of its good news. The self is the temple of God, and "What profit would a man show if he were to gain the whole world and destroy himself in the process?"[42] This dedication to the self grounds a constellation of Christian positions that debase the life of action and transform a potentially worldly agent into a pilgrim on earth, a *Homo viator*.

Arendt's indictment of Christianity from the perspective of the world consists of three interrelated charges. First, Christianity rejected those classical viewpoints that fostered worldly engagement. It reversed the early Greek vision of reality, of mortals in an immortal universe where great accomplishments were motivated because these provided the only opportunity for achieving the immortality awarded by remembrance of city and people. This striving for greatness entailed a heroic contempt for one's own life. For Christianity, the single living individual is born with immortality into a universe that is mortal: "It is the world that will pass away: men will live forever."[43] Desire for an earthly immortality became "futile and unnecessary."

The victory of Christianity over ancient culture was probably due to the sacredness and immortality that it conferred upon individual life, an undreamed-of hope for people who felt that their world was in fact passing away.[44] In addition to the reversal of Greek experience, there was an inversion of Roman experience. Christianity undermined the republic's emphasis on the past that had invited a citizen to achieve fulfillment by contributing to the public reality initiated by the state's founders. With Christianity, human life was directed to the future, to the eternity that will be enjoyed beyond the world: "man was only a pilgrim on this earth, and what he was actually looking forward to was life after death."[45] Christianity's repeal of the classical world's perspective did not lead, however, to a revision of the primacy that Greek philosophy gave to the life of contemplation over that of action. The contemplative vision of God, which will be the joy of life after death, functions as a Christian standard for the evaluation of the relative merits of contemplation and action during earthly life.

The second charge in Arendt's indictment proceeds from these principles. Christianity necessarily demeans the life of political action for it proclaims a negative freedom to people, a "freedom from politics," a freedom that is "politically perhaps the most relevant part of our Christian heritage."[46] The experience of inner freedom that Christian thinkers make their paradigm is a derived and distorted form of political freedom. This distortion results from the alienation through which "worldly experiences were transformed into experiences within one's own self."[47] The virtue of interior freedom is tied to a liberty from secular involvements, a mentality that provides the "reason why Christian churches could remain so indifferent to the question of slavery while clinging fast to the doctrine of the equality of all men before God." To the extent that Christianity deals with political issues, it must subordinate them to a conception of the common good that is foreign to the public realm, namely, the "salvation of one's soul as a concern common to all."[48] That this separation from an authentic public interest is intrinsic to Christianity is fortified for Arendt by her consideration of the task central to the discipleship of Jesus: the pursuit of goodness. Goodness must hide from being seen or heard if it is to preserve its purity of intention. As Jesus said: "Why callest thou me good? None is good, save one, that is, God."

In contrast to the public identity that comes to the person of action, the Christian dedication to good works drives its adherents to anonymity. From the perspective of the public domain, the Christian is comparable with the criminal: "Both are lonely figures, the one being for, the other against, all men; they, therefore, remain outside the pale of human intercourse and are, politically, marginal figures who usually enter the historical scene in times of corruption, disintegration, and political bankruptcy." Good works are performed for the sight of God alone and thus "truly are not of this world."[49]

The third count in Arendt's indictment is that far from Christianity being only indifferent to the public realm, it is actually the source or support of values that are destructive of political life. As a result of the Christian belief that the Absolute has incarnated itself in history, historical reality has never again been free from institutions and individuals who seek to apply absolute standards to the public domain. Its conceptualization of revelation as truth clashes with a political model of life that rejoices in the necessary diversity of opinions due to the different perspectives of human beings. Christianity's conception of law as divinely enunciated commandments to which obedience is owed is in conflict with the political qualities of constant, mutual agreement and freedom.[50]

Finally, the lingering legacy of Christian values on human civilization supports the tendency for certain moral experiences such as compassion and pity to dictate human conduct in the political realm. In Arendt's interpretation, however, such virtues, when introduced into politics, abolish the distance of the worldly space that sets limits to what can be done to and on behalf of others. The violent excesses of a Robespierre and modern revolutionaries in general have their source in the victory of moral feelings over political virtues. Faced with overwhelming suffering and unrestrained by limited political objectives, revolutionary compassion "will shun the drawn-out wearisome processes of persuasion, negotiation, and compromise, which are the processes of law and politics, and lend its voice to the suffering itself, which must claim for swift and direct actions, that is, for action with the means of violence."[51]

In the light of her critique of Christianity, it is hardly surprising that Arendt was opposed to any attempt to transcend secularity and directly reintroduce religious viewpoints and passions as such into public-political affairs. For the political realm such a return would risk the injection of a fanaticism utterly alien to the very essence of freedom and would encourage an escapism from politics by promoting a search for unworldly solutions to worldly problems.[52] The return would be no less dangerous for religion itself, which would face the threat of being perverted into an ideology and being made into an instrument of coercion.

The amalgamation of religion and politics has an attractiveness for many as a result of two inaccurate presumptions. First, it is incorrectly assumed that the crisis of our age is religious in nature and not political. Those who seek in religion a way of arresting the decline in tradition, authority, and personal responsibility fail to appreciate that Christianity's historical importance for these areas was due to its borrowing of Greek and Roman understandings at the time when, with the collapse of the Roman Empire, it assumed responsibility for Western culture. The second inaccurate assumption is the hope that a religious sanction can be restored to political conduct, that life will be lived once again in the shadow of a Final Judgment. Such an expectation fails to confront the reality that religion is an ever-diminishing force in Western communities and no longer affords the possibility of directing the thought and action of a majority.[53]

Certainly Arendt's criticism of Christianity needs to be contested. It is undeniable that Arendt has identified unworldly features within Christianity that have become dominant forces at different points in its history. There has been a tradition that counseled a radical disengagement from the world because it was depicted as a place of temptation, evil, and corruptibility, unworthy of human love. The human being was *Homo viator*, needing salvation from the "shipwreck of the world." Viewed against the background of this tradition, it is not surprising that Arendt would conclude, in reference to the experience of action among America's founding fathers, that it was "nothing less than the weight of the entire Christian tradition which prevented them from owning up to the rather obvious fact that they were enjoying what they were doing far beyond the call of duty."[54] What is surprising, however, is that her critique ignores the far more prominent and influential traditions of world affirmation that are also part of religious history.[55] I believe that this disregard is due to three factors: the excessive authority exercised over her both by Kierkegaard's vision of religion and by her teacher Rudolf Bultmann's radical disjunction of the self's existence from a sinful world; second, as I have already mentioned, her conviction that no religion could furnish a universal foundation for our culture's confrontation with the contemporary political crisis; finally, her view that religion was bound to be dogmatic and lack that "broad-mindedness" required by our pluralistic culture.

In fact, however, her thought's covert theology demonstrated the potency of certain religious understandings for a renewal of action and of the political faith upon which such renewal would rest. Many others ought not to have been disregarded.[56] Arendt failed to appreciate how the religious emphasis on the care of one's unique soul generated a sense of individuality that was a resistance to the destruction of plurality, the disappearance of the many into a mere mass, the "One Man of gigantic dimensions" that characterized totalitarianism.

It is precisely this individuality that inhibits the corruption of religious compassion into the destructive pity that was such a feature of the French Revolution:

> To Dostoevski, the sign of Jesus's divinity clearly was his ability to have compassion with all men in their singularity, that is, without lumping them together into some such entity as one suffering mankind. The greatness of the story, apart from its theological implications, lies in that we are made to feel how false the idealistic, high-flown phrases of the most exquisite pity sound the moment they are confronted with compassion.[57]

Within the religious vision, each person possesses an equal human dignity that transcends any utilitarian considerations. As creatures of the same Creator, each individual is also related to all others in an ontological relationship that is called to concretize itself in mutual commitments. This relationship is the context for all other communities, including the political, and has sustained the training for community that has been such an important contribution of religion to Western culture. Arendt disregarded this contribution—that religion, certainly in America, was a "school of political democracy," giving to people the actual experience of what it meant to be a member of a community while recognizing that there was a plurality of such communities.[58]

Certainly, major political movements within contemporary America—civil rights, antiwar, and the challenge to nuclear policy—testify to the continuing potency of political action originating in and supported by ecclesial communities. However, other movements, especially of the conservative right, would alarm Arendt because they assault political discussion. In addition, she did not appreciate how religious asceticism was a means of promoting communal and political awareness. Its call to simplicity of life was not necessarily a rejection of the world's goods as such, but rather a sensitive awareness of the conditions necessary for freedom. As she recognized in her examination of the desire for wealth and consumption, there is a fundamental incompatibility between freedom and luxury.[59] By focusing attention on the more permanent realities, religious asceticism fostered an education in worldliness, a regard for the superiority of the durable over the passing.

If Arendt had not been so adamant in her judgment regarding religious hostility to the public realm, she might have found within religious experience resources for resolving one of her own philosophy's persistent problematics: its dualism between society and polity. The division is intelligible in terms of her analysis of the destruction that takes place in the public realm when it is subordinated to economic ambitions and values. Nevertheless, the isolation of politics from the economy renders her theory irrelevant to the material conditions without which freedom cannot be achieved. Although Arendt echoes the Bible's warnings on the dangers of wealth, she does not take up its vision of justice for the poor. The biblical theology of creation and covenant demands a strict stewardship of the world's goods, which are the property of all. Within such a vision, the poor are liberated from the obscurity into which their poverty has thrown them, and recognition is given to their right to become participants in the sphere of action.

In acknowledging an ontological bond among all humans, religious faith grounds a collective responsibility that can never be satisfied by mere political respect but necessarily includes a task of economic justice. At the same time, however, this task, which is motivated by a regard for human dignity, does not degenerate into that economic domination of human life and purpose that Arendt properly decried. It does involve, however, an extension of the meaning of the political realm to embrace the necessary conditions for participation in its freedom. No matter how sublime her depiction of the political realm, if it were to be bereft of economic justice, Arendt would have presented a mere mirage.

Arendt's tendency to have her distinctions isolate essentially related realms shows itself in her radical disjunction of politics and religion. While not wishing to deny the obvious differences that exist between her *amor mundi* and religious faith, I have attempted to show how they can be thought of as complementary, an alliance invited by the crisis of the world itself. If religious experience provides Arendt with some of her philosophy's major categories, her thought offers religion a path toward a renewed worldliness, an opportunity to shape a presence in the full light of public life. The closest she ever comes to an articulation of a religious community's specific responsibility for that life is in her reflections on two popes, Pius XII and John XXIII. Her reaction to Hochhuth's controversial drama about Pius, *The Deputy*, is a searing indictment of a Christian leader's alleged unworldliness and of the disastrous absence of political capabilities to which it leads: judgment, speech, action. Pius is portrayed as lacking that most worldly of mental faculties, judgment. He is accused of failing to understand what was taking place around him and of a "rigid adherence to a normality that no longer existed in view of the collapse of the whole moral and spiritual structure of Europe." This loss of a feeling for reality was exhibited in the "flowery loquacity" of Church statements which attempted to hide its overwhelming silence, its failure to speak publicly against the fate that was engulfing European

Jewry. Fearing its unpredictability, the spokesman of Catholicism refused to act.[60]

If the Church's conduct during World War II demonstrated to Arendt the calamity that can result from an unworldly life lived in the world, Pope John XXIII manifested for her both the promise and the danger of a true Christian's appearance in the public realm. His "astounding faith" liberated him from all utilitarian attitudes and bestowed a confidence that enabled him to treat all as his equals and to present himself to the world exactly as he was.

In response, the world paid him the tribute of carefully attending to his words and acts and the honor of capturing his existence as a permanent reality through the countless stories told about him and passed on for future generations. Despite her deep admiration for his virtues, however, Pope John also represented the danger of Christian life, its capacity to shake the world. She liked to cite Luther's remark on the fearful consequence of an authentic proclamation of biblical faith, that the "most permanent fate of God's word is that for its sake the world is put into uproar. For the sermon of God comes to change and revive the whole earth to the extent that it reaches it."[61] In her essay on Pope John, Arendt expresses the awareness that Christian detachment can be both a rich worldly presence as well as a potentially dangerous transcendence of the world as it is. She is correct in that a monotheistic faith must refuse to absolutize anything, the world included. A religious *amor mundi* can never be an uncritical love, but there is no reason, contrary to much of what Arendt says, that it must be an unloving criticism.

The religious person's tension between a love for the world and a recognition of its limitations was Hannah Arendt's own experience and the gift of her Jewish faith. *Amor mundi* does not entail an *amor fati*; quite to the contrary, it demands the preservation of a certain distance, the willingness not to conform, the permanent status of what Arendt called the conscious pariah.[62] As was the case with her friend Waldemar Gurian, every person who attempts to love and act in the world is also always a "stranger in the, world, never quite at home in it": "His whole spiritual existence was built on the decision never to conform and never to escape which is only another way of saying that it was built on courage."[63] It is in that same region of courage where Arendt's *amor mundi* and religious faith can meet. It is a courage to love the world not because there is an ideological vision of its potential perfection but because it is greater than the storms of evil that pass over it. It is this awareness of evil and sin that guides faith and sustains democratic communities. Manifesting a face scarred by evil, the world appears more vulnerable but also more real and more lovable.

Conclusion

I mention above how important forgiveness is in Hannah Arendt's understanding of human action. I would like to conclude with an acknowledgment of how significant a confession of guilt and the seeking of forgiveness are for the dialogue between Christians and Jews, between Jesuits and Jews. We Catholics have come to appreciate the need for a penitential voice with regard to the Holocaust and our conduct during that period of mass murder as well as in the history of anti-Semitism that preceded it. Pope John Paul II's pilgrimages to Auschwitz (1979), the Synagogue of Rome (1986), Mauthausen Concentration Camp (1988), and finally Jerusalem (2000) were the model for the journey of confessing sinfulness to which the pope called all Catholics. Several bishops' conferences in Europe followed his example and, perhaps, it is now time for the Society of Jesus to join that penitential voice.

In a recent essay I attempted to give some sense of the difficult history of Jesuit-Jewish relations that needs to be recognized.[64] Most Jesuits are unaware of this history, but it is important that they come to appreciate that for some scholars it is central to how the Society is perceived. Hannah Arendt herself identifies anti-Semitism as the special charism of the Society: "It was the Jesuits who had best represented, both in the written and the spoken word, the anti-Semitic school of the Catholic clergy."[65]

Jesuit preaching of the Gospel too often turned out to be bad news for the Jews. And we might have expected it to be so different. Perhaps our greatest source of pride as a religious society is that we carry the name of Jesus himself. We know that Ignatius of Loyola's desire for intimacy with his Savior even included an actual sharing in the Jewish lineage (*secundum carnem*) of Jesus and Mary. Yet we excluded Jewish converts from our ranks for over three hundred years. And yet perhaps, within the perspective of faith, Ignatius's holy desire may have been granted, for we often came to mirror for our enemies the despised face of the Jew.

Jesuits and Jews were the most frequent victims for those who sought a total, diabolical explanation for how history operated. They formed, as one writer has said, a "tragic couple," both demonized in infamous documents: the *Monita Secreta* for the Jesuits, the *Protocols of Zion* for the Jews. Their diabolical character was charted on the axes of space and time. Spatially, they operated outside any specific territory and aspired for domination over the world; they lurked behind thrones at the same time that they were quite willing to overthrow those very kings and nations. Jews and Jesuits were preeminently people of the city and hence were accused of being allied to wealth, loose morality, and a cunning, deracinated intelligence that was contemptuous of the traditions of the rural past. Temporally, they were at home in periods of decadence and collapse and hence they were perceived as devotees of modernity: the same spectacles that detected the Jesuits as fathering the French Revolution saw the Jews as the creators of the Russian one.

This history echoed in Germany in the years leading to and during the period of the Third Reich, and it may be a badge of honor for the Society that Hitler carried a hatred for Jesuits that seems even to predate his obsession with Jews. And we paid a price: some eighty-three Jesuits were executed by the Nazis, another forty-three died in concentration camps and twenty-six more died in captivity or of its results. Decree 5 of General Congregation 34 ("Our Mission and Interreligious Dialogue") stated that dialogue "with the Jewish people enables us to become more fully aware of our identity as Christians." Perhaps it also leads into a deeper understanding of ourselves as Jesuits and of Ignatius's desire for us in relationship to the people of Jesus and Mary. Not embracing Ignatius's love of Jesus' people certainly damaged the Jewish people. But, as history has shown, that refusal did not lead Jesuits to a safer spiritual, moral, or political place for themselves. Seeking reconciliation between Jesuits and Jews on the basis of historical knowledge will bring us to a new place, certainly one far more promising than those we leave behind. Arendt would have celebrated that.

What Might Israelis and Jews Learn about Christians and Christianity at Yad Vashem?

David M. Neuhaus, S.J.

Why am I giving a talk on the presentation of Christians and Christianity in the new Yad Vashem museum in Jerusalem at a congress that is devoted to the theme of the relevance of modern Jewish thought for Jewish-Christian relations? My presentation here is an attempt to read Yad Vashem as a contemporary Jewish "text" that is saying something about Jewish-Christian relations. This "text" has been "written" by those working at Yad Vashem, and I propose to take them seriously as contemporary Jewish thinkers. Striking is the fact that the "text" has recently been "rewritten"—a new museum has replaced the old one. The following presentation is one Christian's "reading" of the new museum.

Many Israeli and foreign Jews (as well as non-Jews) make their way to Yad Vashem not only to learn about what happened to the Jewish people at one of the darkest moments of its history but also to commemorate the murdered millions. In particular, youth (schoolchildren, soldiers, and university students) are regularly taken through the museum and surrounding shrines and memorials as part of their education. Yad Vashem might be considered one of the most important places for the formation of Jewish identity in Israel today. In this sense, it is also formative for the Jewish encounter with Christians and Christianity. What might Israelis, Jews, and others learn about Christians and Christianity at Yad Vashem? Have there been any changes in the "text" when one compares the new museum to the previous one?

The Yad Vashem museum and surrounding shrines and memorials that commemorate the Shoah were established in 1953 by an act of the Knesset, the Israeli parliament. Yad Vashem ("a memorial and a name," a reference to Isa. 56:5) is situated alongside Mount Herzl, where the founder of political Zionism, Theodor Herzl (1860–1904), was laid to rest in 1949. There, too, one finds the tombs of many of Israel's prominent political leaders and the most important of Israel's military cemeteries. The entire area of Mount Herzl and Yad Vashem constitutes a central civic pilgrimage site that commemorates foundational events in the history of the Jewish people and the State of Israel in the twentieth century, particularly the Shoah and the establishment of the state. Yad Vashem is not just a place for documentation of historical facts but also a shrine promoting remembrance of this darkest hour. The command to remember, often evoked at Yad Vashem in biblical terms of "remember what Amalek did to you" (Deut. 25:17), is the fundamental purpose of the shrine and museum.[1] In the 1998 Vatican document on the Shoah, "We Remember: A Reflection on the Shoah," this aspect of memory was also central:

> We invite all men and women of good will to reflect deeply on the significance of the *Shoah*. The victims from their graves, and the survivors through the vivid testimony of what they have suffered, have become a loud voice calling the attention of all of humanity. To remember this terrible experience is to become fully conscious of the salutary warning it entails: the spoiled seeds of anti-Judaism and anti-Semitism must never again be allowed to take root in any human heart.[2]

On March 15, 2005, a new Yad Vashem museum was inaugurated in a lavish ceremony that brought tens of world leaders to Jerusalem, including high-ranking representatives of the countries in which the Shoah took place (Germany, Poland, Russia, Ukraine, Hungary, Rumania, France, etc.). The Catholic Church was represented by cardinals Jean-Louis Tauran and Jean-Marie Lustiger.[3] The new museum, built alongside the old one it replaces, is dramatic in its structure and uses the modern pedagogical means of presentation available today. Designed by the renowned Israeli architect, Moshe Safdie, it is a long, triangular-shaped tunnel covering 4,200 square meters, most of it underground.

Whereas the old Yad Vashem was a conventional museum, displaying exhibits that evoked the horror of those years, the new museum emphasizes individual experience through the testimonies of survivors alongside the documentation and display of artifacts and personal possessions. Wherever the visitor turns, he or she is confronted with television screens, about a hundred spread throughout the museum, on many of which survivors recount their own personal stories. The museum itself leads the visitor through ten distinct halls where the history of the period unfolds step by step. Other writers on this subject might discuss the historiography involved in the constitution of the new museum, its presentation of the facts mingled with highly personal testimonies, and the formative ideas and ideologies that have produced this monument. Some might compare it with the Holocaust Museum in Washington, DC. Still others might analyze the philosophy of memory and its particularist and universalist overtones at Yad Vashem or the relationship between memory and healing, healing and pardon, pardon and reconciliation.

My own aim is more modest: to read, impressionistically and personally, the "texts" in the museum that present Christians and Christianity within the context of the story of the Shoah, wondering how they might be formative for the encounter of my Jewish fellow countrymen and -women with Christians. The new museum has kept the format of the old museum, presenting step by step the unfolding story of the Shoah. In this story, Christians and Christianity are secondary to the theme of Jewish suffering, and this should not be forgotten in what follows. I stop and meditate only the "texts" that evoke Christians and Christianity.

A Christian visitor to Yad Vashem is confronted with the darkest side of the history of Christendom, one that often arouses denial in Christians. In this regard, the Vatican document "We Remember" encouraged Christians to confront the facts: "The fact that the *Shoah* took place in Europe, that is, in countries of long-standing Christian civilization, raises the question of the relation between the Nazi persecution and the attitudes down the centuries of Christians towards the Jews."[4]

Here I am more interested in what Jews might learn about Christians and about relations between Jews and Christians in the contemporary world in which we must work together so that events like the Shoah never happen again. I remember being struck each time I visited the old Yad Vashem by the overwhelmingly negative image of Christianity and Christians conveyed by the museum. The stereotypes of a traditional Jewish education that saw Christians and Christianity as essentially anti-Jewish were reinforced as Christian Europeans at the time of the Shoah were presented as either collaborators with the Nazis or indifferent to the fate of the Jews. One had to step outside the previous Yad Vashem museum to realize that not all Christians in Europe at the time of the Shoah were either active supporters of the Nazis or passive observers. In 1963, the Avenue of the Righteous from among the Nations was established at Yad Vashem. This was later extended into a garden. As of January 2005, Yad Vashem had recognized 20,757 "righteous Gentiles" (with about 2,000 trees and 18,000 inscriptions). Among these righteous Gentiles are many who risked their lives in rescuing their Jewish brothers and sisters exactly because they were faithful Christians, following Jesus and the teachings of the Christian faith. Yet at the old Yad Vashem, the specifically Christian identity, faith, and motivation of many of these righteous men and women seemed largely unrecognized.

To what extent does the new museum present the complexities and diversity of Christian reactions during the period of the Shoah? To what extent does it distinguish between Christianity and the history of Europe? To what extent does it reinforce, reform, or combat the stereotypical thinking and prejudices that Israeli and Diaspora Jews might have with regard to Christians and Christianity? Most important, does it reflect any echoes of a new relationship between Jews and Christians forty years after *Nostra Aetate* and almost sixty years after the establishment of a state where Jews are the majority and Christians are a tiny and often embattled minority?

The first direct confrontation with Christianity in the museum comes almost immediately one enters the first exhibition hall, dedicated to the theme "From Equals to Outcasts." Right after the presentation of the 1933 rise of Hitler, there is a section on traditional Christian anti-Judaism. This is the most troubling, the most explicit, and the most formative of the material on Christianity in the museum. Between representations of the two well-known figures from the thirteenth-century entrance to Strasbourg Cathedral, proud Ecclesia and downcast Synagoga, an imposing headline broadcasts a statement by St. Augustine "Slay them (the Jews) not, scatter them abroad." The text that introduces the visitor to Christianity and the Jews is the following:

> Since its inception Christianity was ambivalent towards Judaism. It recognized the Jews' uniqueness as divinely chosen bearers of God's Word. However, Christianity developed a hatred of the Jews for rejecting Jesus as the Messiah who preached a new redemptive gospel and it blamed them collectively and forever for his death. Fifth century Christian theology determined that the Jews should not be killed, rather they should be kept in their humiliated status until they accept Christianity. In the Middle Ages, the negative image of the Jews became entrenched with the charge of deicide. This charge led to popular outbursts and blood libels against the Jews, especially in times of crisis. In its theological struggle against Judaism and the Jews, Christianity perpetrated and spread this negative image over the centuries and wherever European Christian culture reached.[5]

This text, harsh as it is, does allude to an ambivalence that has characterized Christian attitudes to the Jewish people. The text is illustrated with a number of images. In addition to the statues from Strasbourg Cathedral, there is a 1475 altar piece showing the Jews draining the blood of the child Simon of Trent (a medieval blood libel); an illustration of Hell (1175), showing the Jews in a cauldron, and a typical medieval illustration of Judas Iscariot receiving payment from the Pharisees (dressed as medieval Jews) in return for the betrayal of Jesus. In a display case below there are ashtrays engraved with the "*Judensau*," the Jewish pig, and Jews suckling the pig, mother of the Jews, in this repugnant image. The ensemble is shocking. However, is this not a rather stereotypic presentation of Christianity, portrayed as simply the incarnation of anti-Judaism? Where is the expression of the "ambivalence" mentioned at the beginning of the text? To what extent does this initial presentation negatively influence the perception of Christians and Christianity in the rest of the museum? A presentation of the Shoah as if it were simply the natural outcome of the teachings of Jesus of Nazareth and his followers betrays the far more complex history of Christians, Jews, their relationship in Europe, and what happened in the Shoah. Furthermore, is such a presentation constructive in promoting relations between Jews and Christians today in the State of Israel, where Jews are the empowered majority?

The sensitive visitor will note, however, that this exhibit on Christianity's anti-Judaism is separate from what follows, a more expansive presentation of modern racial anti-Semitism. The saga continues, telling the story of the Nazis' establishment of power in Germany. In a series of fourteen photographs showing how Hitler was welcomed by German society, three, placed at the top center of the collection, are images of high clergy welcoming Nazism, including one that shows Hitler greeting Catholic religious leaders. Mitigating this overall negative image of Christian hierarchy is the adjacent highlighted quotation of Protestant pastor Martin Niemöller, echoing a different perception of what was happening in Germany:

First they came for the Jews and I did not speak out because I was not a Jew.
Then they came for the Communists and I did not speak out because I was not a Communist.
Then they came for the trade unionists and I did not speak out because I was not a trade unionist.
Then they came for me—and there was no one left to speak out for me.

Dare one hope that Niemöller's reflection be understood as that of a committed Christian, a very different fruit of the long centuries of Christian teaching and history? Likewise, the text that documents the establishment of the Dachau concentration camp mentions that there were clergymen, hopefully understood by the visitor as Christian opponents of Nazism, among its inmates.

Although this first hall is overwhelmingly focused on the increasing persecution of the Jews in Germany, mentioned also are the gypsies, mentally handicapped, homosexuals, and Jehovah Witnesses who were also rounded up, persecuted, and put to death. This attention to the fact that the Nazi genocidal violence was not only directed at the Jews is another important, if understated, undercurrent in the new museum. In the section devoted to the Auschwitz death camp, which comes later in the visit, figures are given for deaths at the camp, showing that although the Jews were the main victims, they were not the only ones. The death statistics given are as follows:

Jews 1,100,000
Poles 70,000
Gypsies 25,000
Russian prisoners 15,000

The exhibition halls that follow the first one have very little explicit material about Christians during the Shoah. In a section consecrated to the invasion of Poland, an attentive visitor will notice that among the photos of people rounded up, there is one image of a priest in full cassock, he, too, victim of the Nazi occupier. In the hall which starkly documents the mass murder of Jews, the first large image is of a fire raging, and in the background one sees a golden-domed Russian Orthodox Church, a perhaps ambiguous image that might suggest the devastation visited on all of Eastern Europe by the Nazi invasion.

Not all Christians reacted in the same way to the Nazi horror. It would seem important to stress this in the presentation of Christians in the Shoah. Otherwise, division between Jewish victims and Christian victimizers locks both Jews and Christians into sterile stereotypes that obstruct dialogue and the building of new relationships. In the hall on the theme of "Between Walls and Fences," documenting the implementation of Nazi anti-Jewish policy throughout Europe, the introductory text to this hall stresses that there were differences in application of Nazi policy according to attitudes toward the Jews among the local population. The text mentions the difference between Western and Eastern Europe, an important complexity implying that each context must be examined and that Europeans reacted in different manners to the fate of the Jews. Dare one hope that sensitive educators might indeed make more explicit these texts as they take their charges around the museum? The most striking text on this theme is in a final panel in the hall dealing with rescue and resistance:

> The fate of Jews in occupied countries was decided not only by German policy but also by the stance of the majority society. The local population reacted in *diverse ways* [author's emphasis] to the environment of violence and terror in which the Jews were a target of persecution and murder. Some took part in the murders along with the Germans, while others helped Jews. Many people gloated over their plight and sought some profit by informing on them, blackmailing them or looting their property. In most cases the local population reacted with apathy to the murder of Jews. Both traditional and modern anti-Semitic feelings, the atmosphere of fear the Nazis imposed and conformism led most Europeans to consciously deny the obvious crimes

against their Jewish neighbors who had lived in their midst for centuries.

Although introducing a nuance that some Christians helped Jews, the text still does not grapple with the specifically Christian elements in much resistance and heroism. Furthermore, the sensitive visitor might here reflect on the universal applicability of this analysis of human reaction to catastrophe. Collaboration with evil is odious. However, apathy and the inability to identify evil are dangers to our humanity in all situations where people are being victimized and persecuted.

The new Yad Vashem does not overlook the controversial figure of Pope Pius XII. The text on the pope is overwhelmingly hostile and critical of his behavior during the Shoah. He is castigated for his silence in the face of Nazi crimes, his dialogue with the Nazis in spite of what was going on, and his failure to do anything to protect the Jews, especially in Rome. He is accused of abstaining from signing an Allied document protesting the extermination of the Jews. The only nuances in the text are the mentions of the pope's protests to the leaders of Hungary and Slovakia about the deportations. Not mentioned is the fact that in these two countries, unlike in the rest of Europe, the leaders were practicing Catholics and thus possibly more amenable to the words of a pope who was otherwise largely ignored by the civic authorities. Nowhere is there any mention of possible motives for the pope's position, the general context of silence, or, more important, the involvement of the Catholic Church in saving Jews through hiding them in monasteries, convents, and churches, a fact mentioned later on in the same hall. Likewise, there is no mention of the prodigious activity of Pius XII's successor, Mgr. Giuseppe Roncalli (later John XXIII) serving in these dark years successively in Bulgaria, Turkey, and France. He is credited elsewhere with saving thousands of Jews by issuing false documents by which Jews could escape the clutches of the Nazis. The debate about Pius XII rages on, and perhaps that text will be amended with more and more nuances as Jewish and Catholic historians work together to document the truth about the pope's role in those dark days.

In the new museum, there is one hall that more than any of the others does echo a new tone in Jewish-Christian relations. The documentation of the story of "Resistance and Rescue" gives numerous examples of Christian heroism during the Shoah. One striking example is that of the Roman Catholic archbishop of Nice, Paul Remond (1873–1963), who gave cover to two Jews, Odette Rosenblatt and Moussa Abadi, who saved Jews by placing them in Catholic institutions, providing them with certification that they were Christians. In this hall also commemorated and honored are the Belgian priest brothers Louis and Hubert Celis and the Italian priest Don Gaetano Tartalo, and the Jews they saved. Another central exhibit here focuses on the case of Le Chambon-sur-Lignon and its vicinity, where thousands of Jews were saved by Protestants led by Pastor André Trocmé. A citation of this pastor dominates the exhibit: "I do not know what a Jew is, we only know what human beings are." Likewise, the case of Denmark is documented although no mention is made of the Christian faith that stimulated the heroic resistance to the Nazis and the joint efforts of the king and the Danish people to ensure the safe escape of the Jews to Norway. In slight contrast to this, a general comment on the situation in Italy states that although many Italians collaborated with the Nazis or were indifferent, "many other Italians, particularly priests and nuns, helped Jews find hiding places."

Undoubtedly, the most dramatic rescue story by Christian leaders presented in the new museum is that of the Jews of Plovdiv in Bulgaria, retold by a survivor on one of the television screens. She describes the rounding up of the Jews, the visit of the local bishop, and his successful efforts to get them released, concluding her testimony with a homage to the people and the Church of Bulgaria. The story of Bulgaria and the role of the leadership of the Bulgarian Orthodox Church is documented in a written text too. In a special placard devoted to Metropolitans Stefan and Kiril, the visitor can read:

> They were among the heads of the Bulgarian Orthodox Church. They and all the members of the Holy Synod took a forceful stance by protesting the Bulgarian government's anti-Jewish laws. During the preparation for the deportation of Plovdiv's Jews, Metropolitan Kiril visited them and promised that he would do all in his power so that they would not be deported. On May 24, 1943, a Bulgarian holiday, Metropolitan Stefan delivered a public address and even sent an appeal to the King, calling for an end to the unjust persecution of the Jews. Both, but especially Metropolitan Stefan, had a personal relationship with the King which influenced the government's decision not to deport the Jews from Bulgaria itself.

The case of Bulgaria, presented here very prominently, raises again the issue of Christianity and Christians, showing a different face from the dominant one in the museum. This "little remnant" that resisted the Nazis, risking death to save Jews at that fateful hour, did so because they were faithful disciples of Jesus Christ and committed members of the Church. This is not fully explicit in the museum and hence might not create the necessary balance to the overwhelmingly negative initial introduction to Christianity.

A peculiarity at the entrance to the hall on "Resistance and Rescue" is that in the section devoted to partisan resistance, one corner focuses on the figure of Oswald Rufeisen, a German-speaking Polish Jew, who infiltrated the German administration and had a central part in saving Jews from the Mir Ghetto. A televised interview with the man and his fellow resistance members tells the story. However, it is nowhere mentioned that this same Oswald Rufeisen is none other than the well-known Carmelite Brother Daniel, a convert to Catholicism, about whom all Israelis learn when they study the question of "Who is a Jew?" in the history of the State of Israel.[6] It is interesting, though, that elsewhere the new Yad Vashem makes explicit mention of the fate of Jewish converts to Christianity. Whereas Christians have come to know the story of Edith Stein, declared one of Europe's patron saints by Pope John Paul II, Jews have tended to ignore the fate of thousands of converted Jews, regarded as apostates by their own people but as Jews by the Nazis. In the section of the museum that reconstructs a street of the ghetto in Warsaw, a placard is consecrated to the converted Jews in the Warsaw Ghetto:

> Around 2000 Jewish converts to Christianity, who had cut themselves off from their Jewish roots, were also locked inside the walls of the Warsaw Ghetto. There they strictly observed separate religious ritual in the remaining churches and were helped financially by church aid organizations. Some of them held key positions in the *Judenrat* and its institutions. Yet, their self-imposed segregation and different lifestyle estranged them from the Jewish community at large. With the deportations to the Treblinka death camp, the converts' fate was the same as that of the Jews.

The final exhibition hall is dedicated to the "Return to Life." Another painful episode alluded to here is the fate of some of the Jewish children hidden in convents and monasteries or with fervent Christian families. Emphasized here are the legal battles inaugurated by surviving family members to get the children back after they had been baptized and had lived as Christians during the war. These cases do indeed throw a shadow on the saving of Jewish children. It might be worthwhile to point out, though, that some priests, including Father Karol Wojtyla (later Pope John Paul II) refused to baptize children who had been placed with Christian families, understanding fully the betrayal involved in coercing Christian practice in Jewish children confided to Christians for safekeeping.

After passing through two spaces consecrated to the memorial of the victims, the visitor, exiting the museum, is confronted with a breathtaking view over the Judean hills and the Jewish neighborhoods that surround modern Jerusalem. The message seems to be a resurrection message. The people put to death in the camps during the Shoah have come back to life in the State of Israel. It is clear that the Shoah and the State of Israel (the themes of our previous meetings together in Krakow and in Jerusalem) are major themes in our dialogue with the Jewish people. They are perhaps not primarily theological themes but touch upon our shared history in a world of conflictual relations. Studying these themes together often brings us to a point where there is "a parting of the ways," painful to admit to one another and yet essential to reflect on if we are indeed to move forward to a more mature and deeper understanding of self and other. Only thus can we build relationship founded on firm rock rather than on sand. The new museum, read as a "text," is indeed more sensitive in its presentation of Christians and Christianity than the old one was. Clarifying the difficult and sensitive issues in ongoing dialogue between Jews and Christians is essential, though. This dialogue helps us not only truthfully present the past but also form new generations for a future in which the horrific errors of the past are not repeated. Reading Yad Vashem as a contemporary Jewish text reveals that there is still much work to be done in a Jewish-Christian dialogue about our often divergent readings of history and the implications of that history for a shared future in a better world.

Contributors

Rabbi Tovia Ben-Chorin

Rabbi Tovia Ben-Chorin, son of the famous Israeli rabbinic scholar Shalom Ben-Chorin, is the retired rabbi of the Jüdische Liberale Gemeinde *Or Chadash* in Zürich, Switzerland. He was formerly rabbi of Jerusalem's Har-El congregation, Israel's first Reform synagogue, founded by his father. He is chair of the Central Conference of European Rabbis and vice president of the Federation ARTZA-Suisse.

James Bernauer, S.J.

Fr. James Bernauer, S.J., is Professor of Philosophy at Boston College. He is the author of Michel Foucault's *Force of Flight: Toward an Ethics for Thought.* He has edited *Amor Mundi: Explorations in the Faith and Thought of Hannah Arendt* and most recently *Michel Foucault and Theology: The Politics of Religious Experience.*

Peter Du Brul, S.J.

Fr. Peter Du Brul, S.J., is an American Jesuit who volunteered for the Near East Province when he was too young to know better. But the marriage stuck. He has been teaching and chaplaining in Palestine since 1974, mostly at the University of Bethlehem, administered by the La Salle Christian Brothers. His field is philosophy, but he teaches both religious (Scripture) and cultural studies (the great books) as well. His research is centered on the Apocalypse, the Quran, and nineteenth-century Jesuit explorer of Central Arabia, William Gifford Palgrave.

Harold Kasimow

Harold Kasimow is the George Drake Professor of Religious Studies at Grinnell College, where he has taught since 1972, especially in the areas of comparative religion and Judaism. Professor Kasimow has written a number of articles on interfaith dialogue and on Abraham Joshua Heschel that have been published in the United States, Poland, England, India, China, and Japan. He is coeditor, with Byron L. Sherwin, of *No Religion Is an Island: Abraham Joshua Heschel and Interreligious Dialogue* (1991) and *John Paul II and Interreligious Dialogue* (1999), both published by Orbis Press. His latest coedited book is *Beside Still Waters: Jews, Christians and the Way of the Buddha*. Kasimow is completing a book titled *The Search Will Make You Free: A Jewish Dialogue with World Religions*, to be published in English and Polish by Wydawnictwo Wam, the Jesuit publishing house in Krakow. He serves on the editorial boards of several scholarly journals.

Thomas Michel, S.J.

Fr. Thomas Michel, S.J., is an American Jesuit of the Indonesian Province and serves as Secretary for Interreligious Dialogue for the Society of Jesus. His published works include his doctoral thesis from the University of Chicago, *Al-Jawab al-Sahih: Ibn Taymiyya's Critique of Christianity.* He has taught extensively in Indonesia, Turkey, and Italy and in 2000 delivered the D'Arcy Lectures at Oxford University, in Oxford, England, on Christian-Muslim relations.

Donald Moore, S.J.

Fr. Donald Moore, S.J., is Professor Emeritus of Theology at Fordham University and has published extensively on the writings of Martin

Buber and Abraham Joshua Heschel. Since January 2000 he has also been engaged in interfaith dialogue and in work for justice and reconciliation through the Pontifical Biblical Institute in Jerusalem.

David M. Neuhaus, S.J.

Fr. David Mark Neuhaus, S.J., is an Israeli Jesuit who teaches Scripture at the Seminary of the Latin Patriarchate of Jerusalem and in the Religious Studies Department at Bethlehem University. He is also a research fellow at the Shalom Hartman Institute, Jerusalem. He completed a BA, an MA, and a PhD (Political Science) at Hebrew University, Jerusalem. He then completed degrees in Theology and Scripture in Paris (Centre Sèvres) and Rome (Pontifical Biblical Institute).

Stanisław Obirek

Stanisław Obirek studied Polish philology at the Jagiellonian University in Krakow and in 1976 entered the Society of Jesus. In 1994 he submitted his doctoral thesis in Krakow. Among his publications are *The Vision of Church and State in the Sermons of Piotr Skarga, S.J. (1536–1612)* (1994), *The Jesuits in the Commonwealth of Poland-Lithuania, 1564–1668* (1997), and *What We Have in Common? Dialogue with Nonbelievers* (2002). In September 2005 he left the Jesuit order and is now teaching at the University of Łódź in the Faculty of International and Political Studies.

Marc Rastoin, S.J.

Fr. Marc Rastoin, S.J., was born in 1967. After studies in Political Science with an essay on the religious parties in modern Israel, he entered the Society of Jesus in France in 1988. He completed a PhD on Galatians under the direction of Prof. Jean-Noël Aletti in 2002 in Rome (published in 2003 as "Tarse et Jérusalem. La double culture de l'apôtre Paul en Ga 3,6–4,7" in *Analecta Biblica* 152), is currently teaching biblical theology at the Jesuit Faculty of Theology in Paris, and is engaged in Jewish-Christian dialogue in Paris.

Christian M. Rutishauser, S.J.

Fr. Dr. Christian M. Rutishauser, S.J., has been since 2001 a codirector of the Lassalle-Haus Bad Schönbrunn Centre for Spirituality, Interreligious Dialogue, and Social Responsibility (Switzerland). His main field of work is adult education, retreats, spiritual guidance, history of spirituality, and interreligious dialogue. He is also Lecturer in Jewish Studies at the Jesuit Faculty of Philosophy in Munich and at the Cardinal Bea Centre at the Gregorian University in Rome.

Jean-Pierre Sonnet, S.J.

Fr. Jean-Pierre Sonnet, S.J., is Professor of Biblical Exegesis at the Institut d'Etudes Théologiques in Brussels and also teaches at the Institut Lumen Vitae in Brussels and at the Centre Sèvres in Paris. After gaining a license in Sacred Scripture at the Pontifical Biblical Institute (Rome), he specialized in literary approaches to the Bible at Tel Aviv University and Indiana University (Bloomington). Narrative exegesis and theology, biblical hermeneutics, and Jewish tradition are his primary fields of interest. Among his publications are *The Book within the Book: Writing in Deuteronomy* (Leiden, 1997), *L'analyse narrative des récits de l'Ancien Testament* (Paris, 1999, with J.-L. Ska and A. Wénin), and a collection of poems, *Le corps voisé* (2002). He translated Robert Alter's *Art of Biblical Narrative* and *Art of Biblical Poetry* into French. Since 2004, he has been in charge of the Jesuit publishing house Lessius.

Notes

INTRODUCTION
Harold Kasimow

1. *Decree 5: Our Mission and Interreligious Dialogue, Documents of the Thirty-Fourth General Congregation of the Society of Jesus* (St. Louis: Institute of Jesuit Sources, 1995), 12 (149).

2. *Nostra Aetate: Declaration on the Relation of the Church to Non-Christian Religions*, proclaimed by His Holiness Pope Paul VI on October 28, 1965, no. 2.

3. Ibid., no. 2.

4. Ibid., no. 4.

5. Ibid., no. 1.

6. Quoted on the cover of Augustin Cardinal Bea, *The Church and the Jewish People*, trans. Philip Loretz (New York: Harper & Row, 1966).

7. Abraham Joshua Heschel, "Choose Life," in *Moral Grandeur and Spiritual Audacity: Essays by Abraham Joshua Heschel*, ed. Susannah Heschel (New York: Farrar, Straus and Giroux, 1996), 253.

8. Thomas Merton, *Turning toward the World: The Journals of Thomas Merton, Vol. 4 (1960–63)* (New York: Harper Collins, 1996), 61–62.

9. Reinhold Niebuhr, quoted in Byron L. Sherwin, "Abraham Joshua Heschel," *The Torah* (Spring 1969): 7.

10. Ibid.

11. John C. Haughey, "A Jewish Prayer: A Share in Holiness," *America* 128:9 (March 10, 1973):219–20.

12. *America* 128:9 (March 10, 1973):202.

13. Quoted in Robert E. Kennedy, *Zen Spirit, Christian Spirit: The Place of Zen in Christian Life* (New York: Continuum, 1995), 14.

14. "Testimonials," Morning Star Zendo, http://members.tripod.com/~kennedyzen/.

15. "Kennedy's Dharma Successors," Morning Star Zendo, http://members.tripod.com/~kennedyzen/.

16. J. Kakichi Kadowaki, *Zen and the Bible: A Priest's Experience*, trans. Joan Rieck (London, UK, and Boston: Routledge & Kegan Paul, 1980).

17. Published in translation as *The Jewish People and Their Sacred Scriptures in the Christian Bible* (Rome: Pontifical Biblical Commission, 2002).

18. Ibid., sect. 84, para. 1.

19. Ibid., sect. 22, paras. 3 and 4.

20. See Edward Kessler, *Bound by the Bible: Jews, Christians and the Sacrifice of Isaac* (Cambridge, UK: Cambridge University Press, 2004).

From Windfall to Fall: The *Conversos* in the Society of Jesus

Marc Rastoin, S.J.

1. I wish to thank two of these historians for their assistance with this paper: James W. Reites, S.J., both for polishing my English and for his comments on an earlier draft of this paper; and Francisco de Borja Medina, S.J., for his advice and observations. All mistakes must, however, be considered as mine.

2. See James W. Reites, S.J., "St. Ignatius and the Jews," *Studies in the Spirituality of the Jesuits* 13 (1981):1–48; Reites, "Ignatius of Loyola and the Conversos," in *Columbus, Confrontation, Christianity: The European-American Encounter Revisited*, ed. Timothy J. O'Keefe (Santa Clara, Calif.: Forbes Mill Press, 1994), 57–68; Jean Lacouture, *Les Jésuites*, 2 vols. (Paris: Seuil, 1991), 1:196–212; Francisco de Borja Medina, S.J., "Ignacio de Loyola y la 'limpieza de sangre,'" in *Ignacio de Loyola y su tiempo*, ed. Juan Plazaola, S.J. (Bilbao: Mensajero, 1992), 579–615; Eusebio Rey, S.J., "S. Ignacio de Loyola y el problema de los Cristianos Nuevos," *Razon y Fe* 153 (1956):173–204; John W. O'Malley, S.J., *The First Jesuits* (Cambridge, Mass.: Harvard University Press, 1993), 188–92; and now the article from J. Aixalá and J. Escalera, "Cristianos nuevos," in *Diccionario histórico de la Compañia de Jesús* (Madrid: IHSI/Comillas, 2001), 1:1002–1005; James Bernauer, S.J., "The Holocaust and the Catholic Church's Search for Forgiveness: An Invitation to the Society of Jesus?" *Studies in the Spirituality of the Jesuits* 36/2 (2004). This very famous sentence is reported by Pedro de Ribadeneira, S.J., the first biographer of Ignatius, and seems to be confirmed by several other witnesses. Cf. *Monumenta Historicum Societatis Iesu* (*MHSI*), *Ribadeneira*, 2:375 (and *Fontes narr.* 2:476).

3. Because the appendix to this chapter contains biographical information on Jesuits from *conversos* families, I shall not follow for them the conventions of the *Archivium Historicum Societatis Iesu (AHSI)* and provide information in notes for the relevant Jesuits. The word *converso* is kept here even if it can be contested. It would be better to speak of "Judeo-convert," but I use the term *converso* in the common sense of a Christian of Jewish origin.

4. For a good presentation and summary, see O'Malley, *First Jesuits*, 188–92; and Antonio Dominguez Ortiz, *Los judeoconversos en la España moderna* (Madrid: Colecciones Mapfre, 1932), 152–54: "Había nacido ésta con un talante protestario, diríamos hoy . . . en cambio fueron muchos los conversos que acudieron a ella. . . . Esta afluencia de conversos no podía dejar de irritar."

5. We must remember that from 1580 to 1640 Portugal was under the sovereignty of the Spanish king and that the decree of suppression was adopted during that period (1593). According to Medina, Father General Claudio Acquaviva and the Italian assistant Lorenzo Maggio (b. 1531 Brescia; SJ 1555; d. 1605 Rome) greatly favored the decree (Medina, "Ignacio de Loyola," 609–13).

6. The full text of decree 52 can be found in John W. Padberg, S.J., Martin D. O'Keefe, S.J., and John L. McCarthy, S.J., eds., *For Matters of Greater Moment: The First Thirty Jesuit General Congregations* (St. Louis: Institute of Jesuit Sources, 1994), 204.

7. Padberg, O'Keefe, and McCarthy, *For Matters of Greater Moment*, decree 53, 204–5. Only two delegates voted against it: José de Acosta and Francisco Arias (cf. *Diccionario*, 1:11). Antonio Astráin, S.J., *Historia de la Compañia de Jesús en la Assistencia de España*, 7 vols. (Madrid: Sucesesores de Rivadeneyra/Razón y Fe, 1902–1925), 3:605, writes: "Podemos decir que la Congregación Quinta no tuvo en la práctica ningún resultado pernicioso para el Instituto de la Compañía"!

8. According to John P. Donnelly, S.J., "The decision to exclude men of Jewish and Moslem [*sic*] descent needs further study"; Donnelly, "Antonio Possevino and Jesuits of Jewish Ancestry," *AHSI* 55 (1986) 9.

9. Antonio Dominguez Ortiz, *La clase social de los conversos en Castilla en la edad moderna* (Granada: Universidad de Granada, *Archivum*, 1991 [1955]) 62–73, a *reelaboración* of Dominguez Ortiz, *Los judeoconversos*. On page 43 of *La clase social*, Dominguez Ortiz writes: "El Estatuto de Toledo tuvo inmensa resonancia en toda España." See also Reites, "St. Ignatius," 20; and Albert A. Sicroff, *Les controverses des statuts de pureté de sang en Espagne du XVème au XVIIème siècle* (Paris: Didier, 1960). See also Yosef Kaplan, *Jews and Conversos. Studies in Society and the Inquisition* (Jerusalem: Magnes Press, 1985).

10. According to Dominguez Ortiz, "No cabe duda de que en todas las Órdenes se planteaba con agudeza la cuestion de los conversos, por lo

menos en la primera mitad del siglo XVI"; Dominguez Ortiz, *La clase social*, 68. See also William V. Bangert, S.J., *Jerome Nadal, S.J., 1507–1580: Tracking the First Generation of Jesuits*, ed. Thomas M. McCoog, S.J. (Chicago: Loyola University Press, 1992) 103–104.

11. According to Astráin, *Historia*, 2:357, on November 15, 1551, "Despues le llamó a parte [al Dr. Torres] y lo dijo que el non tenía enemistad con la Compañía ni la queria mal, pero que el hacia esto porque en la Compañía se hiciese el estatuto que el habia hecho en la iglesia de Toledo . . . y que si esto se hace en la Compañia, que hará y no habrá mayor amigo que el y que más la favorezca." See also *MHSI*, *Epistolae Mixtae* (*Epp. Mixtae*), 2:626. Siliceo did not want to speak to Villanueva either because he doubted the purity of the Jesuit's blood (Reites, "St. Ignatius," 25), or because this Jesuit had not yet been ordained, or because of his social background. We note that the archbishop came from a very poor family and suspected that the great noble families married *conversos* for economic reasons. In fact Dominguez Ortiz shows that many of Spain's great families had married *conversos* at the end of the fifteenth century. Opposition to the *conversos* was deeply rooted in poor *Cristianos viejos*. Interestingly, Astráin occasionally defined families of the *conversos* as being "gente poderosa" (on Polanco's family, see Astráin, *Historia*, 1:211) or "hombre rico y poderoso" (ibid., 1:309). When he wrote of other families, he liked to say "de noble linaje" (ibid., 1:315, with a curious reference to Gaspar de Loarte) or "nobilisimo joven" (ibid., 1:303). Francisco de Villanueva was not from the nobility, "un pobre extremeño, hijo de humildes labradores" according to Astráin (ibid., 1:259), but his name may have seemed suspect to Siliceo. Regardless, the social dimension of the attitude toward the *conversos* is very important. On relations between the archbishop and the Jesuits, see also Bangert, *Jerome Nadal*, 108–109. See, e.g., Astráin, *Historia*, 1:348–65. The text is in *Epp. Mixtae* 2:626. See also Albert A. Sicroff, *Los estatutos de limpieza de sangre* (Madrid: Taurus, 1985), 315–27. The nuncio was Cardinal Poggio (Astráin, *Historia*, 1:356 and 362).

12. Ignatius's reply, as reported by Astráin, was very direct: "De venir a concierto con el arzobispo, aceptando sus diseños y applicando nuestras Constituciónes a las suyas, no es menester pensar: *bástele á el entender en lo que está á su cargo!*" (Astráin, *Historia*, 2:360). See also Reites, "St. Ignatius," 26. In fact, as the nuncio had promised that the novitiate in Alcalá, situated within the archdiocese of Toledo, would not accept *conversos*, Ignatius was obliged to accept this restriction but he considered it simply a temporary provision so that the Society could continue to work in all areas of Spain. He wrote, "Y en señal de que tenemos á vuestra Señoría Rma. por Señor y padre . . . , yo escribo á los Nuestros que allá están, que en Alcalá ó en otra parte de ses reino *no acepten persona ninguna* para la compañía que no sea conforme á la intención ó muestra de Vuestra Señoría Rma . . .

de Roma, 1° de Junio 1552"; *Ignat. Epist.* 3:68. Meanwhile novices could be sent to Rome. On this point, see Bangert, *Jerome Nadal*, 106. For the same policy by Borgia, see note 33.

13. B. 1516 Vergara (Guipúzcoa); SJ 1538 Roma; d. January 30, 1573 (Madrid). He was the son of a brother of Ignatius's sister-in-law, Magdalena de Araoz. He was also the first professed Jesuit after the first ten companions and had a very important position in Spain.

14. For a good account of Araoz's attitude, see Bangert, who has some strong words about Araoz: "Evasive and aloof, he made clear that . . . he was, as Nadal found, untouchable"; Bangal, *Jerome Nadal,* 224. See, esp., ibid., 275–76: "Nadal began to lose his battle against suspicious thoughts about Araoz. . . . During conversations with Araoz, Nadal discovered that Antonio [Araoz] was convinced Lainez was not the general of the Society. . . . Nadal came to the harsh conclusion that *Araoz honored the machinations of the Spanish court more than he did the Institute of the Society.*" He had just before explained that the court, and especially the powerful Count Rui Gómez, wanted not only to limit the powers of the visitors from Rome (in this case Nadal) but also pressure the Society to adopt the *Estatutos de limpieza* and that Araoz agreed on that policy: "Rui Gómez . . . once more opened the rift between the court and the Society on admission of New Christians into the Jesuit ranks. Urgently he pressed for exclusion of men of Jewish ancestry"; ibid., 225. He also affirms that they (the court, and probably Araoz too, as Nadal increasingly believed) wanted to get rid of Laínez. He writes, "a chance to remove Laínez, a man known to be of Jewish stock"; ibid., 273. On Araoz's attitude, see also Medina, "Ignacio de Loyola," 599–601. See also Sicroff, *Los estatutos*, 318: "En particular, el padre *Antonio de Araoz . . . no se mostraba hostil a la idea de establecer un criterio de limpieza de sangre* para los miembros de la Compañía de Jesús. Ya en 1549 había planteado la cuestión" (cf. letter of November 5, 1549, *Epp. Mixtae* 2:314) and this very strong expression: "Sin embargo, esto no impidió al padre Araoz menear una *guerra secreta contra los conversos de la Compañía*, actividad que llevaba conjuntamente con sus esfuerzos por hacer mas independiente de Roma a la provincia española [*sic*] de los jesuitas"; ibid., 323. See Astráin, *Historia*, 3:101.

15. Mario Scaduto, S.J., observes that, during the generalate of Diego Laínez, Francisco de Toledo, a famous *converso* and scholar who became the first Jesuit cardinal, was quickly accepted into the Society and sent to Rome. Scaduto comments: "Il suo trasferimento non sollevò in Spagna, le reazioni più tardi provocate da quello improvviso, di Acosta, Mariana, Ros e Ramiro. Forse perche apparteneva a famiglia di estrazione giudaica: ed è risaputo che in alcuni settori della compagnia, *capeggiati da Araoz*, non si vedeva di buon occhio l'ingresso nell'Ordine di cristiani nuovi, che Roma era lieta di accogliere"; Mario Scaduto, *L'epoca di Giacomo Lainez*, 2 vols.

(Rome: La Civiltà Cattolica, 1964–1974), 2:287. Interestingly, José de Acosta himself was most likely a *converso* (O'Malley, *First Jesuits*, 321). On Araoz's opposition, see Reites, "St. Ignatius," 21–23; and Bangert, *Jerome Nadal*, 105.

16. Simão Rodrigues: b. 1510 Vouzela; SJ 1534; d. 1579 Lisbon. Ordained June 24, 1537; Professed December 1544.

17. Josef Wicki, S.J., "Die 'Cristaos Novos' in der indischen Provinz der Gesellschaft Iesu von Ignatius bis Acquaviva," *AHSI* 46 (1977):348.

18. It would be an error to conclude that the admission of *conversos* stopped abruptly after 1559. It continued but with greater difficulty. After 1565 some Spaniards (70 between 1565 and 1580, 5 in 1565, 7 in 1566, 8 in 1567, 9 in 1568, 8 in 1569, 4 in 1570, 5 in 1571, 2 in 1572, 6 in 1573, 1 in 1574, 3 in 1575, 3 in 1576, 1 in 1577, 0 in 1578, 2 in 1579, 6 in 1580) were sent directly to Rome (of course, not all of them were *conversos*). The probability that some of them were *conversos* is real, the proportion being different each year. See the catalogs of the Roman province of the Society. I thank Francisco de Borja Medina, S.J., for this information. On this point, see note 33.

19. See Francisco de Borja Medina, S.J., "La Compañia de Jesús y la minoria morisca (1545–1614)," *AHSI* 57 (1988):3–136, for more detailed information on *moriscos*, Jesuit apostolates in Andalucía, and the role played by the *conversos*. See also Dominguez Ortiz, *La clase social*, 163: "Consta que muchos de sus discipulos fueron conversos."

20. According to Ruiz Jurado, about thirty disciples of Juan de Ávila joined the Society. He gives the names of twenty-six. See Manuel Ruiz Jurado, S.J., "San Juan de Ávila y la Compañia de Jesús," *AHSI* 40 (1971):153–72, esp. 158. Ignatius went as far to write: "que en tanta uniformidad de voluntades y modo de proceder del Mtro Abila y nosotros, que no me pareze que quede sino que, ó nosotros nos juntemos con él, ó él con nosotros, para que la cosas del divino servicio mejor se perpétuen"; *Epp. Ign.* 3, 162, quoted on 160.

21. Diego de Guzmán: b. 1522 Seville; SJ January 1553 Oñate (Guipúzcoa); d. May 8, 1606 Seville. He was a "noble sevillano a quien no tocaba el problema de limpieza de sangre, emparentado con las dos casas más poderosas de Andalucía, Arcos y Medina Sidonia"; Medina, "Ignacio de Loyola," 607. The *Diccionario*, 2:1858, writes: "Era hijo de Rodrigo Ponce de Léon, primer conde de Bailén. . . . Emparentado con las casas más poderosas de Andalucía." The question, however, remains disputable, for many noble families from Andalucía contracted rich *converso* marriages. Nevertheless, I think that Bangert's qualification of Guzmán as a *converso* is an error (cf. Bangert, *Jerome Nadal*, 133). For the explanation of Guzmán's solidarity with Loarte, *Diccionario*, 2:1858 adds: "Convencidos G y Loarte de que el problema provenía del origen judeoconverso *de este último*, pidieron a Araoz (13 julio 1553) la dimisión de la CJ por la falta de espíritu

evangélico que suponía la discriminación respecto de los cristianos nuevos." This attitude Guzmán maintained all his life, for "en repetidas occasiones le expresó [to Father General Acquaviva] su disconformitad con el decreto 52, canon 3 *De Genere*, de la Congregación General V (1593–1594) que excluía de la CJ a los cristianos nuevos de origen judío o musulmán, pidiendo su abolición o mitigación"; ibid. See also Ruiz Jurado, "San Juan de Ávila," 165.

22. Annoyed by rumors that the Society was changing its policy toward *conversos*, Juan de Ávila protested to Jerónimo Nadal. To demonstrate that the Society had not altered its stance, Nadal accepted Santander immediately. See Bangert, *Jerome Nadal*, 107–108; Medina, "La Compañía de Jesús," 54. Loarte's admission had been delayed because he was under investigation by the Spanish Inquisition. For a young and controversial order, it was a mark of great courage or the height of foolishness to accept a man suspected by such a powerful body. On the whole affair, see Ruiz Jurado, "San Juan de Ávila"; and Pierre-Antoine Fabre, "La conversion infinie des *conversos*. Des 'nouveaux-chrétiens' dans la Compagnie de Jésus au 16ème siècle," *Annales. Histoire des Sciences Sociales* 54 (1999/2):875–93; and Medina, "Ignacio de Loyola," 607. We should mention that Ignatius himself had been arrested twice by the Inquisition and subjected to two different inquiries. He knew too well what it could be like.

23. A wave of conversions occurred in 1391 after terrible popular riots against the residents of Jewish neighborhoods, the *aljamas*. Later, new conversions, in Burgos, e.g., came as the result of St. Vincent Ferrer's preaching in 1413 and 1414. For the chronology, see Dominguez Ortiz, *Los judeoconversos*, 267: "1391 conversiones provocadas por el terror. 1413–1414: Disputa de Tortosa. Predicación de San Vicente Ferrer. Nuevas oleadas de conversiones." He notes that: "Diversos indicios hacen suponer que los judíos castellanos estaban más asimilados que los andaluces." Cf. also Léon Poliakov, *Histoire de l'antisémitisme. De Mahomet aux Marranes* (Paris: Calmann-Lévy, 1961), 178: "Il y en eut qui noircirent leurs frères *conversos*: Ainsi ceux de la Vieille-Castille concédaient que ceux d'Andalousie n'étaient que des Juifs ou pire, mais réclamaient pour eux-mêmes la qualité de bons chrétiens."

24. When the Portuguese Franciscans discovered that Henriques was a *converso*, they dismissed him. Rodrigues accepted him into the Society and sent him almost immediately to India (Wicki, "Die 'Cristaos Novos,'" 346).

25. See Poliakov, *Histoire*, 199 and 217. The collective baptism was imposed in Portugal in 1497, but the Inquisition was not created immediately. This helped the formation of crypto-Judaism in Portugal.

26. Dominguez Ortiz, *La clase social*, 83: "Mientras que los conversos españoles representaban la parte del pueblo hebreo que per convecimiento,

codicia o temor abandonó de grado su antigua fe, lo que explica que pocos conservaran su antigua creencia, los portugueses, procedentes del bautismo forzoso [1497], en general . . . eran judios más o menos contaminados de cristianismo . . . para los españoles descendientes de conversos fue una gran calamidad la llegada de estos indeseables huespedes."

27. According to Wicki, only Vaz was professed of the four vows ("Die 'Cristaos Novos,'" 353–55).

28. Alessandro Valignano: b. 1539 Chieti; SJ 1566 Roma; d. 1606 Macao.

29. Wicki, "Die 'Cristaos Novos,'" 353–54. Wicki remarks that such advice, coming from an Italian and such a famous figure, must have had some weight in Rome. Wicki notes that Matteo Ricci expressed similar sentiments in his letter to Father Acquaviva on November 25, 1581 (ibid., 357). The Portuguese were the most determined in the anti-*converso* policy and acted years before the Fifth General Congregation. See, on Rodrigues's policy, Medina, "Ignacio de Loyola," 582–87.

30. Medina, "Ignacio de Loyola," 596, exposes Ignatius's position from 1546 to his death: "Esta posición era favorable a la no exclusión de los nuevos cristianos en la Compañía." Medina continues: "En agosto [1553], Ignacio daba esas normas. . . . Si por otra parte, eran aptos *se debían enviar a Italia*, donde 'no se mira tan sotil de qué raça sea el que se vey ser buen supósito'"; ibid., 601, quoting *Epp. Ign.* 5:335 (Polanco to Araoz, August 14, 1553). This suggestion is repeated in another letter (Polanco to Miron, April 5, 1554; *Epp. Ign.* 6:569–70): "Es uerdad que, si por la disposición de los ánimos de una tierra no fuese cosa edificaua aceptar alguno tal, diestramente *se podría enderezar a otra parte*, si fuese buen supósito"; quoted in Medina, "Ignacio de Loyola," 602, and again in 1555 (letter from Polanco to Borgia, May 29, 1555, *Epp. Ign.* 9:87, quoted in Medina, "Ignacio de Loyola," 604; and letter from Polanco to Borgia, June 13, 1555, *Epp. Ign.* 9:149–50, quoted by Medina, "Ignacio de Loyola," 605). See also Sicroff, *Los estatutos*, 322.

31. See notes 67 and 123.

32. Wicki, "Die 'Cristaos Novos,'" 359: "Die portugiesische Provinzialkongregation vom dez 1584 stellte damals fest, daß in der Provinz keine Cristaos-novos aufgenommen wurden, daß jedoch andere Provinzen das täten." The move began even earlier: "Der Provinzial von Indien, Rui Vicente (1574–1583), von Valignano ernannt, klagte am 1 Dez. 1578 dem General, daß die Obern von Portugal Neuchristen nach Indien abschöben"; ibid., 354.

33. Francisco de Borja (better known in the English-speaking world as St. Francis Borgia): b. 1510 Gandia; SJ 1546; d. 1572 Rome. Priest in 1551, professed in 1548. Borgia's attitude toward the *conversos* was well known, and in 1565 an effort was made to discredit him in order to impede his election as general. Benedetto Palmio (b. 1523 Parma; SJ 1546; d. 1598 Ferrara)

wrote: "Fu presentato a Pio IIII una lunga informazione delle divisioni che si ritrovavano nella Compagnia nate in Spagna et [*sic*] che . . . queste divisioni venivano fomentate dalla moltitudine de [*sic*] novi cristiani che si erano accettati in Spagna da Borgia, mentre era là commissario, et in queste informazioni se conteneva un lungo catalogo de questi novi cristiani, tra i quali ancora erano numerati alcuni, che governavano in Roma la Compagnia et non si sapeva che havessero questa nota . . . pare che tutto questo fusse presentato al papa per impedire che Francesco Borgia fusse generale" (Vitae 164, 19v), in Mario Scaduto, S.J., "Il governo di S. Francesco Borgia 1565–1572," *AHSI* 41 (1972):139. The same scheming failed this time but worked seven years later against Polanco. Palmio made clear that Araoz was probably behind those manipulations, adding: "Non successe l'unione che si desiderava tra lui e Antonio Araozzo, il quale, essendo stato eletto assistente, non volse venire, et in questo veramente fu degno di reprensione; se ben forse non venne, immaginandosi et persuadendosi certo che veniva a continua contentione, perché *il Borgia in tutto il suo generalato perseverò* nei suoi ditami *d'accettare* molti colegii et *molti nuovi cristiani*, anzi, quelli che non volevano accettare in Spagna, li chiamava in Italia et de lí sparse per diverse provincie, cosicché le divisioni di Spagna doventarno comuni a tutta la Compagnia"; ibid., 140. In the last sentence we perhaps see a hint as to why the Italian assistant, Lorenzo Maggio, approved of the decree in 1593.

34. In the General Examen (as in Nadal's questionnaire), one question asks of the candidate to the Society whether he is from old or new Christians, but this is not an impeachment but a question put in order to know the candidate better. See Ignace de Loyola, *Ecrits* (Paris: DDB, 1991), 403: "34.2 Pour mieux connaître les personnes. . . . 34.4. Commençant par son nom, on lui demandera. . . . 36.2. *S'il descend de chrétiens de vieille souche ou de chrétiens récents*. 36.3. Si quelqu'un de ses ascendants a été censuré ou déclaré coupable pour quelque erreur contre notre religion chrétienne et comment." See also the note on the same page explaining that some fathers in the *Observata patrum* discussed the pertinence of the introduction of that demand but that Ignatius, after having it suppressed, put it again in the B text. The question implies that a positive answer does not hinder the candidate's acceptance.

35. For Laínez, see *Diccionario*, 2:1003: "Araoz volvió a insistir en que se adoptaran en la CJ los estatutos sobre la pureza de sangre, pero Laínez se adhirió a las normas establecidas por Ignacio . . . (*Ribadeneira* 2:250–52). El tercer general Francisco de Borja, aunque tenía gran esperiencia en los asuntos y sientimientos españoles, mantuvo abiertas las puertas de la CJ para candidatos cualificados, fuera cual fuese su origen." See also the article "Cristianos nuevos," in the *Diccionario histórico de la Compañia de Jesús* 2:1002–1005. See also Sicroff, *Los estatutos*, 328, letter from Laínez, November 23, 1564 (*Ribadeneira*, 2:374).

The *Diccionario*, 3:2748, adds: "El jesuita morisco más conocido es, sin duda, Albotod, puesto come modelo, junto con el judeo-converso Giovanni B. Eliano, de la universalidad de origen etnico-religiosa en la CJ de *los tres primeros generales*, Ignacio, Laynez, y Borgia, frente a la discriminación posterior que terminó con la absoluta exclusión de la admisión en la CJ."

The exclusion of Mercurian, the fourth General of the Jesuits, appears disputable. For the opinion of Mercurian, see, among others, the sentence quoted, e.g., in Lacouture, *Les Jésuites*, 1:200.

36. This text, "De prognatis genere hebraeorum societatis aditu non excludendis," can be found in *Ribadeneira*, 2:374–84. He voiced his opposition again in 1608. Cf. *Ribadeneira*, 2:247 and following.

37. Cf. *Diccionario*, 2:1004: "La politica de restricciones en la admisión, iniciada por Mercuriano . . . continuó bajo Claudio Acquaviva sobre todo desde 1584 y culminó en la instruccion a los provinciales de España sobre la 'moderación açerca del reçebir gente que tenga raça' (1592/93) en la que también se ordenaba excluir de puestos importantes de gobierno a los ya admitidos de este linaje." For a slightly different chronology, see Francisco de Borja Medina, S.J., "Precursores de Vieira: Jesuitas andaluces y castellanos en favor de los cristianos nuevos," in *Actas Congresso Internacional: Terceiro centenário da morte do Padre António Vieira* (Braga: Universidade Católica Portuguesa, 1999), 504: "Cuatro años atrás, el mismo Acquaviva, antes de cualquier decreto discriminador, había dado órdenes secretas a los provinciales de no admitir a los cristianos nuevos y de excluir de los puestos importantes de gobierno" (with note "Acquaviva a los provinciales de Espana, 18 abril 1590." ARSI, *Inst 184/II,* 366–367; *Hisp*, *89* 78). On the change in the years around 1572, see Sicroff, *Los estatutos*, 324: "La presión ejercitada sobre los jesuitas para que cuidasen más su reputación crecía." That it was a very long battle indeed is confirmed by Medina, "Precursores," 504: "Acquaviva, al menos desde 1586, venía ordenando la exclusión de este linaje e, incluso, la expulsión de los ya admitidos, buscando para ello otras razones aparentes!" It is therefore perhaps not so surprising to notice that some Jesuit *conversos* were described as "depressed" and "melancholic" during the years from 1590 to 1600 (see, e.g., the *Diccionario* entry on Jose d'Acosta), as the specificity and evangelical character of the Society were so blatantly diminished. The beginning of high lobbying for the decree came from Manuel Rodrigues, assistant for Portugal, writing to General Acquaviva in 1584. See Medina, "Ignacio de Loyola," 585: "En este contexto, Rodrigues proponía, como única solución viable, la no admisión de cristianos nuevos en la Compañía al igual que hacían los colegios mayores en las Universidades y las órdenes religiosas" (letter of April 22, 1584, *Inst. 184/II*, 365). Rodrigues tried to pretend that this policy of non-admission of new Christians was Ignatius's intention, as corroborated by Goncalves de Camara and even of Xavier,

using a letter to Barzeus of April 1552 (*Xavier* 2:418–419). This policy had been initiated in Coimbra as early as 1546 by Simon Rodrigues, who was provincial at that time, as Medina, "Ignacio de Loyola," 593, indicates.

38. Even if the context was different two centuries later, it can be argued that the decree of the Fifth General Congregation was the first sign of a fatal compromise that would ultimately lead to the suppression of the Society when the European kings (see note 39) succeeded in forcing the pope to disband this international and too-independent body. At the end of his vast inquiry into the Portuguese Assistency, Alden concludes: "The leadership . . . yielded to the prevailing prejudices of the European governments and societies upon which it was heavily dependent and turned its back on prospective New Christian recruits, despite the fact that some of its early leaders were of Jewish origin"; Dauril Alden, *The Making of an Enterprise* (Stanford, Calif.: Stanford University Press, 1996), 654.

39. In his ninth reason against any change in the Society's *Constitutions*, Ribadeneira wrote: "La 9a esto es contra el parecer de los hombres más santos, más religiosos, más graves y amigos de la Compañia. Más santos, porque *el Padre Maestro Ávila dixo que por dos cosas se podria perder la Compañía; la primera por admitir a ella mucha turba; y la 2a por hacer distinción de linages y sangre*" (*Ribadeneira*, 2:381). See also Reites, "St. Ignatius," 29. Ironically, as the Society adopted the most extreme *statutos de limpieza*, public opinion and the king began to consider relaxing the regulations; instead of resulting in a renewed popularity for the Society, the measures brought a decrease in vocations and criticism from the laypeople attached to the Society. See Medina, "Precursores," 1:501, 506–10. Ávila predicted fateful consequences for the Society if it accepted this policy. Ribadeneira cited this prophecy and claimed that the final suppression of the Society by the European Bourbon dynasty it had so loyally served was the fulfillment of this prophecy. On the role of the Bourbon family, see *Diccionario*, 1:878–84, which evokes "un cisma de los Estados borbónicos" (879) and even a "frente borbónico" (882). The irony is that the price to be paid to the last monarchy to defend the Jesuits, the Austrian one, was the hand of Marie-Antoinette for the French dauphin: "María Teresa capituló . . . y dejó a los jesuitas a merced de los Borbones, habida cuenta de su política matrimonial, y sobre todo de la derivada del relativamente reciente enlace de su hija María Antonieta con el delfín de Francia, futuro Luis XVI"; ibid., 883. The social and political context of those final years of the Society in Spain is well depicted in Philip Trower, *A Danger to the State* (San Francisco: Ignatius Press, 1998).

40. Cf. the letter from Fr. Juan Ramirez of the college of Córdoba to Fr. General Borgia, September 1, 1572. ARSI, cod. *Epistolae hispaniae* (*Epist Hisp*), 18, B, fol. 314, quoted in Astráin, *Historia*, III, 591: "[La nobleza de Córdoba] no entra hombre de ellos en la Compañía, sino todos se entran en

San Pablo . . . y la razón de esto es porque nuestro colegio está muy infame entre los caballeros, de que no entran en él sino judios." Also see O'Malley, *First Jesuits*, 190. Regarding one of the early Society's most outspoken critics, Melchior Cano, O.P., Dominguez Ortiz comments: "Aun más fuerza me hace la consideración del odio con que el iracundo dominico distinguió a la recién fundada Compañía de Jesús, *que en sus primeros años fué refugio de muchos conversos*," *La clase social*, 170 (emphasis added). This reaction from the Cordobans was echoed in Rome when the Romans assimilated the Spanish priests with Jews. Cf. Poliakov, *Histoire*, 175: "D'autres [*conversos*] allaient judaïser à la cour pontificale . . . (l'opinion commune du petit peuple de Rome finit par conclure que tous les Espagnols étaient Juifs)."

41. Reites, "St. Ignatius," 21. We shall see that it was part of Nadal's questionnaire in the communities, for example in Alcalá, but that no answer remains (cf. note 58).

42. Dominguez Ortiz, *La clase social*, 153.

43. Astráin, *Historia*, 1:313; Wicki, "Die 'Cristaos Novos,'" 350.

44. Reites, "St. Ignatius," 23. Cf. *Diccionario*, 2:1003: "Uno de los más persistentes críticos era Antonio Araoz. . . . Con discreta franqueza escribió a Ignacio en 1545: 'Padre, hasta estar la Compañía algo más conocida y fundada en Castilla, parece muy conveniente mirar sobre recibir *gente verriac* [en vasco nueva], porque para muchos sólo eso es veneno'" (*EpMix* 1:241). Ignatius answers through Polanco: "'Del no aceptar cristianos nuevos no se persuade Nuestro Padre sería Dios servido, pero bien le parece se debría tener con los tales más circonspección'" (*Chronicon* 3:371). See also Medina, "Ignacio de Loyola," 599.

45. Wicki, "Die 'Cristaos Novos,'" 357. This method was used by Matteo Ricci in writing to the general in 1581.

46. Concerning his trial by the Inquisition in Alcalá, Ignatius writes: "Otras observancias del sábato las ignoro, ni en mi tierra suele haber judíos," Fontes Narrativi (Fontes Narr.). The same observation appears in Sicroff, *Los estatutos*, who observes that saying "*vizcayno*" was an indirect way to say "old Christian." By the end of the fifteenth century, the Basque province of Guipúzcoa had already adopted a policy forbidding the residence of *conversos* in the province and also forbidding marriage to *conversos*; Sicroff, *Los estatutos*, 117. This policy was enforced by law after 1527 (cf. footnote 47).

47. Wicki, "Die 'Cristaos Novos,'" 346. The Basques were known for their strong anti-*conversos* feelings, as shown by the *ordenanzas* of Guipúzcoa, promulgated in 1527.

48. Loyola to Ávila, Rome, February 7, 1555, *Epp. Ign.*, 8:362–63.

49. O'Malley, *First Jesuits*, 54–55.

50. See the wording of Dominguez Ortiz, *Los judeoconversos*, 263: "La Compañía de Jesús que en aquella epoca era asilo de conversos."

51. Cf. Scaduto, *L'epoca*, 1:124. Four of the seven children were religious.

52. Cf. Astráin, *Historia*, 1:313: "En los años siguientes fueron entrando otros muchos, entre los cuales llamaron la atención dos grupos de hermanos que vistieron nuestra sotana. Fueron éstos, por un lado, cuatro hijos del buen Rodrigo de Dueñas, llamados Mateo, Bernardino, Gabriel y Gaspar, y por otro, cinco hijos de Antonio de Acosta y Ana de Porres, que fueron Diego, maestro de teología en Roma y provincial de Andalucía; Bernardino que trabajó largos años en Méjico; José, el más joven y el más célebre de todos, aunque su celebridad sea en parte tan triste como á su tiempo veremos; Cristóbal, que murió al poco tiempo de entrar en religión, y Jerónimo, el más viejo de todos, pero que entró el último en la Compañía y la sirvió en varios cargos importantes," The *converso* origin of the Acosta family is well known but not totally certain. Dominguez Ortiz, *La clase social*, 313, mentions the famous *converso* Rodrigo de Dueñas, a rich merchant who was the father of four Jesuits. The allusion to the ill-fated José is due to his presumed role in the Fifth General Congregation. According to Astráin, he was linked to the *perturbadores*, who were against the authority of the general.

53. This expression describes how much Spanish society was dominated by the shame/honor pairing. The most important thing for a hidalgo was to keep his rank and his honor. Spiritual texts of the time, such as that of St. Therese of Avila, spoke about the necessity to overcome the "*punto de honor*," this excessive preoccupation with personal social honor; see "Autobiography," sec. 3., especially 26: "*punto de honor*," in Thérèse d'Avila, *Œuvres complètes*, French ed. (Paris: DDB, 1964), 139. See also Sicroff, *Los estatutos*, 328: "Limpieza de sangre, honor y nobleza estaban estrechamente elazados en el sistema de valores que gobernaba la sociedad española del siglo XVI."

54. Dominguez Ortiz, *La clase social*, 173: "Dos hermanos de don Diego fueron frailes carmelitas, uno calzado, uno descalzado. . . . *Conociendo la inclinación de los conversos a la vida religiosa*, no solo no vemos nada de extraño en que ingrasaran en una Orden que no tenía estatuto de limpieza sino que lo reputo como otro indicio del hebraismo . . ." (emphasis added). We can even specify that many were interested in Bible studies, and this dimension was very much welcome by Ignatian evangelical spirituality; see Dominguez Ortiz, *Los judeoconversos*, 205: "Un campo preferido por los conversos de las primeras generaciones fue el de los estudios biblicos." A good example is the translation of the Bible from the Hebrew to Castillan, done by a converted Jew, Martín de Lucena, in 1450.

55. Dominguez Ortiz, *La clase social*, 38; and Lacouture, *Les Jésuites*, 197 and following. Dominguez Ortiz analyzes the spirituality of the *conversos* in Spain in the first part of the sixteenth century. They insisted on the

importance of preaching to the people as well as a faith rooted in a personal encounter with Christ. Early Jesuits developed both aspects in their apostolates. On the basis of his study of Nadal's *responsa*, Father Medina notes that almost all Jesuit *conversos* expressed an interest in Scripture in their answers to Nadal's inquiry on the origin of their vocation to the Jesuits. Nadal's *responsa* contain a wealth of information on the social origins of early Jesuits. With the exception of Thomas V. Cohen's not-readily-available doctoral dissertation, "The Social Origins of the Jesuits, 1540–1600," 2 vols. (Ph.D. diss., Harvard University, 1973); and T. V. Cohen, "Why the Jesuits Joined, 1540–1600," in *Historical Papers* 9 (Canadian Historical Association, 1974): 237–58, few have studied this material. There is nothing, however, in the article about the *converso* question.

56. This refers to urbane, learned young intellectuals who had completed advanced studies and were attracted to the missions, to preaching, to humanist studies, and to the teaching profession. Cf. the accurate description from Linda Martz, "Converso Families in Fifteenth- and Sixteenth-Century Toledo: The Significance of Lineage," *Sefarad* 48 (1998):117–96: "The upper and middle echelons of the Toledo converso society were intelligent, educated, talented and dedicated to achievement. . . . The same abilities make their lineage extremely difficult to trace if the families were concerned with concealing their origins and a great many Toledo conversos had a great many reasons for trying to conceal their origins after the arrival of the Inquisition," 119. Sicroff, *Los estatutos*, 321, speaks explicitly about this attraction of the *conversos* to the Society and the rage that this provoked in Siliceo: "mientras seguía demostrado una predilección notoria [toward the Society] por ciertos *spirituali* cristianos nuevos."

57. Many *conversos* were among the clerical elite in Spain. In his introduction to Dominguez Ortiz's work (*Los judeoconversos* [1993], 2nd ed.), Francisco Villanueva commented: "Lejos de veleidades judaizantes, la *élite* conversa del siglo XV no habia tendido sino a la más completa asimilación y de hecho se alzó bajo Juan II a una posición de jefatura intelectual de la Iglesia castellana. . . . Conversos como don Alonso de Cartagena, fray Hernando de Talavera [Archbishop of Granada] Álvarez Gato, Juan de Encina, Sánchez de Badajoz y tantos otros documentan el noble ensueño de un cristianismo capaz de causar el desarme interior de la sociedad española dentro de un espíritu de libertad y de paz cristologicamente orientado. . . . El tema del amor divino fue una clara invención de los conversos" (xviii). It would be difficult to find a more Christologically oriented text than Loyola's *Spiritual Exercises*!

58. I have been through Nadal's questionnaire (FG 77, I, II, III, IV in the Jesuit Curia archives and *Nadal* 2:527–89) to search for *conversos*' answers to the inquiry that Nadal was conducting all over Europe. The Jesuits who answered Nadal's questionnaire are classified not by nation or community or year but by alphabetical order of their Christian names. The answers

are mostly spread through the decade from 1559 to 1569, with the majority of them having no indication of date. The Spaniards clearly constitute the main group of those who answered. The questions, called "communes interrogationes," are very similar to those of the General Examen (in the prelude to the *Constitutions*, n. 34–51). We have the answers of some notorious *conversos*, but like all the others, they answer the question "¿de que provincia y de que lugar?," which is the first version of the questionnaire, which is found in the Jesuit Curia archives under the classification FG 77, I, 5.6, which has "cuius nationis et . . . provincia . . . et patria." In such a way, we have the answers of Alphonsus Pisanus (Jesuit Curia Archives FG 77, I, 53, "Hispanus ex civitate toletana"), José de Acosta himself (FG 77, III, 311, "de Castilla, de Medina del Campo"), and Luis de Santander (FG 77, IV, 61, "de Andaluzia de Eçija"). According to Bangert, *Jerome Nadal*, 234: "The second questionnaire, of thirty-two questions, was secret. Each Jesuit answered orally." Bangert says, following Nadal (1, 791): "communes de todos más en particular"; ibid., 1:791; "examinis secreti interrogations quibus non scripto, ut plurimum, sed verbo respondebatur" explain the editors of *Nadal*. FG 77, I, 7, which is presented with the mention of "Alcalá," as if Nadal used the questionnaire during his visitation in that city, has, like the General Examen, those two questions: "*3: Sies de cristianos viejos o no.* 4: Si fueron notados sus padres o parientes por Inquisiçiõ." This version is repeated on page 8 (with "Inquisición") and page 9. The fact that in those first years the matter was already a potential problem for community life is suggested by question 23 of the Alcalá copy (77, I, 7): "Si han hablado en linages, ó naciones, juzgando eso." The matter was so delicate that it was secret and could not be talked of, even if the fact was well known among some fathers (such as Loarte and Pisa). Of the other *converso* Jesuits from whom we have answers, I will note: Alonso Romã (Roman), FG 77, I, 41 ("Castilla . . . Toledo . . . Yllescas"); Balthasar Loarte, FG 77, I, 241; Cipriano Soarez, FG 77, I, 352 ("del reyno de Toledo y de Ocana"); Ferdinando Jaenus (de Jaén), FG 77, II, 57 ("Hispanu. Boeticj. Cordube"); Francisco de Angulo, FG 77, II, 72 ("Andaluzia de tierra de Cordova de un lugar q se dice Luçena"); Geronimo de Acosta, FG 77, II, 346. Such an absence of written documentation is in itself very revealing. During the years when the matter was hotly discussed between Rome and Spain (1588–1594) and when orders came not to discuss the subject in the communities, there were no potentially embarrassing files to be destroyed "for the sake of peace." The rumors only continued.

59. See "Juan de Ávila," in *Diccionario* 1:305–306. See also *Diccionario*, 4:3499: "Su admisión [Santander], a propuesta de Ávila, constituyó la prueba dada por Nadal a este último para disipar sus temores sobre la sinceridad de la CJ en afirmar que no hacía distinción de linajes, lo que Ávila dudaba después del caso de Gaspar Loarte." The same opinion, unsurprisingly, appears in Medina, "Ignacio de Loyola," 607.

60. For the similarities between Ávila's vision of religious life and the Society, see Ruiz Jurado, "San Juan de Ávila," 160. According to this author, Ávila's bad health was the main reason he did not join the Society. Cf. ibid., 169. Of course, not all *conversos* were perfectly religious. For the intellectual susceptibility of a Francisco de Toledo, for example, see Scaduto, *L'epoca*, 2:283 and 290–92. The social origins of some of them *may* explain their position in the *Memorialistas* dispute.

61. Indeed, Francis Borgia's mentality displays a real change between his beginnings in Gandia and his time in Rome. We need to compare the Borgia of Gandia to the Ignatius of Manresa and the Borgia of Rome to the Ignatius of Rome. For Araoz's spiritual attitude, see the complaints from Nadal. For Oviedo and Borgia, see Ignatius's letters to Oviedo on March 27, 1548 (*Epp. Ign.* 2, 54–56) and to Borgia on September 20, 1548 (*Epp. Ign.* 2, 233–37) and again in July 1549 (*Epp. Ign.* 12, 632–54).

62. See the good conclusion from Albert A. Sicroff, *Los estatutos de limpieza de sangre*, rev. ed. (Madrid: Taurus, 1985), 315: "Ninguna comunidad religiosa importante de la España del siglo XVI sufrió más agudamente las penosas consecuencias de la preocupación con la limpieza de sangre que *la Compañía de Jesús concebida como fue con la colaboración enérgica de cristianos nuevos.*"

63. Cf. Medina, "Ignacio de Loyola," 613. The Jesuit Robert Persons gives some interesting comments on the reception of the decree in Spain as an Englishman familiar with Jesuit life in Spain. See Francis Edwards, *Robert Persons* (St. Louis: Institute of Jesuit Sources, 1995). Persons made two interesting points. First, he confirmed the anti-*converso* trend at the king's court at the time of the Fifth General Congregation, and second, he described resistance among some Jesuit provinces. See ibid., 171: "The decrees of the Fifth General Congregation reached Spain by late spring of 1594. Persons concluded, 'they all make a good impression except the third about the Hebrew race.' . . . 'It is scarcely decent to exclude any race of Christians from a means which our Lord left for their salvation, namely, the religious life, if they are incurring danger in the world.' . . . Some of the royal ministers had spoken to Persons on occasion, intimating that such a decree would be a good thing. Persons brought many reasons against it."

64. Throughout the sixteenth century, the Holy See was in fact trying to oppose and limit the *estatutos de limpieza*.

65. Even if there were no direct link between the decree and the activities of "*los perturbadores*" in 1593 (a connection maintained by Astráin, *Historia*, 3:468–651 and Rey, "S. Ignacio de Loyola"), as some suggest, the decree could not but appear as a concession made to Iberian national feelings. Should this, however, be interpreted as a defeat for Claudio Acquaviva despite his apparent personal support for the decree? Or was he willing to concede to Iberian prejudices to please King Philip II in order to gain

victory on constitutional matters? The fact that some of the *perturbadores* were *conversos* could easily have been powerfully used by the supporters of the decree. An answer requires further investigation of Acquaviva's generalate.

66. F. Medina supports the idea according to which Acquaviva played a decisive role in favor of the decree. It is also the opinion of Aixalá and Escalera in the *Diccionario*, 2:1004, who wrote: "Acquaviva contribuyó, en la CG [1593], de modo decisivo al decreto de linaje que prohibía taxativamente la admisión en la CJ." This may be true, but even in that case his motivation would probably be the same as the reason advanced by the Spanish supporters of the decree, namely to make the Society more acceptable to Iberian worldly standards and the wishes of Philip II. After receiving the letter of protest from Possevino, General Acquaviva answered that he was obliged to act that way. Donnelly, "Antonio Possevino," 11, writes: "Acquaviva's reply . . . is dated November 7, 1598 [*Congr.* 26, 38]. The General admitted quite frankly that a major consideration in passing the decree . . . was pressure from Spain: important people had warned him that 'we will never have peace with the King, with his principal ministers and with the Inquisition nor would the Society ever have the status it deserved unless the decree was passed.'"

67. I have added four Italian men who were not technically *conversos*: Antonio and Alessandro Possevino (whose family was already Christian); Eliano, who came from a pious Jewish family in Italy; and Paolo Mentuato, also a Jew by birth. Technically the term "*conversos*" applied only to Spanish and Portuguese Christians of Jewish origin. Future researchers should peruse pre-1565 Spanish catalogs for Spanish Jesuits with typical *converso* names who had entered the Society as priests and had worked overseas. Cf. Mario Scaduto, S.J., *Catalogo dei Gesuiti d'Italia (1540–1565)* (Roma: IHSI, 1968). A more thorough examination of Nadal's *responsa* would probably help refine the number. Apart from those whose origin is fairly certain, I have made another list of sixty-three Jesuits whose Jewish origins are highly probable. Regarding this group, I have considered diocese of origin, name, preadmission studies, preadmission clerical status, and country of ministry. In order not to lengthen this paper, I do not include this second list.

68. The main sources used are O'Malley, *First Jesuits*; Wicki, "Die 'Cristaos Novos'"; Medina, "La Compañia de Jesús"; and Joszef Fejér, S.J., *Defuncti primi saeculi Societatis Iesu*, 2 vols. (Rome: Institutum Historicum Societatis Iesu, 1982).

69. This group is made of the names that are given in the different articles and dictionaries. It groups the Spaniards together (including one Frenchman of Spanish origin, Alexandre de Rhodes). I have chosen alphabetical order as being easier to consult.

70. Made his profession in 1570. Inscribed in the province of "la India occidental." He returned to Spain in 1590 and was present at the Fifth General Congregation. Donnelly, "Antonio Possevino," 8, so describes his role in 1593: "Acosta is famous in Jesuit history for quite another reason. He tried to enlist the support of Philip II of Spain to secure more autonomy for the Jesuits in Spain. The result was a crisis of authority within the Society and the convocation of the Fifth General Congregation, the first one called not to elect a new general. A severe power struggle ensued in both Spain and Rome. Suffice it to say that the forces behind Acquaviva were victorious . . . rather different judgments have been made on this congregation, but the subject has not had the monograph that it deserves." See Claudio M. Burgaleta, S.J., *Jose de Acosta (1540–1600): His Life and Thought* (Chicago: Loyola Press, 1999); *Diccionario*, 1:10–12: and *Nadal, MHSI* 2:569. I am not convinced by Burgaleta's arguments that Acosta was not a *converso* after having read Appendix 1, 126–27. In fact Burgaleta argues more against an old presentation (Lobotegui) than against the last arguments used in the *Diccionario.* So I am inclined to drop his suggestion that Acosta was not a *converso.* About Acosta's role in the Fifth General Congregation, the *Diccionario* is very cautious, 1:11: "Actuó con buen celo y por el bien de la CJ, pero equivocadamente."

71. He made his profession in 1568 in the province of Castilla La Vieja. See *Nadal*, 2:544.

72. Astráin, *Historia*, 1:313: "Jerónimo, el más viejo de todos, pero que entró el último en la Compañía y la sirvió en varios cargos importantes." Professed in 1570 in Segovia.

73. Cf. *Diccionario*, 1:40: "De origen neoconverso." On this Sevillan family, see the interesting comment by Ruth Pike, *Aristocratas y comerciantes. La Sociedad Sevillana en el Siglo XVI* (Barcelona: Ariel, 1978), quoted by Dominguez Ortiz, *Los judeoconversos*, 184–85: "El estigma de su origen era cuidadosamente escondido mediante cuadros genealógicos hábilmente trazados. Uno de los mejores ejemplos fue la familia de los Alcázar, en la que hubo muchas generaciones de comerciantes, eclesiásticos, funcionarios y escritores."

74. Cf. *Diccionario*, 2:1003: "Por la misma razón [being *conversos* like Ferrer] Vasco Baptista y Gaspar Vaz fueron removidos de las cátedras de la universidad (ARSI, *Lus.* 68, f. 51)." Typical *converso* name. His mother was Leonor de Lucena; cf. João Pereira Gomes, S.J., *Os professores de filosofia da Universidade de Evora* (Evora: Câmara municipal, 1960), 113. Cf. Fejér, *Defuncti*, 2:21.

75. Cf. *Diccionario*, 1:707: "Hijo de Hernando Fernández de Castro y Juana de Aranda, bienhechores del colegio de Sevilla, era cristiano nuevo y hermano mayor de Gaspar y Melchor, tambíen jesuitas."

76. Cf. Medina, "*Precursores*," 509: "Melchor de Castro, catedrático del colegio de Sevilla y su rector, apuntaba a la incongruencia que suponía

el que un superior tuviera que negar la admisión en la Compañia por la misma razón por la que él mismo no debía ser recibido. Argumento que el P Esteban de Hojeda esgrimía para excluir del cargo de provincial a los notados, entre ellos el propio Melchor de Castro de quien advertía: 'Sería cosa ridícula aver decretado tan estrecho de limpieza para los que an de ser rescibidos y ser la cabeça que los a de rescebir y tractar de sus informaciones tan notada porque es cosa muy notaria.'" He had two brothers in the Society.

77. See *Diccionario*, 2:1005: "Pariente de Juan de Ávila, era licenciado en filosofía por la Universidad de Alcalá . . . cuando entró en la CJ . . . partió de Lisboa para el Japón." A beatification process was open in 1901.

78. Died in Montilla according to Fejér, *Defuncti*, 2:66. He and Juan do not belong to the family of Rodrigo de Dueñas.

79. One of the four sons of Rodrigo de Dueñas (Bernardo, Gabriel, Gaspar, and Mateo). Cf. Fejér, *Defuncti*, 2:66: and Astráin, *Historia*, 1:313. Martz, "Converso Families," evokes several times the large families ("given the large number of children and the close intermarriage among converso families"; ibid., 131) that she calls "clans." In Toledo they are "the Madrid clan" (ibid., 149), "the Palma clan" (ibid., 155), and "the de Herrera clan" (ibid., 143). Rodrigo de Dueñas was a rich merchant who founded the college of Medina del Campo. It is interesting to note that he helped the other order that did not adopt the *Estatutos*: the reformed Carmelites. Cf. Dominguez Ortiz, *Los judeoconversos*, 180: "Como era habitual en los conversos ricos, ejerció un generoso patrocinio religioso del que se benefició Santa Teresa para sus fundaciones."

80. Died in Seville according to Fejér, *Defuncti*, 2:66.

81. Cf. Fejér, *Defuncti*, 2:78. For Miguel Ferrer, who died in France, see ibid. Also see following note.

82 Cf. *Diccionario*, 2:1003: "El tercer general Francisco de Borja . . . nombró a Paulo Ferrer, un cristiano nuevo, canciller o rector de la Universidad de Évora . . . (ARSI, *Lus*. 63, f. 82)." Cf. Fejér, *Defuncti*, 2:78. Wenceslao Soto Artuñedo, S.J., mentions together two other Ferrers of the same city of Malaga in the establishment of the college here. See Wenceslao Soto Artuñedo, "Fundación del colegio Jesuítico de San Sebastián en Málaga," *AHSI* 70 (2001):95–172, 121, n. 135: "Pedro Paulo Ferrer . . . Miguel Ferrer . . . Juan Bautista Ferrer." We have the answer from Paulo in FG 77, IV, 303. He indicates thirty-two years, a priest, and from Malaga. So in his case, the questionnaire was made in 1561. We should notice that Ferrer was sent by Borgia to Portugal with "Fernão Peres," born in Córdoba and perhaps a *converso* too (b. 1530; SJ 1559; d. 1595). See Francisco Rodrigues, S.J., *Historia da Companhia de Jesus na Assiténcia de Portugal*, 2 vols. (Porto: Apostolado da Imprensa, 1931), 1:464.

83. "Einige Neuchristen wurden, wie schon erwähnt, auch Obere in Indien, keiner Rektor des Paulskollegs oder Provinzial. In Japan stand jedoch

in schwieriegster Zeit P. Pedro Gómez, Spanier, als Vizeprovinzial . . . den Jesuiten 1590 bis 1600 vor"; Wicki, "Die 'Cristaos Novos,'" 356 and 359. See *Diccionario*, 2:1774. We have his answer in FG 77, IV, 310. He was twenty-six, a priest, and had one brother studying medicine. He says that one of his brothers was also a Jesuit but does not give the name.

84. Cf. *Diccionario*, 2:1923: "Se graduó en artes y teología. . . . Ya sacerdote, entró en la CJ. . . . Fue uno de los 'memorialistas.'" The author of the entry has this very strange concluding statement: "No es posible apreciar lo que pudo influir en su conducta y sensibilidad religiosa el atavismo converso de su familia"; ibid., 1924. Martz, writes: "J. Román de la Higuera. It is very likely that the Jesuit chronicler was, in fact, a descendant of the majordomo of the cardinal Mendoza, which would explain why he is so well informed about the Jarada family"; Martz, "Converso Families," 137. He was a disciple of Juan de Ávila. Cf. Ruiz Jurado, "San Juan de Ávila," 158.

85. Cf. *Diccionario*, 3:2146: "De origen converso, era hijo de Francisco Méndez y Leonor Arias." In 1594, he had to face an Inquisition trial: "En el proceso . . . los inquisidores recordaron a J su ascendencia neocristiana y la condena a la hoguera de su abuelo, añadiendo: 'mirad por vos que tenéis el fuego muy cerca que podrá ser os chamusque.'" Died in Seville; see Fejér, *Defuncti*, 2:109.

86. Scaduto, *L'epoca*, I,124. He joined in December 1547, was ordained in 1556, dismissed by his brother in August 1556, reaccepted by Borgia in 1567, dismissed again in 1571. M. Scaduto concludes: "Si ha notizia di una terza riammissione ad opera del P. Acquaviva, col quale finalmente si placò et poté morire nell'ordine"; ibid., 124. But Fejér, *Defuncti*, does not have his name. See, however, Scaduto, *Catalogo.*

87. Cf. Scaduto, *L'epoca*, 1:123–25. His parents were Juan Laínez and Isabella Gómez de León. See *Diccionario*, 2:1601: "descendia (probablemente en cuarta generación) de un judío converso."

88. Scaduto, *L'epoca*, 1:124, n. 7; and Fejér, *Defuncti*, 1:140. According to Fejér, *Defuncti,* 2:118, a priest called "Franciscus Laínez" died in Baeza in 1581.

89. Cf. Fejér, *Defuncti*, 2:124. He was a brother of Gaspar, as he himself indicates in his answer to Nadal's questionnaire: "Tengo un ho en la Compa y es el doctor Loarte rector en genova" (FG 77, I, 241). We do not know, however, if Juan de Loarte came from the same family. See Nigel Griffin, "A Curious Document: Baltasar Loarte and the Years 1554–1570," *AHSI* 45 (1976):56–94.

90. Cf. Scaduto, *L'epoca*, 2:617, on his entrance. The "no" of Araoz and the "yes" of Ignatius. His companion, a disciple of Juan de Ávila, as he was himself, was Diego de Guzmán who, according to M. Scaduto, was from a "noble" family, son of Rodrigo Ponce de León and Blanca de Sandoval. See also Medina, "La Compañia de Jesús," 41.

91. Cf. Wicki, "Die 'Cristaos Novos,'" 351. Cf. Fejér, *Defuncti*, 2:164.

92. See *Diccionario*, 3:2960, where the author of the entry uses only this euphemism, "born into a rich family": "Nacido en una familia acomodada, tuvo diez hermanos, dos de ellos jesuitas: Esteban (1566–1636) y Gabriel (d. 1594)." See Fejér, *Defuncti*, 2:171. Died in Toledo.

93. Cf. Fejér, *Defuncti*, 2:171. Died in Huete.

94. This Luis de la Palma, S.J., is mentioned in Dominguez, *La clase social*, xxi (and in Astráin, *Historia*, vol. 3). There were three de la Palma brothers in the Society. Luis became provincial of Toledo. Cf. Medina, "*Precursores*," 515: "Todavía, en 1625, [The General] encargaba lo mismo al provincial de Toledo Luis de La Palma, de conocido linaje converso toledano que, al parecer, había recibido gente de linaje sospechoso."

95. Cf. Medina, "*Precursores*," 502: "Méndez no podía ocultar su aversión a los cristianos nuevos. Se había ventilado, poco hacía, el caso de uno de ellos, Diego Pareja natural de Córdoba." Fejér, *Defuncti*, 2:172, lists three men named Pareja in the Society, three priests and a brother.

96. Made his profession in Augsburg in 1561 in the German province with Canisius. Died in the Polish province; cf. Fejér, *Defuncti*, 1:196, "(Pol) Calissii." Cf. O'Malley, *The First Jesuits*, 189: "Alfonso de Pisa, a well-known medical doctor and mathematician." See his formation and his activities in Scaduto, *L'epoca*, 2:283. See also *Diccionario*, 4:3146–48; and *Nadal*, 2:531. This important Toledan *converso* family is noted by Dominguez Ortiz, *Los judeoconversos*, 222: "Al linaje Pisa, muy relacionado con otros de notorios conversos, perteneció Francisco de Pisa." One "Ioan. Dominicus Pisanus" died in Napoli in 1604, according to Fejér, *Defuncti*, 1:196.

97. Cf. *Diccionario*, 4:3168 ("sobrino de Juan Alonso"). I wonder if some *converso* "*Memorialistas*" did not hold the hope of avoiding the adoption of the decree by having a closer relation to the king, believing that Acosta and others could counterbalance at the court the pressure for the adoption of the *limpieza* within the Society. In fact, it is during this period that the monarchy began its efforts to attenuate or suppress the *estatutos de limpieza*.

98. The only other Polanco who died in the Society (except a scholastic, Juan, who died in 1623). See Fejér, *Defuncti*, 2:184.

99. Cf. Dominguez, *La clase social*, 72, who explains how the king of Portugal tried to veto him as fourth general of the Society because he was a *converso*. The Jesuit Leão Henriques (1522–1589; *Diccionario*, 2:1899) asked the king, Sebastián, and Cardinal Infant D. Henrique to write a letter to veto Polanco. Cf. *Diccionario*, 4:3168, for the name of the king. See also *Diccionario*, 2:1004: "en las cartas del rey Don Sebastián al papa Gregorio XIII era la de interponer un veto a la elección de algún cristiano nuevo o que favoreciera su admisión en la CJ (Rodrigues, 2/1:345–59)." Polanco

was from the well-off family of Burgos (*conversos* since the end of the fourteenth century). See Dominguez Ortiz, *Los judeoconversos*, 178: "Entre esos grandes mercaderes burgaleses figuraban los Maluenda, Bernuy, Astudillo, Vitoria, Curiel, Polanco, Salamanca, Quintana-Dueñas, la Moneda, Brizuela, López del Peso." He adds "de la familia de los Vitoria procedió el ilustre Francisco de Vitoria, y de la Polanco el che estuvo a punto de ser el cuarto General de la Compañía de Jesús y que no lo fue precisamente por su ascendencia."

100. Cf. O'Malley, *The First Jesuits*, 189; and Astráin, *Historia,* 1:210. Born in 1515 or 1516: "Donde debió nacer por los años 1515 ó 1516" (Astráin, *Historia*, 1: 210).

101. His name is given by A. Possevino writing to the general Acquaviva trying to convince him to cancel decree 52 of the Fifth General Congregation. Cf. Donnelly, "Antonio Possevino," 10–11. See *Diccionario*, 4:3289; and Fejér, *Defuncti*, 2:190, "in Japonia." The only one of that name in Fejér.

102. Cf. *Diccionario*, 4:3342: "Sus abuelos, de probable origen judío (se llamaban de Rueda), emigraron de España a Avignon." Being of Spanish origin, he fits well in the *converso* category *stricto sensu.*

103. Cf. *Diccionario*, 4:3168.

104. Cf. *Diccionario*, 4:3345: "Era hijo del jurado toledano Álvaro Husillo Ortiz de Cisneros y de Catalina de Villalobos, ambos de origen converso. Tomó el nombre de sus antepasados maternos, procedentes de Galicia (Riba de Neira)." See also J. Gómez-Menor, "la progenie hebrea del P. Pedro de Ribadeneira," *Sefarad* 36 (1976):307–32. His masterwork is the first biography of St. Ignatius, *Vita Ignatii Loyolae*, published in 1572. The work of Gómez-Menor has been confirmed by Martz, "Converso Families," 135, who writes: "Catalina de Villalobos, married to Alvaro Husillo. . . . For posterity, it is his first marriage and his daughter Catalina de Villalobos that are the most memorable, as one of her children was to become the famous Jesuit, Pedro de Rivadeneira." She adds ironically: "One wonders if he would have achieved such prominence had his surname been Jarada, San Pedro or Husillo."

105. His origin is given by Medina, "La Compañia de Jesús," 53: "De origen judio." He entered as a priest in Gandia in 1549 and made his profession in 1559. In 1572 he was the third professed Jesuit transcribed in the province of Aragon. See also *Diccionario*, 4:3402, "de origen judeocristiano." Fejér, *Defuncti*, 2:203. See also *Nadal*, 2:533.

106. Luis de Santander, born near Seville in 1527, disciple of Juan de Ávila, admitted as a priest by Nadal in 1554 to show Juan de Ávila both the goodwill of the Society and that the Society was not accepting the *limpieza* statutes, even after the hesitations about Loarte. Superior of Segovia in 1559, of Alcalá in 1572. Made his profession in 1564 and was also transscribed to the province of Aragon. Died in Valencia in 1593. Medina, "La

Compañia de Jesús," 54, mentions his origin: "De origen judio." He was one of the protesters against the decree of 1593. See *Diccionario*, 4:3499: "Sacerdote de origen judeocristiano y discípulo de Juan de Ávila. . . . Fue uno de los de Andalucía que protestó al general contra el canon 3° de la Congregación General V (1593). . . . Personalmente, fue víctima de esta política discriminatoria."

107. This name was provided to me by Professor Bernard Vincent (EHESS of Paris). Santofimia's family was involved in a trial for *limpieza de sangre*. He is the only Jesuit of that name; cf. Fejér, *Defuncti*, 2:216. See also Soto Artuñedo, "Fundación," 145, n. 239.

108. According to F. Medina, he was most probably a *converso* (personal conversation, March 23, 2001). See also *Diccionario*, 4:3593: "Era maestro en artes. . . . Quizá por pertenecer a una familia de conversos ('por los quatros costados' según un contemporáneo), pasó a Lisboa, donde pidió entrar en la CJ." Cf. Fejér, *Defuncti*, 2:225.

109. Cf. *Diccionario*, 4:3654: "Examinaron su doctrina Juan de Mariana y Juan de Sigüenza en España, y en Roma *su tío*, Francisco de Toledo." The *converso* origin of the uncle is well known, but it is striking how often that of the nephew goes unnoticed by his biographers.

110. According to F. Medina, this Jesuit (cf. Fejér, *Defuncti*, 2:229) came from a very well-known *converso* family (personal conversation with F. Medina, March 23, 2001).

111. Cf. O'Malley, *The First Jesuits*, 189. He made his final profession in Rome in 1564. See *Diccionario*, 4:3807–808. Martz, "Converso Families," 148, writes: "Toledo was a very popular surname with the Toledo conversos." See Dominguez Ortiz, *Los judeoconversos*, 221: "El famoso cardenal jesuita Francisco de Toledo: nació en Córdoba, 1532 . . . todos sabían allí que su padre fue un escribano sambenitado. Incluso se rumoreaba que su madre y su hermana habían perecido en la hoguera [ver el artículo de F. Javier Rodríguez en *Archivo Teológico Granadino*, 52:1989]."

112. Cf. Alden, *The Making of an Enterprise*, 257. Cf. Fejér, *Defuncti*, 2:230.

113. Born in 1534 near Ávila, joined as a priest in 1557, made his profession in 1570, died in 1603. Medina, "La Compañia de Jesús," 94: "De origen judeoconverso." See *Diccionario*, 4:3911: "En 1573, confió ser cristiano nuevo al P. General Everardo Mercuriano cuando le rogaba que no le nombrase rector de ninguno de los tres colegios principales de Andalucía (Sevilla, Cordóba, Granada): 'Yo soy hijo de un çapatero pobre *ex christianis neothericijs*, que es cosa que en España tanto se aborrece' (AHSI *Hisp 119* 113)."

114. Joined after the decree. Cf. Medina, "*Precursores*," 515: "De uno de ellos, Rodrigo de Vida—el mismo apellido lo delataba—la provincia pidió la dispensación, que el general mostró dificuldad en solicitarla."

There was another one: "Del otro, Paulo de Morales, no hubo evidencia. Vitelleschi ordenó silencio. . . . Ambos perseveraron en la Compañia"; ibid.

115. Cf. *Diccionario*, 4:4057: "De ascendencia neocristiana, era bachiller en artes. . . . Buen teólogo."

116. Cf. *Diccionario*, 1:81–82: "De familia de cristianos nuevos, se graduó en medicina." Cf. Wicki, "Die 'Cristaos Novos,'" 349. See Fejér, *Defuncti*, 2:7.

117. Cf. Wicki, "Die 'Cristaos Novos,'" 351; and *Diccionario*, 1:90. See Fejér, *Defuncti*, 2:8.

118. Mentioned by Wicki, "Die 'Cristaos Novos,'" 355, who deduced the name from a letter written by Valignano. Died in Brazil according to Fejér, *Defuncti*, 2:14.

119. Cf. Wicki, "Die 'Cristaos Novos,'" 351. Cf. Fejér, *Defuncti*, 2:25 (the only one of that name).

120. As Henriques, he had been a member of another order before joining. Cf. *Diccionario*, 1:707: "Hijo de un rico platero de origen judío . . . llevó unos meses el hábito franciscano, pero no siendo admitido por ser cristiano nuevo, embarcó (1547) para Goa, y Javier lo aceptó en la CJ." The same can be said of Antonio Belo.

121. Cf. Wicki, "Die 'Cristaos Novos,'" 350. Died in "Chaul," according to Fejér, *Defuncti*, 2:61.

122. Italian. On this fascinating figure, perhaps the only practicing and educated Jew (being the grandson of Rabbi Elia Levita) who entered the Society during Ignatius's lifetime, see the article presenting his autobiography, José C. Sola, S.J., "El P. Juan Bautista Eliano, un documento autobiografico inedito," *AHSI* 4 (1935):191–221. Sola writes: "Entrado en la Compañía se llamó tambien Romano . . . Solo el [catalogo] de 1577 le pone Jo. B. Elianus," 303. See *Diccionario*, 2:1233; and Fejér, *Defuncti*, 1:82.

123. Cf. Wicki, "Die 'Cristaos Novos,'" 349. See Fejér, *Defuncti*, 2:72 ("in Aethiopia").

124. Mentioned by Wicki, "Die 'Cristaos Novos,'" 355. In a letter the aristocrat F. de Meneses lamented about this Jesuit whose uncle had been tried by the Inquisition. Died perhaps as a martyr in the Moluccas. Fejér reports "occisus, in Moluccis 24 09 1580"; Fejér, *Defuncti*, 2:74.

125. Cf. Wicki, "Die 'Cristaos Novos,'" 352. Disappeared from the catalog in 1567. Another Figueiredo, Melchor (b. 1530), entered the Society in Goa in 1554 and died in Japan in 1581 (see *Diccionario*, 2:1416).

126. Mentioned by Wicki, "Die 'Cristaos Novos,'" 355. The name is explicitly quoted by Valignano. Gomes died in 1591, according to Fejér, *Defuncti*, 2:93, who says "Bazain? Feb 1591." Bassein was a Portuguese stronghold on the Indian coast in the present state of Maharashtra.

127. Made his last vows in 1564 in Coimbra. According to Valignano (quoted by Wicki, "Die 'Cristaos Novos,'" 353), he could not be made provincial because he was partially *converso* on one side. Same situation as that of Pedro Gómez. He died in 1590, according to Fejér, *Defuncti*, 2:12.

128. Was a Franciscan before joining. Dismissed, already a deacon, for *limpieza*, he was admitted by Rodrigues and sent to Xavier. Cf. Wicki, "Die 'Cristaos Novos,'" 346. See *Diccionario*, 2:1900. See Manuel Lópes.

129. Cf. *Diccionario*, 3:2416: "Era hijo del médico Simão Lopes y de Isabel Henriques, conversos del judaismo, y hermano de dos jesuitas, uno de ellos el téologo Enrique Henriquez. . . . Entre sus parientes cercanos por la línea materna de los Bentalhado, perseguidos por la Inquisición portuguesa, se cuentan el fundador de la communidad judía de Amsterdam y su nieta, la madre del filósofo Baruch Spinoza." See also Griffin, "A Curious Document," 92.

130. The *Diccionario*, 3:2416, informs us that there was a third brother from the same family as Manuel Lopes ("hermano de dos jesuitas") and Enrique (or Henrique—both spellings are used) Henriquez (Lopes).

131. Cf. *Diccionario*, 3:2620: "Al no ser admitido en la CJ de Portugal, probablemente por su ascendencia judía, viajó a Roma para lograrlo del P. General. Aceptado en la provincia de Toledo." Sent as missionary to Mexico.

132. Italian. Cf. Scaduto, *L'epoca*, 2:410: "Un infermo, l'ebreo convertito P. Mentuato, mori poco dopo." Died in Ferrara.

133. Cf. Wicki, "Die 'Cristaos Novos,'" 350. Does not appear in Fejér.

134. Cf. Wicki, "Die 'Cristaos Novos,'" 348. Fejér, *Defuncti*, 2:161, calls him "Michael" while mentioning another Fr. Emmanuel de Nobrega who died in Brazil in 1570.

135. "Nach Meneses P L. Pinheiro der im Verdacht stand, Neuchrist zu sein, weil in Cochin gegen ihn, ein gehässige Schmähschrift zu lesen war. Als er 1581 Vizerektor des Paulskollegs war, wurde er 'voce populi' abgesetz"; Wicki, "Die 'Cristaos Novos,'" 356. He died in 1590 or 1591, "in India," according to Fejér, *Defuncti*, 2:181.

136. This Jesuit was among the few who managed to join after the decree: "En 1622 llegaron a Roma noticias sobre su linaje y se puso en duda la validez de su admisíon . . . varios padres, entre ellos Luis de la Puente, intercedieron a su favor. . . . Para mayo 1623, se recibió en Roma la información firmada por el Inquisidor General de Portugal. . . . Pinto era hijo de cristianos nuevos per ambas partes. A su padre, no obstante la notoriedad de su linaje, se le había hecho la gracia de admitirlo por médico del Rey. . . . Andrés Pinto, a pesar de los órdenes del General, perseveró en la Compañía"; Medina, "*Precursores*," 514.

137. Italian. Died as a scholastic in Perugia. Cf. Fejér, *Defuncti*, 1:200.

138. Italian. For his life and his fight against decree 52 of the Fifth General Congregation, see Donnelly, "Antonio Possevino." He made his profession in 1569 and was transcribed to the province of Aquitania in 1572. For another part of his life, see John Patrick Donnelly, S.J., "Antonio Possevino, SJ, Papal Mediator between Emperor Rudolf II and King Stephan Báthory," *AHSI* 69 (2000):3–56.

139. Cf. Medina, "*Precursores*," 505: "Se trataba del H. Enríquez de Quadros, nacido en Tánger en 1561 y admitido en la Compañía, en Andalucía, en 1579 o 1580. . . . Según se decía, su padre había recibido el bautismo de mayor. El provincial se lamentaba de tener un buen surtido de este linaje debido al recibo de su predecesor (Diego de Acosta, hermano de José)." He could, however, be of *morisco* origin. Died in Madrid, according to Fejér, *Defuncti*, 2:188. Two priests of that name died in the Society, one in Goa in 1572 ("Antonius") and one in Malacca ("Ioannes").

140. Cf. Wicki, "Die 'Cristaos Novos,'" 347; and also Medina, "Ignacio de Loyola," 588. Cf. Fejér, *Defuncti*, 2:200.

141. Cf. *Diccionario*, 4:3486: "Estaba dedicado al comercio en el oriente y tenía conocimientos músicos e de cirugía." Cf. Fejér, *Defuncti*, 2:211 ("Arias"; died "in India").

142. Wicki writes "D. de Sande, Verwandter des Obern dessen Großmutter Neuchristin gewesen sei. . . . Sande war tatsächlich ein Neuchrist und konnte unter Valignano als Provinzial die feierliche Profeß von 4 Gelübden am 15 Jan 1584 in Goa ablegen"; Wicki, "Die 'Cristaos Novos,'" 355–56. He died in Macao. See Fejér, *Defuncti*, 2:213; and *Diccionario*, 4:3495.

143. Cf. Wicki, "Die 'Cristaos Novos,'" 349. Fejér, *Defuncti*, 2:216 has only one "Santos. (de los) Bartholom," who died in Mexico in 1610.

144. Cf. Alden, *The Making of an Enterprise*, 257. Fejér, *Defuncti*, 2:221.

145. Cf. Wicki, "Die 'Cristaos Novos,'" 348. See also Medina, "Ignacio de Loyola," 83: "cristiano nuevo." Scaduto, *Catalogo*, 144.

146. Cf. *Diccionario*, 4: 3821: "E. septiembre 1569, Cádiz, España. Perteneciente, casi con certeza, a una familia portuguesa de cristianos nuevos de origen judío con negocios en Flandes, donde vivió bastante tiempo." Entered as a widower, he offered himself repeatedly for missions overseas. The *Diccionario* adds an interesting story: "En Ragusa los judíos le tendieron una trampa: Le ofrecieron en matrimonio a una bella joven con 25.000 ducados de dote, a cambio de abrazar la ley mosaica. T rechazó enérgicamente la propuesta. . . . Amenazado de muerte, volvió a Roma con el hijo del gran rabbino, que había ganado para el cristianismo." He died as a chaplain of the Great Armada by the Irish coast. See Soto Artuñedo, "Fundación," 145, n. 243: "b. 1537 Portugal; SJ 1573 Cadiz; d. 20.ix.1588 en el galeón San Marcos, frente a Irlanda." See also Francisco de Borja Medina,S.J., "Jesuitas en la armada contra Inglaterra," *AHSI* 58 (1989):3–42, 35, "con toda probabilitad de origen neocristiano."

147. Cf. Wicki, "Die 'Cristaos Novos,'" 350. Cf. Fejér, *Defuncti*, 2:239 (died in Goa).

148. Cf. *Diccionario*, 4:3910: "Se graduó de bachiller en teología (30 abril 1592) y enseñó esta disciplina. Pero siendo de ascendencia judía, fue apartado de la docencia, y no hizo el doctorado." Died in Lisbon, according to Fejér, *Defuncti*, 2:240.

149. The most important and able of all, according to Wicki, "Die 'Cristaos Novos,'" 351: "Seine Grosseltern wären von der Inquisition verbrannt worden." See also *Diccionario*, 4: 3910: "Era cristiano nuevo, cuyos abuelos fueron quemados en la hoguera de Serpa. . . . Fue el primer cristiano nuevo en hacer la profesión en Goa." Cf. Fejér, *Defuncti*, 2:240 (called "Gomesius"; died in Lisbon).

150. Cf. *Diccionario*, 4:3917: "Por ser cristiano nuevo, surgieron dificultades para su entrada en la CJ; pero fue admitido en atención a su padre, doctor Tomás Rodrigues da Veiga, profesor de medicina en la Universidad de Coímbra y bienhechor de los jesuitas. . . . Concluidos los estudios, partió a la provincia de Polonia. . . . Después, estuvo en el Colegio Romano." See Fejér, *Defuncti*, 1:263 (died in Rome).

Reflections on the Dialogue between Jew and Non-Jew in the Bible and in Rabbinic Literature

Rabbi Tovia Ben-Chorin

1. Nelson Glueck, *Das Wort Hesed im altestamentlichen Sprachgebrauche als menschliche und göttliche gemainschaftsgemässe Verhaltungsweise* BZAW, 17 (Giessen, 1927); published in English as *Hesed in the Bible*, trans. Alfred Gottschalk (HUC, Cincinnati 1967).

2. Yizhak Heinemann, "Hesed" in *Biblical Encyclopedia* (Hebrew), Bialik Institute (Jerusalem, 1958).

The Goal of the Ignatian Exercises and Soloveitchik's Halakhic Spirituality

Christian M. Rutishauser, S.J.

1. For biographical details, cf. Shulamith Meiselman, *The Soloveitchik Heritage: A Daughter's Memoir* (Hoboken, NJ: 1995); Menchem D. Genack, *Rabbi Joseph B. Soloveitchik. Man of Halakhah—Man of Faith* (Hoboken, NJ: 1998); Aaron Rakeffet-Rothkoff, *The Rav: The World of Rabbi Joseph B. Soloveitchik* (New York: 1999); Christian M. Rutishauser, *Josef Dov Soloveitchik: Einführung in sein Denken* (Stuttgart: 2003), 21–45.

2. Ignatius de Loyola, *Spiritual Exercises*, no. 91–100.

3. Joseph Dov Soloveitchik, *Halakhic Man* (Philadelphia: 1983), 3.

4. Ibid., 36.

5. James W. Reites, "St. Ignatius of Loyola and the Jews," *Studies in the Spirituality of Jesuits* 13 (1981):1–48; "Die Juden: Perspektiven ignatianischer Weltsicht," in *Ignatius von Loyola und die Gesellschaft Jesu 1491–1556*, ed. Andreas Falkner and Paul Imhof (Würzburg: 1990), 417–30; John W. O'Malley, *Die ersten Jesuiten* (Würzburg: 1995), 220–24.

6. Autobiography, no. 61.

7. Rutishauser, *Josef Dov Soloveitchik*, 135–56.

8. *Family Redeemed*, 16.

9. *The Synagogue*, 325.

10. Ibid., 324.

11. Ignatius, *Spiritual Exercises*, no. 1; Soloveitchik, *Halakhic Man*, 52.

12. Ignatius, *Spiritual Exercises*, no. 23.

13. Ibid., no. 101–109.

14. Ibid., no. 230–37.

15. "Confrontation," *Tradition* 6/2 (1964):17–21.

An Ignatian Perspective on Contemporary Jewish Spirituality
Donald Moore, S.J.

1. Judith H. Banki and Eugene J. Fisher, *A Prophet for Our Time* (New York: Fordham University Press, 2002), xiv, xvi.

2. "*Nostra Aetate:* Declaration on the Relation of the Church to Non-Christian Religions," in *Vatican Council II: The Conciliar and Post-Conciliar Documents*, ed. Austin Flannery (Collegeville. Minn.: Liturgical Press, 1975), 738–42, paras. 2 and 4.

3. Donald Moore, S.J., *The Human and the Holy* (New York: Fordham University Press, 1989), 6.

4. Ibid., 7.

5. Abraham Heschel, "From Mission to Dialogue?" *Conservative Judaism* (Spring 1967):1–11, 9–10.

6. Maurice Friedman, *Martin Buber's Life and Work*, vol. 3 (New York: E. P. Dutton, 1983), 291.

7. Martin Buber, "Interpreting Hasidism," *Commentar*y (September 1963):218–25, 218.

8. Friedman, *Martin Buber's Life and Work*, 299.

9. Martin Buber, *Hasidism and Modern Man* (1958; New York: Harper Torchbooks, 1966), 130–36.

10. Martin Buber, *Tales of the Hasidim: Early Masters* (1947; New York: Schocken, 1961), 127.

11. Buber, *Hasidism and Modern Man*, 138.

12. Abraham Heschel, *Who Is Man?* (Stanford, Calif.: Stanford University Press, 1965), 36.

13. Ibid., 39.

14. Buber, *Hasidism and Modern Man*, 140.

15. Ibid., 139.

16. Buber, *Tales of the Hasidim: Later Masters* (1947; New York: Schocken, 1961), 284.

17. Buber, *Hasidism and Modern Man*, 139–40.

18. Heschel, *Who Is Man?* 118.

19. Louis J. Puhl, S.J., *The Spiritual Exercises of St. Ignatius* (Westminster, UK: Newman, 1960), 1.

20. Herbert Alphonso, *The Personal Vocation* (Rome: Centrum Ignatianum Spiritualitatis, 1990), 14, 18.

21. Buber, *Hasidism and Modern Man*, 141.

22. Martin Buber, *I and Thou* (New York: Charles Scribner's Sons, 1970), 143.

23. Buber, *Hasidism and Modern Man*, 163, 166.

24. Heschel, *Who Is Man?* 108.

25. Ibid., 114.

26. Martin Buber, *Ten Rungs: Hasidic Sayings* (New York: Schocken Books, 1947, 1962), 15.

27. Buber, *Hasidism and Modern Man*, 170–73.

28. Ibid., 127.

29. Buber, *Tales of the Hasidim: Later Masters*, 173.

30. Buber, *Tales of the Hasidim: Early Masters*, 122.

31. Buber, *Hasidism and Modern Man*, 49–50.

32. Ibids., 43.

33. David Stanley, *A Modern Scriptural Approach to the Spiritual Exercises* (Chicago: Loyola University Press, 1967), 149.

34. Ibid., 154.

35. Janos Lukacs, "The Incarnational Dynamics of the Constitutions," *Studies* (Winter 2004): 36–38.

36. Peter-Hans Kolvenbach, "Politics and Mysticism in Ignatius of Loyola," *Ignatiana* (June 1991):1.

The Jewish Theology of Abraham Joshua Heschel as a Challenge for Catholic Theology

Stanisław Obirek

1. S. Ronen, *In Pursuit of the Void: Journeys to Poland in Contemporary Israeli Literature* (Krakow: Judaica Foundation, 2001), 45–46.

2. J. Carroll, *Constantine's Sword: The Church and the Jews* (Boston: Houghton Mifflin, 2001), 47.

3. Ibid., 50.

4. John C. Bennett, "Heschel's Significance for Protestants," in *No Religion Is an Island. Abraham Joshua Heschel and Interreligious Dialogue*, ed. H. Kasimow and B. L. Sherwin (New York: Orbis Books, 1991), 124–25.

5. All the quotations by Heschel are from essays in *Moral Grandeur and Spiritual Audacity: Abraham Joshua Heschel*, ed. Susannah Heschel (New York: Farrar, Straus and Giroux, 1996), 246.

6. Ibid., 245.

7. Ibid., 238.

8. Ibid., 237.

9. Ibid., 236.

10. Cr. J. C. Merkle, "The Pathos of Divine Concern," in *Abraham Joshua Heschel: Exploring His Life and Thought*, ed. John C. Merkle (London: Collier Macmillan, 1985).

11. Heschel, *Moral Grandeur and Spiritual Audacity*, 243.

12. Ibid., 243.

13. Heschel, *Moral Grandeur and Spiritual Audacity,* 243.

14. Ibid., 268–85.

15. Ibid., 272.

16. Ibid., 274–75.

17. Ibid.. 278.

18. Ibid., 278.

19. Abraham Joshua Heschel, *The Sabbath* (Boston, Shambhala Library, 2003), 55.

20. Elie Wiesel, *And the Sea Is Never Full* (New York: Knopf, 1999), 398.

21. Cf. the last book by Rabbi Irving Greenberg, *For the Sake of Heaven and Earth: The New Encounter between Judaism and Christianity* (Philadelphia: Jewish Publication Society, 2004).

From Midrash to Rashi to Contemporary Narrative Exegesis (R. Alter, M. Sternberg, et al.): Continuity in Jewish Biblical Reading

Jean-Pierre Sonnet, S.J.

1. Emmanuel Lévinas, *Éthique et infini. Dialogues avec Philippe Nemo* (Paris: Fayard, 1982), 13.

2. I am echoing here the presentation of the debate in Robert Alter, *The Art of Biblical Narrative* (New York: Basic Books, 1985), 17–19.

3. Menakhem Perry and Meir Sternberg, "The King through Ironic Eyes: Biblical Narrative and the Literary Reading Process," *Ha-Sifrut* 1/2 (Summer 1968):263–92 (in Hebrew).

4. Menakhem Perry and Meir Sternberg, "Caution: A Literary Text," *Ha-Sifrut* 2/3 (August 1970):608–63 (in Hebrew).

5. See Meir Sternberg, *The Poetics of Biblical Narrative* (Bloomington: Indiana University Press, 1985), 190–229.

6. Robert Alter, *The Art of Biblical Narrative* (New York: Basic Books, 1981); Alter, *The Art of Biblical Poetry* (New York: Basic Books, 1985).

7. See Martin Buber and Franz Rosenzweig, *Scripture and Translation*, trans. L. Rosenwald with E. Fox (Bloomington, Indiana University Press, 1994), 114–50.

8. Erich Auerbach, "Odysseus' Scar," in *Mimesis: The Representation of Reality in Western Literature*, trans. Willard R. Trask (Princeton, N.J.: Princeton University Press, 1953), 3–23.

9. Hans W. Frei, *The Eclipse of Biblical Narrative. A Study in Eighteenth and Nineteenth Century Hermeneutics* (New Haven, Conn.: Yale University Press, 1974).

10. Frei, *Eclipse*, 16.

11. Jean-Louis Ska, "La 'Nouvelle Critique' et l'exégèse anglo-saxonne," *Recherches de Science Religieuse* 80/1 (1992):29–53.

12. Sternberg, *Poetics*, 518. See also Alter, *Art of Biblical Narrative*, 6: "The Bible on its part has a great deal to teach anyone interested in narrative because its seemingly simple, wonderfully complex art offers such splendid illustrations of the primary possibilities of narrative."

13. Sternberg, *Poetics*, xiii–xiv.

14. Ephraim A. Speiser, *Genesis*, The Anchor Bible Commentary Series (New York: Doubleday, 1964), 299; quoted in Alter, *Art of Biblical Narrative*, 3.

15. Alter, *Art of Biblical Narrative,* 10–11.

16. David Stern, "Midrash and the Language of Exegesis," in *Midrash and Literature*, ed. G. H. Hartman and S. Budick (New Haven, Conn.: Yale University Press, 1986), 122.

17. Alter, *Art of Biblical Narrative*, 12.

18. *Pirkei de Rabbi Eliezer. The Chapters of Rabbi Eliezer the Great*, trans. G. Friedlander (New York: Sepher-Hermon Press, 1981; 1916). I owe this observation to Elliott Rabin in an unpublished essay "Midrash as Literature: A Case Study in the Rabbinic Art of Rewriting."

19. See David A. Glatt, *Chronological Displacement in Biblical and Related Literatures*, SBL Dissertation Series 139 (Atlanta, Ga.: Scholars Press, 1993), 3–6.

20. As Sternberg has shown, the fundamental option of the biblical narrative is nevertheless to present the macro sequence of history in order; see Meir Sternberg, "Time and Space in Biblical (Hi)story Telling: The Grand Chronology," in *The Book and the Text: The Bible and Literary Theory*, ed.

R. Schwartz (Oxford, Basil Blackwell, 1990), 81–145; see esp. 82 apropos of the rabbinic rule.

21. See Menakhem Perry, "Literary Dynamics: How the Order of a Text Creates Its Meanings," *Poetics Today* 1–2 (1979):35–64, 311–61.

22. Alter, *Art of Biblical Narrative*, 11.

23. See Meir Sternberg, "How Narrativity Makes a Difference," *Narrative* 9 (2001):115–22.

24. See Adele Berlin, *Poetics and Interpretation of Biblical Narrative* (Winona Lake, Ind.: Eisenbrauns, 1994), 17–18.

25. See *Baba Bathra* 14b–15a.

26. *Baba Bathra* 15a; translation by Sternberg, *Poetics*, 61.

27. Sternberg, *Poetics*, 61.

28. See Jean-Pierre Sonnet, "Y a-t-il un narrateur dans la Bible? La Genèse et le modèle narratif de la Bible," in *Bible et littérature. Dieu et l'homme mis en intrigue*, Le livre et le rouleau 6 (Brussels: Lessius, 1999), 9–27; Sonnet, "Narration biblique et (post)modernité," in *La Bible en récits: L'exégèse biblique à l'heure du lecteur*, ed. D. Marguerat, Le Monde de la bible 48 (Geneva: Labor et Fides, 2003), 253–63.

29. *bT, Shab.*, 63a; *Yeb.*, 11b and 22a. S. Kamin's publications have thrown a new light on the relation between midrash and *peshat* in Rashi's exegetical project; see esp. Sarah Kamin, "Rashi's Exegetical Categorization with Respect to the Distinction between Peshat and Derash," *Immanuel* 11 (1980):16–32; and Kamin, *Rashi's Exegetical Categorization in Respect to the Distinction between Peshat and Derash* (Jerusalem: Magnes Press, 1986) (in Hebrew). Kamin shows that far from opposing the two methods, as his grandson, Samuel Ben Meir (Rashbam) will do (by consecrating the autonomy of *peshat*), Rashi always worked with the commentaries of "our masters" in front of him, and endowed them with a new authority by combining them with the contextual sense of Scripture. Rather than creating a distance between Scripture and tradition, he endeavored to have them mutually renew each other. See Marcel Dubois and Jean-Pierre Sonnet, "S. Kamin, lectrice de Rashi. De la cohérence et de la pertinence d'un projet exégétique," *Nouvelle Revue Théologique* 112 (1990):236–49.

30. Michael Signer, "Rashi as Narrator," in *Rashi et la culture juive en France du Nord au moyen âge*, ed. G. Dahan, G. Nahon, and E. Nicolas (Louvain: Peeters, 1997), 106; Signer emphasizes Rashi's art in this respect: "The reader is drawn into the biblical text both through the Rabbis and through Rashi" (106); in some instances, Signer adds, "the fusion of biblical lemmata with rewritten rabbinic *midrash* is completely seamless" (107).

31. Joseph Kara, Samuel Ben Meir [Rashbam], Rashi's grandson, Eliezer of Beaugency, and Joseph Bekhor Shor are particularly worth mentioning.

32. Uriel Simon, *Reading Prophetic Narratives* (Bloomington, Indiana University Press, 1997), xvi.

33. André Wénin, *Isaac ou l'épreuve d'Abraham. Approche narrative de Genèse 22*, Le livre et le rouleau 8 (Brussels: Lessius, 1999).

34. Both comments figure in Wénin, *Isaac*, 38.

35. *Miqra'ot Gedolot, ad loc.*

36. Robert Alter, *The World of Biblical Literature* (New York: Basic Books, 1992), 15.

37. Sternberg, "The Art of Persuasion," in *Poetics*, 441–80; and Sternberg, "Ideology, Rhetoric, Poetics," in *Poetics*, 482–515.

38. Robert Alter, "Northrop Frye, between Archetype and Typology," in "Northrop Frye and the Afterlife of the Word," special issue, *Semeia* 89 (2002):9–21.

39. Northrop Frye, *The Great Code: Bible and Literature* (New York, Harcourt, 1982).

40. Alter, "Northrop Frye," 20.

41. Ibid., 20.

42. Ibid., 21.

43. R. Ben Bag-Bag, *Pirqei Abot*, 5, 22.

44. *Sifre* on Deut. 17:19.

45. See David Banon, *La lecture infinie: Voies de l'interprétation midrachique* (Paris: Seuil, 1987), 219–45.

46. See Alter, *Art of Biblical Narrative*, 11–12.

47. Ibid., 157.

48. Ibid., 189.

Inscribe the New in the Old: Inner-Biblical Exegesis (M. Fishbane) and the Hermeneutics of Innovation (B. Levinson)
Jean-Pierre Sonnet, S.J.

1. M. Fishbane, *Biblical Interpretation in Ancient Israel* (Oxford: Clarendon, 1985); for a succinct presentation of this approach, see Fishbane, "Inner-Biblical Exegesis: Types and Strategies of Interpretation in Ancient Israel," in *The Garments of Torah: Essays in Biblical Hermeneutics* (Bloomington: Indiana University Press, 1989), 3–18 ; see also B. D. Sommer, "Inner-Biblical Interpretation," in *The Jewish Study Bible*, ed. A. Berlin and M. Z. Brettler (New York: Oxford University Press, 2004), 1829–35.

2. R. Bloch, "Écriture et tradition dans le Judaïsme. Aperçus sur l'origine du midrash," *Cahiers Sioniens* 8 (1954):9–34; see also Bloch, "Midrash," *Supplément au Dictionnaire de la Bible* 4 (1957):1263–81.

3. A. Gélin, "La question des 'relectures' bibliques à l'intérieur d'une tradition vivante," *Sacra Pagina* 1 (1959):303–15.

4. The two sections that follow are inspired by B. M. Levinson, *L'herméneutique de l'innovation. Canon et exégèse dans l'Israël biblique*, Le

livre et le rouleau 24 (Brussels: Lessius, 2005), which expands Levinson's seminal article, "'You Must Not Add Anything to What I Command You': Paradoxes of Canon and Authorship in Ancient Israel," *Numen* 50 (2003):1–51.

5. Translation from W. G. Lambert, "The Fifth Tablet of the Erra Epic," *Iraq* 24 (1962):122.

6. The translation is B. Levinson's; cf. H. A. Hoffner, Jr., *The Laws of the Hittites: A Critical Edition*, Documenta et Monumenta Orientis Antiqui 23 (Leiden: Brill, 1997), 21.

7. B. M. Levinson, *Deuteronomy and the Hermeneutics of Legal Innovation* (Oxford: Oxford University Press, 1997).

8. I summarize here the analysis by Levinson, *Deuteronomy*, 23–52.

9. See the divine institution of ritual slaughtering in Gen. 9:4 ("Only you shall not eat flesh with its life, that is its blood"); see also the narrative of 1 Sam. 14:31–35, which tells of the attempt to slaughter without an altar.

10. In modern exegesis, the equivalence was first proposed by L. de Wette in *Dissertatio Critica* (1805).

11. Does the narrative in 2 Kings 22 indeed recount the rediscovery of Deuteronomy (in its original form)? Was "the book of the Torah" indeed "lost," or does the invention of the document represent a stratagem of its authors or sponsors (other cases of pious frauds have been identified in ancient Mesopotamia)? See in this regard my study "'Le livre trouvé': 2 Rois 22 dans sa finalité narrative," *NRT* 116 (1994):836–61. It seems that the editing of the original Deuteronomy does indeed go back to the period of the royal reformers, Hezekiah (716–687) and Josiah (640–609). Accordingly, the Code of the Covenant, which serves as a canonical "matrix" for the Deuteronomist code, can be dated from before the seventh century.

12. See E. Otto, "Aspects of Legal Reforms and Reformulations in Ancient Cuneiform and Israelite Law," in *Theory and Method in Biblical and Cuneiform Law: Revision, Interpolation, and Development*, ed. B. M. Levinson, JSOTS 181 (Sheffield, Sheffield Academic Press, 1994), 195.

13. The definition in Exodus does not derive from the Code of the Covenant (Exod. 21–23) and therefore does not provide the matrix for the Deuteronomic rewriting.

14. Fishbane, *Interpretation*, 135–36.

15. Levinson, "You Must Not Add," 25–47.

16. It is noteworthy that Deuteronomy cites the text of Exodus but reverses the sequence, beginning with the affirmation that God is faithful with which Exod. 20:5–6 ends. This phenomenon of a reversed citation, characteristic of biblical rewriting, is called Seidel's law, after the scholar who uncovered the principle, M. Seidel, in his study "Parallels in Isaiah and Psalms," *Sinai* 38 (1955–1956):149–72, 229–40, 272–80, 335–50 (in Hebrew).

17. As the NRSV correctly translates it.

18. Levinson, "You Must Not Add," 39–41.

19. One must cite here, other than Levinson, J. Kugel, Y. Zakovitch, S. Bar-On, M. Brettler, H. Najman, B. Sommer, and others, without forgetting the pioneering work of N. Sarna.

20. N. M. Sarna, "Psalm 89: A Study in Inner Biblical Exegesis," in *Biblical and Other Studies*, ed. A. Altmann, Brandeis University Studies and Texts, 1 (Cambridge, Mass.: Harvard University Press, 1963), 29–34; reedited in Sarna, *Studies in Biblical Interpretation* (Philadelphia: Jewish Publication Society, 2000), 377–94.

21. L. Eslinger, "Hosea 12:5a and Genesis 32:29: A Study in Inner Biblical Exegesis," *Journal for the Study of the Old Testament* 18 (1980):91–99.

22. G. Scholem, "Revelation and Tradition as Religious Categories in Judaism," in *The Messianic Idea in Judaism* (New York: Schocken, 1971), 282–303.

23. Levinson, "You Must Not Add," 47.

24. Ibid., 49; see the bibliographical indication in n. 81.

25. See particularly R. B. Hays, *Echoes of Scripture in the Literature of Paul* (New Haven, Conn.: Yale University Press, 1993).

26. Levinson, "You Must Not Add," 48.

27. Ibid., 50.

28. Ibid., 50.

29. T. Mann, "Freud und die Zukunft," in *Gesammelte Werke* (Frankfort: Fischer, 1960), 4971; cited in Fishbane, *Interpretation*, 1.

A Catholic Conversation with Hannah Arendt
James Bernauer, S.J.

1. See Elisabeth Young-Bruehl, *Hannah Arendt: For Love of the World* (New Haven, Conn.: Yale University Press, 1982), 33–36, 62, 82. Visitors to Arendt's personal library, preserved at Bard College, will be struck by the number of specifically theological texts contained in her collection. The 1929 dissertation finally appeared in English in 1996 as *Love and Saint Augustine*, ed. J. V. Scott and J. C. Stark (Chicago: University of Chicago Press, 1996). Nevertheless, I do not want to deny the significance of Greek and Roman experience for Arendt. A helpful discussion of that influence is in Jacques Taminiaux, "Athens and Rome," in *The Cambridge Companion to Hannah Arendt*, ed. Dana Villa (Cambridge: Cambridge University Press, 2000), 165–77.

2. George Kateb, *Hannah Arendt: Politics, Conscience, Evil* (Totowa, N.J.: Rowman and Allanheld, 1983), 158, 165. At the same time I do agree with Richard Bernstein, who points out that Arendt never studied Jewish

tradition with the same seriousness as she did Christianity. See Bernstein, *Hannah Arendt and the Jewish Question* (Cambridge, Mass.: MIT Press, 1996).

3. John Dewey, *A Common Faith* (New Haven, Conn.: Yale University Press, 1934). For a recent collection of essays exploring Arendt's relationship with America, see Winfried Thaa and Lothar Probst, eds., *Die Entdeckung der Freiheit: Amerika im Denken Hannah Arendts* (Berlin: Philo, 2003). My presentation is heavily indebted to an earlier work: James Bernauer, "The Faith of Hannah Arendt," in *Amor Mundi: Explorations in the Faith and Thought of Hannah Arendt,* ed. James Bernauer (Dordrecht: Martinus Nijhoff, 1987), 1–28.

4. Hannah Arendt, *The Origins of Totalitarianism*, 3rd ed. with new prefaces (New York: Harcourt Brace Jovanovich, 1973), 473.

5. Arendt, *The Human Condition* (Chicago: University of Chicago Press, 1958), 247.

6. Arendt, "Remarks" to the January 21, 1973, Meeting of the American Society of Christian Ethics. In *The Papers of Hannah Arendt* at the Library of Congress, container 70, 01183 8–0118 39.

7. Arendt, "What Is Authority?" in *Between Past and Future* (New York: Penguin, 1977), 94–95. Arendt claims that the modern loss of faith itself is not religious in origin; Arendt, *Human Condition*, 253–54.

8. Arendt's 1967 notes for a lecture on Dostoyevsky's *The Possessed*, in *The Papers of Hannah Arendt*, container 69; Arendt, *Origins of Totalitarianism*, 446.

9. See Arendt, "Religion and Politics," *Confluence: An International Forum* 2, 3 (September, 1953):112.

10. Over thirty years ago Philip Rieff first suggested this approach to *The Origins of Totalitarianism* in Rieff, "The Theology of Politics: Reflections on Totalitarianism as the Burden of Our Time," *Journal of Religion* 32 (April, 1952):119–26.

11. Arendt, *Origins of Totalitarianism*, viii–ix, 459, 124.

12. As examples of such interpretations, cf. Rieff, "Theology of Politics"; and Benjamin Schwartz, "The Religion of Politics," *Dissent* 17 (March-April, 1970):144–61. As an example of this tendency in Arendt, see Arendt, *Origins of Totalitarianism*, 452.

13. Arendt, *On Revolution* (New York: Viking Press, 1963), 90, also 76–83; as well as Arendt, "Christianity and Revolution," *Nation* (September 22, 1945):288–89; and Arendt, "Waldemar Gurian," in *Men in Dark Times* (New York: Harcourt Brace Jovanovich, 1968), 241–42.

14. Arendt, *Origins of Totalitarianism*, 445.

15. Ibid., 189–91.

16. Joseph Conrad, *Heart of Darkness* and *The Secret Sharer* (New York: Signet, 1950), 144, 143, 113, 131, 143.

17. See Arendt, *Human Condition*, 243–44; Arendt, *On Revolution*, 195. For more on the specific image of exodus and its political utilizations, see Michael Walzer, *Exodus and Revolution* (New York: Basic Books, 1985).

18. Arendt, *Human Condition*, 254.

19. Arendt, *On Revolution*, 74: Arendt, *Origins of Totalitarianism*, 307, 315.

20. Arendt, *Human Condition*, 236–47.

21. Ibid., 237.

22. Ibid., 245.

23. While Arendt recognized the theoretical influence of the biblical covenant on political conceptions, she always insisted that its nature as a compact between God and humanity made it inherently unpolitical because it was not a compact between equals. I think that her interpretation underestimates the radical novelty of the biblical covenant, but in any case, my point stands. For her discussion of this matter, see Arendt, *Human Condition*, 243–44; Arendt, *On Revolution,* 166–76, 309–10; and Arendt, "Remarks."

24. Arendt, *Human Condition*, 238–39. Arendt cites Matthew 6:14–15, 18:35, and Mark 11:25.

25. Arendt, *Human Condition*, 241.

26. Ibid., 247, 8n1, 247, 318.

27. Arendt, "What Is Freedom," in *Between Past and Future* (New York: Harcourt Brace Jovanovich, 1978), 168.

28. Arendt, *Willing*, vol. 2 of *The Life of the Mind* (New York: Harcourt Brace Jovanovich), 217; cf. Arendt, *Origins of Totalitarianism*, 479; Arendt, *Human Condition*, 177; Arendt, *On Revolution*, 212.

29. Arendt, *Human Condition*, 247; Arendt, "What Is Freedom?" 169.

30. Arendt, "Remarks," 001838. Although it is clear that Hannah Arendt had a personal belief in God (see Arendt, *Men in Dark Times*, 67; Jeannette Baron, "Hannah Arendt: Personal Reflections," *Response* 39 [1980]:62; Alfred Kazin, *New York Jew* [New York: Knopf, 1978], 199), she never identified herself as a member of any denomination: "I am neither a crypto-Baptist nor am I a crypto-Christian? I am by birth a Jew, and as far as religion goes I do not belong to any church, or to any synagogue, or to any denomination"; Arendt, "Remarks," 011828. Judith Shklar has repeated the story that surfaced around the time of the controversy over Arendt's 1963 *Eichmann in Jerusalem*, namely, that Arendt appeared to have been drawn to Roman Catholicism; Shklar, "Hannah Arendt as Pariah," *Partisan Review* 50 (1983), 72. In Arendt's notes for a reply to a question regarding her supposed conversion to Roman Catholicism, she wrote that there "is no truth in it whatsoever. I suppose the rumour has been started in the old hope—*semper aliquid adhaeret.*" Arendt, "Answer to

Grafton," in *The Papers of Hannah Arendt*, container 42, file "Eichmann Case: Correspondence, Periodical, 1963," 13.

31. "Walter Benjamin," 204.

32. Arendt, "What Is Authority?" 126–27.

33. Rieff, "Theology of Politics," 120.

34. For example, in criticizing Arendt, Kateb claims that we "are not at home; we have too much at our disposal merely to construct a home"; Kateb, *Hannah Arendt*, 174.

35. Arendt, "Waldemar Gurian" and "Isak Dinesen" in *Men in Dark Times*, 257, 99, 88.

36. Arendt, "Truth and Politics," in *Between Past and Future*, 264, 90. Arendt, *Human Condition*, 271; Arendt, *Life of the Mind*, 53–65.

37. Arendt, *Human Condition*, 271; Arendt, *Life of the Mind*, 53–65.

38. Arendt, *Human Condition*, 319; on Kierkegaard and Pascal, see Arendt, *Human Condition*, 275–81; and Arendt, "What Is Authority?" 94–95.

39. Arendt, "Religion and Politics," 106; see William James, *The Varieties of Religious Experience* (New York: Collier, 1961), 201–3; Michael Polanyi, *Personal Knowledge: Towards a Post-Critical Philosophy* (New York: Harper and Row, 1964), 299.

40. Arendt's notes for a lecture, "Religion and Politics," delivered at the University of Chicago Divinity school on April 29, 1966. In *The Papers of Hannah Arendt* at the Library of Congress, container 70, 023429.

41. Arendt, "Collective Responsibility," in *Amor Mundi*, 46.

42. Matthew 16:26.

43. Arendt, "The Concept of History," in *Between Past and Future*, 52.

44. Arendt, *Human Condition*, 21, 314.

45. Arendt, "Remarks," 011832.

46. Arendt, *On Revolution*, 284.

47. Arendt, "What Is Freedom," 146.

48. Arendt, "Religion and Politics," 112; Arendt, *Human Condition*, 55.

49. Luke 8:19, as cited by Arendt, *Human Condition*, 75; Arendt, *Human Condition*, 180, 76.

50. See Arendt, *On Revolution*, 195; Arendt, "Religion and Politics," 125; Arendt, *On Revolution*, 190, 199.

51. Arendt, *On Revolution*, 82.

52. Arendt, "Religion and Politics," 126.

53. Arendt, "What Is Authority?" esp. 125; Arendt, "Remarks," 011839.

54. Hugo Rahner, *Greek Myths and Christian Mystery* (London: Burns and Oates, 1963), 383; Arendt, *On Revolution,* 26.

55. See the still classic work of H. Richard Niebuhr, *Christ and Culture* (New York: Harper Torchbooks, 1956).

56. Arendt, "Creating a Cultural Atmosphere," in *The Jew as Pariah*, ed. Ron Feldman (New York: Grove Press, 1978), 92.

57. Arendt, *Origins of Totalitarianism*, 466; Arendt, *On Revolution*, 80, 81.

58. H. Richard Niebuhr, *The Kingdom of God in America* (New York: Harper Torchbooks, 1959), 98. On this inadequacy in Arendt, cf. Robert Nisbet, "Hannah Arendt and the American Revolution," *Social Research* 44 (Spring 1977):69; and Sheldon S. Wolin, "Hannah Arendt: Democracy and the Political," *Salmagundi* 60 (Spring-Summer 1983):14.

59. Arendt, *Human Condition*, 126–35; Arendt, *On Revolution*, 136.

60. Arendt, "*The Deputy*: Guilt by Silence?" was first published in the *New York Herald Tribune Magazine* (February 23, 1964):6–9; republished in *Amor Mundi*, 51–58.

61. Arendt, "Angelo Giuseppe Roncalli: A Christian on St. Peter's Chair from 1958 to 1963," in *Men in Dark Times*, 57–69, 59. In a letter to her best friend Mary McCarthy, she speculated that hierarchical Roman Catholicism might not survive the reforms of John XXIII. Arendt, Letter of December 21, 1968, in *Between Friends: The Correspondence of Hannah Arendt and Mary McCarthy 1949–1975*, ed. Carol Brightman (New York: Harcourt Brace, 1995), 232.

62. See Arendt, "The Jew as Pariah: A Hidden Tradition" in *Jew as Pariah*, 67–90; and Feldman's introduction to this collection, "The Jew as Pariah: The Case of Hannah Arendt," 15–52.

63. Arendt, "Waldemar Gurian," 261–62.

64. James Bernauer, "The Holocaust and the Search for Forgiveness: An Invitation to the Society of Jesus?" *Studies in the Spirituality of Jesuits* 36/2 (Summer 2004).

65. Arendt, *Origins of Totalitarianism*, 102.

What Might Israelis and Jews Learn about Christians and Christianity at Yad Vashem?

David M. Neuhaus, S.J.

1. The message of Yad Vashem might be understood in terms of a quotation from a letter, written by Elkhanan Elkes, leader of the Kovno Jewish Council, to his children, given prominent place on the Internet site of the museum: "Remember both of you that which Amalek did to us; remember everything, do not forget for the rest of your lives and pass on as a holy testament to the coming generations that the Germans killed, slaughtered and murdered us."

2. Commission for Religious Relations with the Jews, *We remember: A reflection on the Shoah* (1998), n. V, http://www.vatican.va/roman_curia/

pontifical_councils/chrstuni/documents/rc_pc_chrstuni_doc_16031998_shoah_en.html.

3. The latter was himself a victim of the Shoah as a young French Jew who later converted to Catholicism. Lustiger lost his mother in the Nazi concentration camps.

4. The ten halls are divided as follows:

    1. The World that Was (an entry area rather than a hall in itself and showing scenes from Jewish life in Europe before the war).
    2. From Equals to Outcasts (focusing on the rise of the Nazis, their taking of power, and the anti-Semitic legislation).
    3. The Awful Beginnings (focusing on the beginning of the war, the success of the German army, and especially the invasion of Poland).
    4. Between Walls and Fences (focusing on the ghettoes of Lódz, Warsaw, Kovno, and Theresienstadt).
    5. Mass Murder (focusing on the mass execution of Jews in Eastern Europe, particularly in the USSR after the Nazi invasion, like the massacre at Babi Yar).
    6. The Final Solution (focusing on the decision to implement a planned extermination of the Jews by setting up death camps and using sophisticated extermination techniques).
    7. Resistance and Rescue (focusing on the opposition to the Nazis and attempts to save Jews).
    8. The Last Jews (focusing on experiences in the camps and the fate of their inhabitants leading up to the liberation of the camps in 1945).
    9. Return to Life (focusing on the stories of those who survived and their difficult reintegration into life).
    10. Facing the Loss (less an exhibition hall than a memorial space for those who perished).

5. *We Remember: A reflection on the Shoah* (1998), n. II.

6. Arriving in Israel in 1959, he was refused immediate citizenship because he was a Catholic despite his insistence that he considered himself Jewish in terms of nationality. He appealed to the High Court of Justice, which in 1962 ruled that for the purposes of the Law of Return, Brother Daniel could not be considered a Jew.

Index

The Abrahamic Dialogues Series

David B. Burrell, series editor

Donald J. Moore, *Martin Buber: Prophet of Religious Secularism.*

James L. Heft, ed., *Beyond Violence: Religious Sources of Social Transformation in Judaism, Christianity, and Islam.*

Rusmir Mahmutćehajić, *Learning from Bosnia: Approaching Tradition.*

Rusmir Mahmutćehajić, *The Mosque: The Heart of Submission.*

Alain Marchadour and David Neuhaus, *The Land, the Bible, and History: Toward the Land That I Will Show You.*

James L. Heft, ed., *Passing on the Faith: Transforming Traditions for the Next Generation of Jews, Christians, and Muslims.*

Rusmir Mahmutćehajić, *On Love: In the Muslim Tradition.*

Phil Huston, *Martin Buber's Journey to Presence.*